Alive Insid

Alive Inside: Unlock Your Leadership Advantage in the Age of AI delivers a groundbreaking leadership framework for reclaiming the distinctly human qualities – compassion, courage, intuition, presence, and storytelling – that keep leaders indispensable in our increasingly automated, AI-driven world.

Blending historical narratives, neuroscience insights, and real-world case studies, Emmanuel Gobillot reveals seven practical principles, from *authenticity over automation* to *stories over structures*, that will transform readers' leadership style and energise their organisational culture. They will discover how vulnerability outperforms perfection, caring becomes a strategic advantage, and attention creates real authority.

Packed with actionable strategies for building the human-centred leadership skills no machine can replicate, *Alive Inside* gives leaders the clarity, capability, and confidence to command trust, inspire teams, and shape cultures that thrive on creativity, connection, and meaning.

Written for current and aspiring leaders, executives, and managers feeling pressured to act like machines, or fearing replacement by them, *Alive Inside* is vital for anyone in rapidly digitising industries seeking to protect their human edge while embracing technological advancement. It is also essential reading for leadership development professionals, business coaches, and students of organisational leadership.

Described as 'the first leadership guru for the digital generation' and 'the freshest voice in leadership today', **Emmanuel Gobillot** is one of the world's foremost thinkers and authorities on leadership. Author of ten UK and US bestselling books and ranked among Europe's most sought-after speakers, Emmanuel consults with CEOs and executives globally. A French national, he moved to the UK in 1985.

Alive Inside

Unlock Your Leadership Advantage in the Age of AI

Emmanuel Gobillot

Routledge
Taylor & Francis Group
NEW YORK AND LONDON

Designed cover image: Mykola Shelepa

First published 2026
by Routledge
605 Third Avenue, New York, NY 10158

and by Routledge
4 Park Square, Milton Park, Abingdon, Oxon, OX14 4RN

Routledge is an imprint of the Taylor & Francis Group, an informa business

ISBN: 9781041161660 (hbk)
ISBN: 9781041161653 (pbk)
ISBN: 9781003683124 (ebk)

DOI: 10.4324/9781003683124

Typeset in Palatino
by Newgen Publishing UK

To you, the reader,
for caring enough to think
and thinking enough to care

Contents

Acknowledgements

The year 2024 felt like a fitting end to my writing career. Routledge had just published my latest book, *This Is Not A Leadership Book*, in which I had condensed over two decades of advising leaders into 20 lessons for success, and De Gruyter Brill had asked me to revise my very first book, *The Connected Leader*, for a brand-new edition. It felt like the circle had been closed, and I could devote myself to my speaking and consulting engagements.

I was sharing this thought with my full-time friend and sometime colleague Shaun O'Callaghan over dinner in a non-descript hotel dining room that could have been anywhere but, on this occasion, was in Denmark, when he challenged me to rethink. We had been discussing leadership and AI, and he felt that this was too important an area for me not to contribute some thoughts on the impact it has had and will have on leadership. His words, 'we are our work', still resonate. I had been thinking about the topic for some time but, as is often the case with Shaun, his challenge spurred me on. I must thank him for it.

Having developed the idea, as I always do, I sought the guidance of Matthew Smith, who has been by my side in different roles (editor, commissioning editor, publisher, and all-round mentor) throughout all my writing endeavours. I owe him more than I will ever be able to repay.

I couldn't have been happier when Meredith Norwich, who had commissioned *This Is Not A Leadership Book*, decided to sponsor this project with her time, effort, resources, and, above all, her wise counsel. No one else has ever been able to challenge me quite as well as Meredith, and few people's words make me think quite as much as hers. So, it has been a delight to once again work with her, Bethany Nelson, Deanna Waistell, and the rest of the team at Routledge. My thanks also go to Louise Smith for her keen eye in spotting mistakes and her kind heart in making suggestions while editing the manuscript. I am so glad to have found a publishing house that feels like a home.

As is the case with all of my books, you would not be reading it if it hadn't been for the patience, advice, and grace (which happens to be her middle name) of my sometime co-author and full-time business partner and wife, Katherine Thomas. She may be annoying in that she gets rid of so many of what I think are my most poetic sentences, but she sure has made the book much less annoying for you to read as a result.

And last, but not least, as I have done from my second book onwards, I want to thank you. It takes readers for a book to be published, which is why I have dedicated this book to you. You have helped me find a career and a voice, and I hope this book will help you with developing yours.

As usual, please do blame me for any mistakes, omissions, or errors in the text and thank the people above without whom there would be many more.

Introduction: If you can't tell the difference, how much do you care?

In April 2025, Sam Altman (chief executive officer of OpenAI) sat side by side with Chris Anderson (head of TED) on the famous circular red carpet. Altman's standing in the tech community should have put at least a third of the audience on his side (the technology part of TED). He is, after all, the CEO whose entire staff threatened to resign unless he was reinstated. Yet, on this spring day in Vancouver, the entertainment and design crowd had other ideas.

About two minutes in, Anderson flashes on screen a cartoon he had instructed Sora (one of OpenAI's models) to generate by prompting it to 'imagine Charlie Brown as a philosophical AI pondering his existence'. He was impressed with the output but, as OpenAI has no agreement with Peanuts Worldwide for the right to use its characters, was less enamoured by what he called a clear case of 'intellectual property theft'.

Altman's somewhat flippant and petulant jab at the agreeing crowd ('you can clap that all you want … enjoy!') made for good viral content. A design and entertainment crowd won't let you get away with copyright infringement.

Yet, as much as I abhor theft and plagiarism, I found it sad that this was the part of the interview that went viral. I guess that his temperament blinded us to his temerity as, in the same

DOI: 10.4324/9781003683124-1

exchange, Altman said something far more controversial, startling, and far-reaching.

When asked what he thought of the cartoon, he gave 'a somewhat meta-answer' (his own description). 'There is really no way to know if it thinks that or if it saw that a lot of time in the training, and if you can't tell the difference, how much do you care?'

It is the very line I chose as the title for this introduction because, unlike Chris Anderson, I felt it deserved some thought. In Vancouver, the remark did not even draw a gasp. There was no follow-up question. There was no challenge. The idea that 'we can't know and shouldn't care' was good enough.

But here is the truth. Sam Altman does know that Sora did not think and could not have thought whatever it wrote. AI does not think. It mimics. His hope, though, by asking you not to care about the difference between probabilistic word association and thinking, is that you will see AI as far superior to what it is.

It is not a conspiracy theory. It is a business model.

Much of the worth of OpenAI, along with the valuation of AI companies in general, relies on achieving the holy grail of disruption that is AGI (artificial general intelligence) – the ability to perform any intellectual task with the same cognitive abilities as a human. That's why every new release is accompanied by headlines such as 'AI is now PhD level' (whatever that means) or 'AI now has an IQ superior to a quarter/half/the entire human population' (which means precisely nothing).

The best shortcut to achieving AGI and reaping the rewards it brings is for you never to worry about the difference between what *is* real and what *feels* real.

If you neither understand nor care about the difference, you neither understand your worth (versus AI) nor care about your agency (over AI). You are relegated to the role of passive user rather than active leader. Passive users make for better business.

It's no surprise then that two narratives have come to dominate AI discussions.

The first is 'the fear narrative', which betrays a lack of understanding of your worth. It goes something like this. AI is better than you. It outsmarts and outperforms you. It will replace you.

The second is 'the co-opted narrative', which betrays a lack of understanding of your agency. It states that AI is like a new colleague. This colleague is very good, with none of the drawbacks of humanity and all of its benefits. If you collaborate with it, it will enhance everything you do.

They may feel like opposites, but their outcome is the same. They paint AI as inevitable and, in doing so, force you to make a false choice. You are either against AI (if you see it as a malevolent competitor) or pro AI (if you espouse the idea that it is a value-added colleague).

This book is neither against nor pro AI, in the same way that it would be absurd to be against or pro the hammer or the tractor. Instead, it aims to provide a new narrative.

AI is an incredible tool. There is plenty of evidence to suggest that it will have a colossal impact on the world in general and a critical one on the business world in particular. Even if you ignore some of the more outlandish claims of the evangelists and account for the fact that our track record of delivering the promise of technology is abysmal, AI is both revolutionary in some fields and radical in most. But it is neither magic nor sentient.

There is no doubt that it will lead to disruption and replacement in the same way that industrial and digital automation has led to some jobs disappearing and some new ones being created. It is not only possible but probable that it will lead to more jobs disappearing, in more fields, than in the past. But, while the tractor replaced many a farmhand, it has never replaced the farmer.

My argument is that we need to resist both fear of obsolescence and facile obedience in favour of the energy, agency, and depth that make us uniquely human. We must recognise that having a lack of control over progress does not make us any less in charge of how it will unfold. We must acknowledge that, while AI can mimic us, it can never replicate the qualities we need to secure the future (presence, values, nuance, wisdom, courage, ethical judgement, and meaning-making).

Despite decades of management thinking, leadership practices have remained static. We have tried to lead like machines. We have sought predictability in a world that is largely probabilistic. We have asserted our power through control, replicability, speed, efficiency, answers, and risk mitigation. We have wanted to be flawless, efficient, emotionless. AI, though, offers a valuable reminder that our curiosity, our compassion, and our imperfections are not faults but the competitive advantages built into our humanity.

The advent of AI is a reminder that we need to restate our unique value and reclaim our agency. AI is a tool, but being alive inside is a choice. AI's adoption, usage, and purpose lie in our hands, not those of the toolmaker.

The argument that underpins this book can be summed up in one sentence: in the age of AI, the leaders who matter most will be the ones who lead most like humans. In an era increasingly shaped by machines that simulate thought, emotion, and even leadership, and where AI can generate, predict, and optimise, to be alive inside matters more than ever.

Being alive is about feeling consequences, holding regrets, and wondering what we are becoming. This is not something AI will ever be able to do. Yet too many leaders are acting more and more as if they too are automated. They are becoming disconnected from emotions, and numb to nuances. Just like the people who are supposed to follow them, they are both more efficient and more disengaged. Organisations are moving faster but feeling more hollow.

To be alive inside is to reawaken the distinctly human capacity for presence, compassion, discernment, and courage that no machine can replicate, no human being should abdicate, and organisations long to duplicate. This book is a call to restore humanity in leadership because the future belongs to those who, rather than fear or co-opt AI, adopt an unapologetic, radically human mindset.

Radical humanity is the recognition that leaders can only succeed by leveraging their humanity in ways they seldom have had to do in the past. It is the conclusion that AI does not need to be beaten (why fight a tractor?). Instead, we need to beat ourselves in the humanity stakes and use all the tools at our disposal for humanity's sake. Radical humanity is the demand that we become even more who we are, in order to thrive where we are.

Human leadership is more relevant than ever. I am as confident that AI will not replace you as I am that, unless you rediscover your humanity faster than AI learns to copy it, a radical human will. This book is designed to decode what radical humanity is and offer you a toolkit to recode your own practices.

To ensure the book is practical and easy to navigate, I have organised it in seven principles. Each is discussed in five chapters covering why the principle matters, what it looks like in practice, and how to implement it.

You can navigate through the book in any order (you bought it, so who am I to say what you do with it). There is, however, a narrative sequence to the principles. In order to make it easier for you to follow it, should you wish to move through the book in a different order, I want to offer you an image to recall what we are about to cover. That image is that of the mundane, cheap, unassuming, and easily disposable paper clip. I want to share with you three very different stories where the paper clip acts as a symbol of our principles. As well as helping you follow the narrative thread, I hope they help you reflect on what you may have stopped seeing and reclaim the moral imagination required to lead in the age of systems that do not care, do not pause, do not reflect, and do not feel.

First, I will talk about Microsoft's cartoon assistant 'Clippy', an example in which our response has morphed from irritation to compliance, as a way to introduce our first three principles.

Principle 1: authenticity over automation

We will travel though the differences between artificial and human intelligence to uncover why, in a world flooded with AI-generated content, where everything is polished and synthetic, being real is a competitive edge. We will discuss how to reclaim your agency over what happens next and assert your worth in making it happen.

Principle 2: moral courage over mere compliance

While we don't know what the future holds, we do know it won't be linear. As AI forces more decisions to be made while accelerating the ability to make them, leaders must pause and do what is right, not just what is easy, expected, or expedient. I will show you why and how radical humanity sees ethics as a compass that will guide you under pressure rather than guidelines to flex as necessary.

Principle 3: intuition over instruction

AI is about data, but leadership is acting on insight. Instinct is a vital form of intelligence. Inner signals are powerful when certainty disappears. Data can provide direction, but they cannot decide. This is why we will discuss why hearing what the data do not say is a critical skill, as well as how your experience and attention create the intuition necessary to lead successfully.

Having covered the first three principles, I will then share with you the second of our paper clips. This time, it is the central premise of a thought experiment posited by a philosopher and intended as a cautionary tale about goal-driven AI and it enables me to introduce the next two fundamental principles of being alive inside.

Principle 4: curiosity over certainty

Our ability to shape the future requires a desire to explore the unknown rather than cling to what we think we know. It requires us to ask the right questions. In this section of the book, we will uncover how radical humanity is about exploring what we don't yet understand rather than knowing more. I will show you how to begin asking better questions to get real breakthroughs.

Principle 5: compassion over calculation

Leadership, however, is not just about results. It's about relationships. AI might help you optimise your organisation, but it cannot create belonging. Human compassion will build the connections necessary for your teams to thrive. People don't follow perfect people. I will show you that compassion isn't a 'soft', nice-to-have extra. It is the strategic foundation for trust and forms the architecture of successful organisations.

Finally, as we progress to our final part of the book, I will take you to wartime Norway, where the humble paper clip became an act of human defiance. This is the kind of defiance that is enabled by the last two principles of being alive inside.

Principle 6: presence over performance

In a world of distraction, plentiful answers, and boundless information, presence is magnetic. Leadership can no longer be just about stagecraft. Real influence comes not from looking the part but from being fully engaged and emotionally available. In a distracted culture, presence becomes a rare and transformative form of leadership. Together, we will uncover how genuine presence creates trust, clarity, and calmness under pressure. I will show you why how polished you appear comes second to how grounded you are.

Principle 7: stories over structures

Finally, when all is said and done, as AI is stripping away the formal levers of power we have clung to, you realise two things. First, policies alone do not move people, and, second, culture is not sustained by handbooks and posters. This is why we will conclude our journey by looking at how metaphors, myths, and meaningful storytelling shape beliefs and behaviours. Stories are not accessories to structure. They are the foundation on which structure stands.

Radical humanity, though, is not just about principles. It is about how you translate them into continuous action. For this reason, at the end of the book, I will introduce a framework for action I call the ALIVE manifesto.

As the world of AI started to unfold, and my research for this book progressed, it became clear that leadership today demands more than the speed and precision AI offers. It calls for human clarity and conscious direction. I have worked to ensure that this structure offers you both. My aim is that, by the time you finish reading the book, you will agree that, while AI will not replace you, it reveals the parts of your leadership that are no longer essential, along with the practices that, if continued, will make you irrelevant. My hope is that you will find this book a useful guide to building new ones.

Finally, I should also mention how this book was written. Over the last few years, publishers have started to ask authors about their use of AI. I suspect this has as much to do with limiting the risk of liability regarding potential copyright infringements as it does with detecting plagiarism. While I welcome the help AI can give to allow people to express their ideas better, I do feel, as an avid reader myself, that, if I am to put effort into reading something, I would prefer that the author had also put effort into writing. That being said, this is a book about AI, and so you would, I think, expect me to know something about the topic.

I have used AI extensively in my research for this book. It did not, however, either complete the research or write the book for me. I have used AI to test some of the ideas I convey by comparing different output. I've also tried to trick the algorithms on certain things to test reliability. I am sure that, as a result, my text is a lot less polished than it could have been had a machine written it, but it does convey my humanity (mistakes, biases, flaws, and bad humour included).

So, let's begin. To lead with purpose, you must stay alive rather than automated inside and, if you can still tell the difference, then you already do care.

Part 1

The obnoxious paper clip

As we start our journey through this book, let me take you back to, or indeed, if you're too young to remember, introduce you to, the late 1990s.

Imagine that you are typing away in Microsoft Word when, suddenly, as you are mid-sentence, a small figure that looks like a paper clip with googly eyes slides into view and bounces on your screen. This was a frequent occurrence back then. Its official name was Clippit, but we all knew it as Clippy. It would always, seemingly randomly, appear and offer to help. For example, it might ask, 'It looks like you're writing a letter. Would you like help with that?', and give you a choice of three options: 'get help with writing the letter', 'type the letter without help', and 'don't show this tip again'. Given that asking if you can help is not a 'tip', that third option should really have been replaced by what we all thought when Clippy appeared – 'can you please just go away?'.

Annoyance was indeed the universal reaction to Clippy. You couldn't shut the blasted thing down fast enough. It was misaligned, interruptive, and grammatically wrong more often than it was helpful or right. It wasn't just that it made mistakes though. Clippy was obnoxious in the same way that people who refuse to read the room and take a hint that their presence is no

DOI: 10.4324/9781003683124-2

longer required are. It came, uninvited, trashed your desktop and refused to leave.

Yet, over time, something fascinating happened. Microsoft retired Clippy in 2001, but its nudging remained. Today, the grammar corrections that once came with a cartoon face appear as thin blue lines (or squiggly red ones if, like me, your spelling is as bad as your typing). Clippy's phrasing suggestions are now embedded in your software. Your writing is no longer evaluated by a pedantic cartoon paper clip but by an invisible force. The difference, though, is that we no longer reject the suggestions. We just accept the prompts, often without thinking and mainly without reading them. Clippy's logic has been internalised.

This is how we change. Our practices, once autonomous, are shaped invisibly by algorithmic logic that we rarely resist because it is both subtle and convenient, even if it is often wrong and never neutral. Our agency and, by default, our leadership disappear through quiet abdication rather than conscious surrender. When we stop noticing how we make decisions, we stop owning them.

The Clippy story is about more than an annoying interface. It is about the slow erosion of human agency and intention. We live in a world where nudges have become norms and in which software makes choices on our behalf, rather than guides our choice. This is how our humanity disappears.

We accept suggestions because they sound correct without ever wondering if they are wise, clear, or empathetic. When everything looks polished, we stop asking if anything is missing. If a sentence is grammatically sound, should we stop wondering if it still carries emotional truth? If a statement is algorithmically made, should we stop registering its ethical weight? If a message is efficiently generated but generic, should we overlook the fact that it no longer speaks in our voice?

The real danger of AI is not that it replaces human work but rather that it erases human will. The risk is that it replaces our willingness to be wrong, to revise, and to care. While Clippy was annoying, it had the grace to be visible. The blue and red lines are silent but everywhere.

What is required now, in the age of AI, are leaders who question the value of technology and the default position that it is inevitable. This is our first principle: authenticity over automation. We need leaders who are unwilling to settle for anything other than what is right and real. This is our second principle: moral courage over mere compliance. And, finally, Clippy shows us the importance of having leaders who eschew default positions in favour of intuition and instinct. This is our third principle: intuition over instruction.

Being alive inside is to be aware of your power and intentional in your values.

Principle 1

Authenticity over automation

Leaders aren't valuable because they're flawless.
They're valuable because they're real.

To explain each of the principles I have written five chapters. To help you navigate the book, should you decide not to read it in one go, you will find below (and on all subsequent principle introduction pages) a five-point outline of the flow (one per chapter).

- Chapter 1: it is a mistake to think that technology is destiny. Leaders have the agency and responsibility to choose whether and how to use AI.
- Chapter 2: to make those choices wisely, they must first understand what AI truly is (and isn't) and how it differs from human intelligence.
- Chapter 3: this will enable them to see that human imperfection, rather than machine-like precision, makes for effective leadership.
- Chapter 4: it is only by embracing and expressing that imperfection that they will build the emotional connections necessary for engagement.

DOI: 10.4324/9781003683124-3

- Chapter 5: in a culture saturated with filters and synthetic signals, knowing how to have genuine presence is the foundation of trust and the hallmark of irreplaceable leadership.

1

The myth of technological inevitability

He may have had a name fit for a king but, on the face of it, or rather on his face alone, Johann Wolfgang Ritter von Kempelen de Pázmánd – Wolfgang for short – never seemed like the kind of man who would impress an empress. But he did.

Don't get me wrong, I am not being shallow by mentioning his looks. I know that looks alone could not make for attraction, even in 18th-century Vienna. I am only trying to find what could possibly make you stand out in the eyes of someone accustomed to looking at the extraordinary. Maybe the fact that Wolfgang was incredibly well educated and had a stellar career was what made him stand out. He had studied law and philosophy while attending universities in Vienna and Rome. He had a keen interest in mathematics and physics, as well as the ability to speak eight languages (German, Hungarian, Slavic, Latin, French, Italian, English, and Romanian). He had moved up the ranks from being a clerk in the Hungarian Court Chamber to retire as the Imperial-Royal Court Councillor.

The truth though is that, however colossal, it wasn't these achievements that attracted the attention of Maria Theresa, archduchess of Austria, queen of Hungary and Bohemia, wife

DOI: 10.4324/9781003683124-4

and empress of the Holy Roman Emperor Francis I. She needed something more, something that she had never seen, which is not easy to give someone who has seen it all.

But Wolfgang had an invention that she, along with Europe's and the Americas' greats (including Napoleon Bonaparte and Benjamin Franklin) could never have imagined, never mind seen. It was a magical device that would go on to become a commercial sensation. It was so revolutionary that, for nearly 84 years after its first unveiling, it would continue to tour the world.

Wolfgang was the father of the so called 'Mechanical Turk'.

To understand 'the Turk', all you need to do is imagine a life-sized model of a human (or rather just a torso), dressed in Ottoman clothing, with a large cabinet in front of it. The mannequin, sporting piercing grey eyes and a black beard, holds a pipe in its left hand while its right rests on a chessboard sitting on top of the cabinet.

More than 200 years before the advent of IBM's Deep Blue and the birth of Garry Kasparov, the Mechanical Turk automaton was able to defeat any and every grand master coming its way. Faced with a challenger, its arm would move the pieces on the board. The time it would take it to win would depend on the quality of its opponent, but win it invariably did.

Transport yourself back to 18th-century Vienna and think about how you would have felt. Here was an intelligent machine, The first of its kind. Amazement, wonder, surprise, or indeed puzzlement and curiosity are all valid emotions to feel. In fact, at the time, just as we do today when faced with AI, anyone who saw the Turk feared it and loved it in equal measure but, above all, was fascinated by it.

Imagine this: an assortment of pulleys, cogs, spokes, wheels, and magnets able to compete against mankind's finest. It was so puzzling that, 66 years after it was first seen, even Edgar Allen Poe published an essay about it, never hiding his scepticism at this, 'the most astonishing of the inventions of mankind'.

He was right to be suspicious. Some 200 odd years later, the Turk reminds us that our fascination with machine intelligence is not new. It also shows us how we overestimate technology's independence while underestimating the human hands that guide it.

It took a bribe from Frederick the Great for Wolfgang to reveal his secret. The automaton may have been mechanically well built but it was no technological marvel. Hidden within its cabinet, tucked away among the mechanical parts needed to move the chess pieces, was a man: a chess master but a man, nevertheless.

Wolfgang's story describes how the artifice of intelligence can become artificial intelligence based purely on what we believe. Just like the Turk, the inevitability of technology is an illusion that rests on carefully curated myths rather than facts.

The illusion of inevitability

These myths are all around us. Spurred on by headlines warning us of the danger of 'being left behind', entrepreneurs being lauded for their ability to 'move fast, break things, and automate everything', and management books warning us to 'adapt or die', we have come to frame technological progress as some kind of Darwinian process. Anyone questioning its application, value, and worth risks being seen as a likely future victim of natural selection.

Rather than a 'fait accompli', the idea that technological progress obeys natural law and that its adoption is the only answer, the presumption of natural selection, betrays a lack of knowledge of how both organisations and evolution work. Technological progress is not shaped by immutable laws of nature. It is shaped simply through countless decisions, all made by human beings.

Decisions that feed our fear of obsolescence, in turn, drive our need for obedience. This herd mentality drives copycat behaviour without clear objectives. It manifests itself in the adoption or announcement of new technology initiatives for the sake of appearing innovative or forward-thinking (especially in front of boards, investors, or the media). You can hear it in the corridors and online meetings when people announce 'our competitors are investing in AI. We have to do something' or 'We can't be the last ones to announce an AI strategy'.

It is, above all, the external manifestation of an internal anxiety that, if you or your organisation don't adopt AI quickly, you will be obsolete. The anxiety is not hard to understand given the endless cycle of reinforcement of that very idea by everyone who has everything to gain by your adoption of AI and a whole lot to lose if you delay it.

Technology has always been fertile ground for our worry that, 'if everyone's doing it, we have to do it too'. Every advert that claims 'AI inside' is just a rescripted one that once was 'web-enabled'. Whether it is the fear of being left behind, or the anticipation of a shareholder backlash at the lack of investment in what is seen as revolutionary, or simply the angst at being seen as anything other than 'cutting edge', the drivers of executive anxiety abound.

But, while it is legitimate to expect our leaders to have a view and be able to argue it, that is not the same as expecting them to blindly follow the herd.

The dangers of abdication

What is legitimate is for leaders faced with any technology to answer three questions in clear and compelling ways: does it make sense for us, for what we want to achieve and who we are? Does it serve our people? Does it solve the right problem or create a new one?

When we treat adoption as inevitable, we stop asking whether it is appropriate. This is when the real damage begins. AI is a reminder that the decisions others make have consequences for our lives more generally and for our organisations most definitely.

We don't have to look very far to spot problems. From the automation of bias to the loss of transparency and accountability via the erosion of human judgement in high-stakes decisions, they are plain to see. These are not kinks that need to be ironed out or bugs that need to be quashed. They are design choices that require the critical eye of those who lead adoption rather than blind implementation.

Don't get me wrong; after over 20 years in business, I am still of the view that people aim to do good. I will never give up on the idea first articulated by the minister Theodore Parker and so eloquently expressed by Martin Luther King Jr that 'the arc of the moral universe is long, but it bends toward justice'.

I will always refuse to be cynical and judge people's intent on the basis of their behaviour. Whether their intent is pure, evil, or pure evil doesn't even matter. What really matters is that they have intentions.

Such people have decided to have ownership of the future. They have made decisions that shape outcomes. But we need to be clear that their agency does not negate yours.

Reclaiming ownership

You own your future as well as the decision to let others have a say in it. As leaders, we should never be either victims or cheerleaders of other people's innovation. We have to drive our own future, as and when, and if and when, it makes sense for us to do so.

We are the stewards of the values, purpose, and culture of our organisations. Our responsibility is to reconcile the often conflicting but never illegitimate needs of the diverse groups of people who form our stakeholder community.

It is our role to make choices, and one of these choices is whether or not to use a tool. We have to filter, to question, and, ultimately, to decide based on our purpose rather than any pressure we may feel under.

There is a simple but effective framework that enables us to shift from fear to agency and guide our approach. I call it the 3 As for alignment, accountability, achievement.

Alignment is about ensuring that whatever action we take is aligned with our objectives and values. Does it make sense for us, for what we want to achieve and who we are?

Accountability is about ensuring that everyone who will be touched by the decision has had a chance to input into it. I am asking you not to abdicate the decision to someone else but rather to ensure you have had a chance to consider the multiple perspectives of your stakeholders. Does this decision serve our people?

Finally, achievement is about whether whatever decision is made is likely to get us closer to our objective faster. This is not about a business case in order to secure funding but rather about surfacing the assumptions made and questioning their validity. Our history of technological innovation tells us that asking the question 'Does it solve the right problem or create a new one?' is never a waste of time.

These three questions (Does it make sense for us, for what we want to achieve and who we are? Does it serve our people? Does it solve the right problem or create a new one?) are legitimate leadership questions. Asking them does not make you a Luddite (by the way, the actual Luddites who gave us the adjective, contrary to the popular myth, were not anti-technology but rather anti exploitation and anti the dehumanisation of work). Asking these three questions ensures you reclaim agency over your own organisation. And reclaiming your agency is the first step to reclaiming your humanity.

But, as we close this chapter, I am mindful not to reduce Wolfgang Ritter von Kempelen de Pázmánd's legacy to his automaton. He was a gifted and genial innovator as well as a researcher. There may well be a link made some day from his research on language and his building of a mechanical language machine to the development of the large language models we know today. What I want to stress is that the Mechanical Turk story is neither about the machine nor the hoax. It is all about the illusion.

AI may feel inevitable today but, like Wolfgang and his chess master, it often hides the most important thing. It hides the human beings making decisions behind the curtain. As a human being, you have the choice to pull the curtain back. As a leader, you have a duty to do so. My question is simply: are you prepared to pull the curtain back?

The fears and wonders of the 18th century haven't left us. We fear that AI will become too human just as Vienna feared the automaton would. Yet, the real risk is different. Your obsolescence is not the risk of the machine replacing you but the risk of you forgetting what it means to be human in the first place.

In Chapter 2, we will pull the curtain back to look behind the polished surface of artificial intelligence to understand the difference between what AI is claimed to be, what it is, and what it isn't. Understanding this difference is the first step to reclaiming what no machine can ever replicate: identity, compassion and real human presence.

2

ABCs: The real difference between us and AI

It is possible to stand out and fit in at the same time. Even a CEO can do this. Tang Yu is proof of it.

Appointed CEO in 2022 to oversee the operations of a tech firm in Hong Kong, Ms Yu stands out as one of the few female leaders in the tech world. But the fact that she does not have a corner office, never shakes hands, nor behaves like a typical CEO also makes her stand out.

Yet, the fact that she is an untypical CEO doesn't mean she doesn't do what CEOs do. She writes memos and issues press releases, analyses data, and makes decisions. You could even say that, given her appointment tipped the company's valuation above US$1 billion despite the fact that she was unknown, these actions are the right ones too.

That she has graced the covers and appeared on the pages of business and lifestyle magazines, as well as received prestigious awards for her work, seals the deal. You can both stand out and fit in.

I would have loved to write that Ms Yu is the living embodiment of leadership being done differently, but she neither is living nor has a body. Tang Yu is the first AI CEO to have ever been appointed.

DOI: 10.4324/9781003683124-5

NetDragon Websoft made headlines around the world when it decided that the future belonged to leaders being able to make impartial decisions, boost efficiency, and reduce human error. Media buzzed. Journalists debated whether Tang Yu was symbolic, experimental, or the start of something bigger. Brushing aside that nothing in AI is impartial, error-free, or necessarily efficiency-boosting, there is no denying that appointing an AI CEO was a good way to raise profile.

Luxury rum producer Dictador was the first in Europe to appoint an AI CEO (another female, called Nika, who was never graced with a surname). Syhunt followed suit by being the first in the cybersecurity world to appoint one (yet another female, this time named Satu Ohara). And Chhatra Sansad, an Indian foundation devoted to youth change makers, eschewed the pointless creativity by simply appointing ChatGPT as its CEO.

I am not sure why three of the above companies decided to make their new CEOs female, nor why two of them chose to give them names with godlike etymologies, but, in the leadership development circles I inhabit, their appointments raised some interesting questions.

If a CEO can be replaced by an algorithm, what exactly are we saying leadership is? Is leadership really only about decision-making and optimisation? Is it about presence or influence? Can logic and polish be enough? Do we lose anything if we simply reduce leadership to data and design?

The problem with these questions is that they are one step ahead of where they should be. Before we even worry about what an AI CEO means for leadership, we should be clear about what we mean by artificial intelligence, how it works, and how it differs from human intelligence. Only when we understand what we are up against, if indeed we are up against anything, can we decide on the most appropriate response.

Artefacts, blueprint, and composition

I often think tech people are the opposite of accountants. This isn't because their respective, if not always respected, professions are different, but because they have an inverted relationship with vocabulary.

Accountants love to use multiple words to describe the same thing, while technologists use the same word to describe many things. These two different strategies share the same intent – sow confusion! If you can't make sense of accounting, you need accountants while, if you don't understand the nature of technology, you're more likely to see it as something much better than it is.

There is money to be made in portraying things as more complex, novel, or advanced than they are. It's a clever strategy but it makes our lives much harder when it comes to understanding AI.

To confuse matters more, technologists love to borrow terms from neurology, despite the fact that we still know very little about how our brain works and everything about how machines operate. They talk about neural networks, synaptic weights, and convolutional neural networks, for example, to make us forget the artificial part of the name.

Ms Yu may well be AI, but so apparently is your toaster, your Netflix account, and possibly the car you drive. This is not a technology handbook but a manual for leadership in the technological age, so I won't go into the intricacies but will rather point to the differences between you and her.

First, let's talk about AI. Its ABC is artefacts, blueprint, and composition. Let's agree that AI refers to systems designed to perform tasks that normally require human intelligence. This could be learning, reasoning, recognising patterns, or making decisions. And, yes, I am still baffled about how any of this could apply to my toaster.

In any case, all AI systems start with artefacts (or data, if you will). In large language models such as ChatGPT, the artefact is called a token (think of it as a small unit of text), and, for Sora (whom we met in Chapter 1), these tokens are bits of pictures called visual spacetime patches.

These artefacts are then put through a blueprint. The blueprint is a set of algorithmic instructions that enable the system to identify patterns and relationships between the data (see enough pictures of cats and you can recreate one, or play enough word associations and you can form a sentence). The system may adjust its internal parameters to interpret, identify patterns, and correlate results, but it is not learning in the true sense of the term. It is maths, not magic, that enables it to make inferences, predictions, or decisions. That's why its output is not reasoning but rather a composition: an assembly of best guesses based on identified patterns.

There are, of course, different levels of data manipulation. Your fridge is unlikely to have the same level of computation as your car or your preferred picture or text generator. So, not all AI is created equal, depending on its purpose, but all obeys the same ABC.

You may hear people refer to narrow AI or reactive machines to try to differentiate different levels of AI capability. Most will talk about narrow or weak AI to describe AI that is designed and trained for a specific task. This includes pretty much all of what we experience today (from Netflix recommendations to Google Maps' directions, Alexa responses, and ChatGPT images and conversations). Weak AI cannot perform beyond its programmed scope or use its input in domains for which it has not been encoded.

You may come across new terms every few months or so (such as agentic AI, for example). If you do, know that these are only there to describe either improvements to, or new uses of, narrow AI in the hope they can be viewed as steps towards AGI.

A more complex form of AI is described as artificial general intelligence (abbreviated to AGI) or strong AI, which I mentioned in the introduction. This is AI with an ability to understand, learn, and apply knowledge across a wide range of tasks, as humans do. This is the level many firms are actively pursuing but none have reached.

You may be tempted to add 'yet' to this last sentence. I have no issues with you doing so. That is provided that you are either involved in the building of AI and use the 'yet' to describe your hopeful intent or that, if you are not a developer, you are able to answer the three questions of our previous chapter to denote your agency. Nothing is inevitable.

If it came to pass, AGI would have the same flexibility in the application of intelligence as humans do. It could solve problems across domains and be completely self-directed in the way it learns. But it would still be artificial rather than human intelligence.

After AGI comes something called artificial consciousness (AC) or self-aware AI. This would be an AI that not only thinks and learns but is self-aware. It would, in effect, have a subjective sense of self, consciousness, and agency, just as humans do. And, while there are plenty of companies working to develop AGI, there is neither scientific consensus on whether AC is possible nor any real-world progress on its development.

But again, the important thing for us to understand at this stage is not so much the how or the why but rather the what. This is because whatever is developed cannot be human by nature. It will always be artificial, and this explains why all the AI CEOs we have met in this chapter are mentioned in the marketing material of their respective firms but are yet to make it on to the 'about us' pages of their website under the 'executive team' section.

Like Wolfgang's automaton, all systems have humans behind them. These humans make choices. They decide on the artefacts that are collected. They design the blueprint that tells the system how to compose.

AI is what Emily Bender, American linguist and professor, called a 'stochastic parrot' to underscore the fact that, while it will generate plausible language, it in no way understands the meaning of that language. Artificial intelligence does not mean that something artificial is intelligent but rather that the intelligence shown by machines is not real. The proverbial monkeys who, given enough time, could write Shakespeare have been given computing power and infinite resources.

You can see now why I mentioned in my introduction to this book that I was dubious about the claims of PhD-level intelligence or greater IQ than half the population. If, by PhD level, we mean being able to know every textbook, then by design they do know. But can they infer anything from these books? It depends on who coded them. And, even if we could agree that

IQ is actually a measure of intelligence (and there is plenty of evidence to suggest it is a poor one, at best), given AI systems are fed all possible data, of course they can have high IQs. Even I could have an above-average IQ if I was given the tests and the answers!

Awareness, body, and culture

Despite the efforts of many a Dubai-based social media influencer, we are not made of silicon. Tang Yu may be the world's first AI CEO, but she will never sit down with a colleague after a crisis and say, 'I don't know what to do but I'm here with you'. That is, unless she is prompted to do so.

The brain as a computer may be an appealing metaphor but it is not a reality. Not only because we know a whole lot more about how computers work than brains but also because there are three key elements that differentiate humanity. We too may be fed artefacts and have a blueprint to analyse them, that's partly what our education is, but our outputs are not mere compositions. We have a different ABC.

We have awareness. We know we exist, and this gives us a level of thinking unavailable to a machine. We feel guilt, empathy, shame, and pride. With awareness, we know when a decision is right not just because it meets criteria but because it feels right. This is not something Tang Yu can do.

Awareness allows us to draw on our personal memories, rich in emotion, and on intuition. We use social nuances to interpret situations in ways Tang Yu cannot. We can *read* a room, sense tension, or feel when silence speaks louder than words.

Along with awareness, we have bodies. Despite our tendency to see bodies as mere vehicles to carry our brains to meetings, our chemistry and physical make-up impact how we understand, interpret, and relate to the world.

Our physical presence as leaders not only feeds our intelligence, it also underscores our impact. Our posture, facial expressions, tone, and touch communicate empathy, vulnerability, and confidence in ways that resonate viscerally. A hand on the shoulder, a knowing glance, or simply standing in solidarity during crises can all be powerful. These are not things Tang Yu can replicate.

Our output is not mere composition; it shapes cultures. We are not clever creatures. We are visceral beings engaged in complex social relationships shaped by our consciousness, our morality, and mortality, as well as our thoughts.

It is true that AI will never second-guess, feel fear, or change its mind, and that there is some motivation within us wanting to emulate these attributes to make ourselves feel stronger or better. But we must remember that Tang Yu will only pause to compute rather than to commiserate. She will only ever search and analyse rather than doubt. She will never stop to question the question, only relentlessly search for the answer, unable ever to master the humility exemplified by the three most human words that build trust in the real world: *'I don't know'*.

When we understand how AI works, we know what it fundamentally lacks. While emotions, experience, judgement, and self-awareness can be mimicked, they can only impact in a human context. Our greatest advantage, to be fully human in the moments that matter most, lies in AI's absence of awareness, body, and culture. These are not bugs in our human system; they are the fuel of social influence.

In the next chapter, we explore why this imperfection, often seen as a characteristic of uncertain and messy humans, is not a flaw to hide. Imperfection is the feature that makes leaders trusted – and irreplaceable. It is no longer a risk for leaders. It is the very thing that sets them apart. That and a pooping duck!

3

The courage to be imperfect

Thirty years before Austrians were amazed by a chess-playing automaton, the French were falling for a duck. Not just any duck, mind you: this duck was changing the way people thought about what it meant to be human.

Jacques de Vaucanson's 'Digesting Duck' quacked like a duck, flapped like a duck, bowed like a duck, and, most astonishingly, ate grain like a duck, digested it like a duck, and excreted it like a duck. But, despite what the popular saying would have us believe, it wasn't a duck. It was a machine made of brass and leather and, just like our Mechanical Turk, it was an ingenious deception.

Enlightenment thinkers were enthralled. The French Academy declared it a triumph of the age. Just like Johann Wolfgang Ritter von Kempelen de Pázmánd would eventually do, Vaucanson became a celebrity. And, as is always the case, this status attracted attention. In fashionable salons, the 18th century's long-form equivalent of TikTok, discussions among the Parisian elite were fierce, fuelled by one key question:

Had man finally built life itself?

Creating life where there is none is a quest as old as humanity itself and one we are hardwired to see, if not to seek. From spotting random faces on the moon or prophets on pieces of toast or simply

DOI: 10.4324/9781003683124-6

allocating human characteristics to cartoon characters, we see life everywhere, even where there is none. Anthropomorphism is the deeply ingrained (no duck pun intended) human habit of projecting our thoughts, our emotions, and our intentions on to things that have none.

Of course, everyone knew rationally that the duck was not a duck. Unlike Wolfgang and his chess-playing automaton, Vaucanson never pretended it was. Yet, despite knowing the duck wasn't real, anyone encountering it couldn't help but behave as if it was.

We still do it today. Even as serious and intellectually superior as I imagine my readers to be, I am sure many of you use the odd 'please' and 'thank you' when interacting with your favourite AI tool. Some argue that it provides further context for AI to mine, thereby leading to better results, but I suspect most do it unconsciously. The fact that managing these unnecessary tokens is costing OpenAI and its competitors millions in additional computing power hasn't deterred Altman from suggesting that it is 'money well spent'. Any practice that encourages users to give AI the sentience it does not have is indeed worth pursuing when you're keen to achieve AGI.

Anthropomorphism is a key part of AI. Listen to the words we use. When AI gives erroneous answers, we don't think 'there is a bug in the code' or 'the algorithm is flawed', we say 'it is hallucinating'. We no longer question the fact that we project our thoughts and feelings on to its composition. We nod in approval.

But ChatGPT doesn't care. The AI assistant you use to innovate isn't curious. The customer service bot that apologises for your online order going missing doesn't feel sorry. Three centuries after Vaucanson, our duck now digests data and excretes decisions, press releases, videos, and cartoons. But anthropomorphism is the least of our worries as leaders. It took Voltaire, the French philosopher, to point out a much more profound insight and lead us to the key question.

An avid observer of the technological advances of the time, Voltaire was fascinated by automation. But, when he encountered the duck for the first time, rather than worry about us projecting our image on to it, he saw how the duck was projecting itself on to us.

In his *Philosophical Dictionary*, under the entry 'Soul', he wrote about 'frail automatons moved by the invisible hand which directs us on this stage of the world' and wondered 'who among us can detect the wire that guides us?'.[1] Voltaire's question remains key today.

Are we beginning to feel the need to mimic AI rather than it mimicking us?

We shouldn't be surprised that, the moment we discovered large language models could write with perfect grammar and impeccable tone, and do so faster than we could, we enlisted their capability. There is nothing wrong with using AI to amplify your voice; there is, however, danger in using it to optimise this.

What we lose in the pursuit of perfection

You only have to spend a few moments on any social media site to see the polished motivational quotes or read the clever insights. You only have to read a press release or a statement from a business to see how effective and efficient this kind of writing can be and also how hollow it is. When you polish your tone, you invariably lose your edge. What your voice gains in precision, you invariably lose in presence. We have now reached a point where the mimicry is mutual. AI is busy learning to mimic our tone as we work hard to mimic its polish.

As I mentioned in the introduction, I see no issue with anyone using AI to make their life easier and output better. Calculators haven't stopped children learning maths, are handy when we are faced with complex calculations, and are indispensable when we are under time pressure. My issue arises from the point when we become so impressed with fast calculations that we forget the purpose of maths in the first place. When we start to behave like AI, with scripted empathy, curated vulnerability, bulletproof confidence, and punchy truisms, we don't become more effective. We become less real.

When we confuse clarity with authenticity, we lose both. Leadership is about impacting and influencing. It is about presence over polish. It is relational rather than performative, and, when synthetic performance overtakes real relationships, we lose trust. The more flawless our leaders become (in politics and business), the more they start to resemble the thing they fear being replaced by (perfection), and the more replaceable they become.

The problem for leaders in the age of AI is not that we see machines as human. That's just what we do. The real problem is that we start expecting humans to be more like machines. We purge humanity from our leadership and replace it with a hollow version of excellence.

In my book *This Is Not A Leadership Book*, I wrote about authenticity. I described my worry that it was too often used as an excuse for poor performance. 'I was just being myself' risks becoming a justification for poor behaviour, a badge of pride for the shameless. I called for authenticity to be skilled. What I meant by skilled was simply that authenticity and intention should work hand in hand. A more skilled version of you is a version that ensures that your intent is reflected in your impact.

This is not the same as saying that leaders must be perfect. We should not mistake skilled authenticity for a need to erase our hesitations, our doubts, or contradictions. But slowly, without even realising it, we are beginning to demand that same frictionless performance from our leaders as we see in our tools. We want our leaders to respond instantly, speak flawlessly, and be always calm, always clear, and, of course, always on. Yet, we don't just want them to be perfect and hollow, we also want them to be real.

The fact that we are capable of building machines in our image doesn't mean we want to reshape our leaders in theirs. From a distance, Vaucanson's duck appeared flawless. It flapped its wings, craned its neck, and, satisfyingly, pooped its grain. But, up close, its brass, leather, and gears were plain for all to see. The duck was a performance, a counterfeit of life, rather than life itself. When leadership seems mechanical, sterile, predictable, even if convincing from afar, it never stays effective up close for very long.

We've all read the corporate messages that sound like they were written by committee. We've received the Q&A documents that only contain answers to the questions we never asked but that leaders were comfortable answering. We have seen the letters, vetted by armies of lawyers, designed to apologise for something for which they cannot bring themselves to admit responsibility. We know they contain all the right words, but they are entirely devoid of human connection.

When, as leaders, we mistake algorithms for engagement or pay more attention to form and function than to feelings, just like our duck, we seem alive but, ultimately, we are mechanical.

Our endless quest to be flawless in message, persona, or timing fails to build trust. The more polished we become, the more people who should be following us worry about what we have to hide. This is not just a leadership issue; it is an organisation problem.

When we no longer trust our leaders are real, we avoid risk. When we no longer believe they have humanity, we hide opinions, questions, and mistakes. Just as in 18th-century Vienna or Paris, leadership becomes a performance, and our organisations become, at best, theatres and, at worst, circuses.

Our credibility has never been built on perfection. It has always been built through presence. Just as I am fond of saying that we will be remembered for what we tolerated rather than for what we did, I am well aware that our success as leaders is seldom based on what we did but rather on how we faced our failures. In this context, authenticity cannot be just about being ourselves. It can't even be just about being more skilful versions of ourselves. It must be about being more of ourselves.

Imperfection as strategy

When Voltaire marvelled at Vaucanson's duck, rather than be focused on or fooled by its mechanics, he was moved by its symbolism. He saw the duck as a mirror that reflected human ingenuity but also as a warning of where it might lead. Three centuries later, we must heed the warning that AI now presents to us.

Humanity was never meant to be polished or flawless, and neither is leadership. It is meant to be human. It is not branding. It is strategy. People may marvel at a duck, but they follow a human. They do not follow a machine. They follow a human who admits they can't be one.

Leadership in organisations tends to be self-selective. It is leaders who appoint leaders rather than followers who choose them. However, looking outside the confines of business to assess who people decide to follow leaves little room for doubt. When so many of our potential leaders start to sound like machines, real presence becomes revolutionary.

We reject people who reject their own humanity. In a world with so much change, so many misconceptions, so many polished social media avatars (human and non-human alike), imperfection becomes an edge. In a world where the bulk of the communication we encounter feels filtered, where most of the brands we trade with feel staged, and most of the leaders we meet feel indistinguishable, our best opportunity to differentiate ourselves is to display our flaws. False authenticity hides them, unskilled authenticity wears them with pride as a badge of honour, but real authenticity simply uses them to signal truth.

Being yourself more is owning mistakes without spin because only then will followers stop hiding theirs. It is about expressing fears and uncertainties without shame because then we give people permission to be open. It is about laughing at ourselves for our quirks because then we give others confidence to accept their own. Imperfection lies at the heart of a culture of trust. Imperfection is what makes your leadership resonant.

The real challenge isn't to outperform AI. Our biggest challenge is to out-concern, out-human, and out-relate it. To do so requires us to do what neither the Turk nor the duck could. We need to hesitate, doubt, reflect, adapt. We will never earn trust by mimicking certainty. Leadership is an intentional act. It is your intention that earns followers' trust. It is your ability to step forward, when you have neither solutions nor answers, that ensures trust remains. Having intention is something Vaucanson's duck could never have. But you can!

In the next chapter, we go deeper into what being 'more of yourself' looks like in practice. We will look at the effect being purposefully human has on leadership impact. We will see that imperfection opens the door to new conversations and, ultimately, to performance. To do so, I invite you to the South Pole.

Note

1 *Voltaire's Philosophical Dictionary*, Carlton House, New York, p. 274.

4

Practising vigorous vulnerability

Having had the chance to interact with thousands of executives, read hundreds of management books, and attended more business conferences than I can count, I have come to rely on a simple rule to measure the worth of any interlocutor. You may not always be able to judge a book by its cover, but you can always judge an author, speaker, or executive by their quotations.

I don't mean the price they charge. In my experience, there is a poor correlation between the worth of something or someone and their price. Instead, I mean the people they choose to quote and the quotations they choose to share.

There is, of course, nothing wrong with using someone else's brilliance to shine light on an argument, even if, I suspect, many use it to throw the spotlight on themselves. But my advice is always to be wary of people who tell you that Darwin wrote, 'it is not the strongest of the species that survives, nor the most intelligent. It is the one that is most adaptable to change', or 'In the long history of humankind (and animal kind, too) those who learned to collaborate and improvise most effectively have prevailed'. You may want to stay clear of people who quote Einstein's 'compound interest is the most powerful force in the universe' or 'Insanity is doing the same thing over and over again expecting different results'. The thoughts are all interesting, but

DOI: 10.4324/9781003683124-7

the quotes and their attribution are entirely made up. Neither Darwin nor Einstein ever said these things. And, if the person who shares them with you couldn't be bothered checking, you have to wonder how costly any other evidence-free advice they are sharing with you could be.

In the leadership circles I inhabit, there's a famous quote that refuses to die.

It is often written or said that, in 1914, when preparing for his Antarctic expedition, Sir Ernest Shackleton placed an advert in a London newspaper (which newspaper varies depending on who relates the story). It's a brilliant advert, in fact, it's possibly one of the most famous recruitment ads in history:

> Men wanted for hazardous journey. Small wages, bitter cold, long months of complete darkness, constant danger. Safe return doubtful. Honour and recognition in case of success.

No wonder it is worth sharing. You can't fault it. It is evocative. It is gritty. It is honest. It is human. But it was never written.

Countless researchers and historians have searched archives and newspaper records. They have trawled through all known documents related to the expedition, and there are many. All have concluded the advert is a myth invented, possibly, decades later and retrospectively attributed to Shackleton.

There is a reason all these quotes and stories keep on being shared, however, and it is a reason that is as old as humanity itself. We want them to be true!

In the case of Shackleton's advert, we want to believe that a leader would speak this plainly. We want to think that great leaders wouldn't hide the hardship they know will come, or sugar-coat the risks they know exist. We want to believe that there are leaders out there who would be able to tell us the worst and still be great enough for us to want to follow them.

But that's the worst part about made-up quotes. For all their attention-grabbing brilliance, they obscure the fundamental character, thoughts, and real lives of the people we pretend said them. Why make up something they said or did when there is so much to learn from the truth? And there is much to learn from Shackleton.

When his ship, the *Endurance*, was trapped and crushed by the ice encircling it, Shackleton faced what, for most of us, would have been an impossible decision to make. His choice was either to leave his men behind while he crossed 800 miles of open sea in a lifeboat, possibly never to return, or to wait and risk freezing to death alongside all of them.

We will never know how his thinking process went or how agonising the moments he took to make his decision were. What history tells us, though, is that he gathered his crew on a barren stretch of Antarctic rock and spoke to them – not to give them a heroic speech as a Hollywood biopic would have him do. He merely admitted the danger and told his men the odds. He never promised success or glory, but he did promise to try and, above all, he promised never to abandon them. He just looked them in the eyes and said 'I will come back'.

It took four months for him to return. And, when he did, not a single man was lost.

Forget the advert. It detracts us from the real leadership lesson. This is a lesson that is relevant to the world we face now and one that brings our journey through authenticity to its rightful conclusion.

Shackleton could not control nature, but he was still in charge of how the future would unfold. He reminds us of the importance of claiming agency we discussed in Chapter 1, even when outcomes appear inevitable.

As we discussed in Chapter 2, he knew that his worth, at the crossroads between obsolescence and success, rested in his humanity.

He also understood that, rather than pretend and make a grand speech, he needed to find a way to ensure his men believed that survival was possible. The answer was authenticity. It lay in his ability not only to be himself but to be the most skilful version of himself. For this to happen, as we saw earlier in this chapter, Shackleton had to give his crew more of himself.

What sets Shackleton apart as one of the greats in the annals of leadership was his foresight that, to be authentically ourselves, we need to show even more of who we are. He shows us that our true differentiator, in an age of synthetic perfection, is our vulnerability.

It was his vulnerability that gave his men their resolve. He didn't rally his team with certainty. He didn't pretend to have control over events he could not control. He showed them fear. He showed them focus. He showed them doubt and determination in equal measure. He showed them authentic humanity. When there is no plan, it is presence that determines the outcome.

Vulnerability underpins engagement

In today's fast-paced, performance-hungry, tech-obsessed, social media-filtered world, vulnerability is either used as posture or mistaken for weakness. Shackleton's act of truth-telling wasn't anything of the kind. It was both necessary and bold. By stating the goal, showing that he had the will to survive, and offering a way to do so, he was being strategic. In dangerous and uncertain conditions, his vulnerability gave his scared crew the one thing they needed. They didn't need someone perfect; they needed someone human and present.

When we try to mimic mechanical perfection, genuine openness is both a rare and strategic act. By being more ourselves, showing our intentions and imperfections in equal measure, we do not lose authority but instead gain credibility and connections.

Somewhere along the line, vulnerability became a marketing tactic. The ability for an executive to shed a tear at the perfect moment became a tool taught by communications consultants. LinkedIn is full of carefully worded 'learning from failure' posts that always end up underscoring some glorious product launch or new career. That's not vulnerability. That's performance. Shackleton didn't share his fear to be relatable. He shared it because it was true, and because his men needed to know he wasn't leading them with blind optimism.

It is natural for leaders to worry that, if they admit uncertainty, they will lose credibility. After all, most owe their position to having demonstrated their ability to do more, faster and better than others. Vulnerability seldom features on a list of desired competencies. We are taught that, if we don't project confidence, we risk losing control.

But think about what Shackleton did. By being his real self, he gave his crew something stronger than false confidence. He gave them a reason to believe in him and, therefore, to hope, not because he had all the answers but precisely because he didn't pretend to have them.

The Zen Buddhist teacher Roshi Joan Halifax articulated this best as 'having a strong back and a soft front', emphasising the importance of maintaining inner strength and resilience (the strong back) while remaining open and compassionate (the soft front). For Shackleton, his strong back, his spine, was his commitment. He had the clarity of purpose, the steady voice documented by his crew in their diaries, and, above all, his refusal to abandon responsibility. But his courage to admit fear without letting it define him was just as important. This was his soft front.

Unfortunately for us, modern leadership often reverses this formula. We preach soft back and hard front. We have come to value posture and scripted messaging while quietly doubting ourselves inside.

The truth is much more powerful though. Showing your vulnerability increases your credibility as much as faking certainty destroys it. It turns out that vulnerability is both emotionally compelling and biologically contagious.

Showing vulnerability activates the circuits in the brain that allow us to experience someone else's emotions. These so-called mirror neurons are the neurological basis for empathy. That's why we sometimes feel uncomfortable around some people without being able to quite articulate why this is. We are wired to feel fakery before we understand it.

Our brains respond more strongly to honest emotions than they do to certainty. In fact, studies in neuroeconomics show that emotion-based content increases our levels of the chemical oxytocin, which fuels social bonding and trust. According to the American neurologist Paul Zak, when people hear a story that includes struggle, vulnerability, or redemption, their brain chemistry changes along with their willingness to trust and follow the person speaking.

That kind of emotional and imperfect leadership builds the culture of safety (in the sense of truth rather than comfort) necessary for high performance.

Practising safe vulnerability

Vulnerability is not something leaders can choose to experience when the moment feels right. We are already, and always, vulnerable. We are vulnerable when we tell the truth at times when it would be easier and more expedient not to, or when we make promises we intend to keep, though we know this will be hard. The question facing every human being is whether or not we are prepared to admit our vulnerability.

All of us are vulnerable. Every leader I have ever met, at every level of every organisation, is carrying uncertainty. We are all uncertain about the direction to take, the decisions we make, the role we are asked to play. The great leaders I meet are all uncertain about themselves.

Those who thrive don't hide that uncertainty but carry it as integrity (the alignment of their public voice with their private thoughts). They thrive because their followers, seeing that their leader is real, become more real themselves, take more risks, and speak the truth. Vigorous vulnerability is how a culture moves from compliance to commitment.

The real risk isn't vulnerability. It is the absence of it.

I am sure you will have seen this in action. I mentioned before the famous Q&A documents that accompany every change programme and answer none of your questions. I am sure you will have witnessed CEOs delivering motivational quotes straight out of a business bingo manual. We know these things are often rehearsed and never real.

Shackleton reminds us that, in the age of AI, what people will remember won't be the mistakes you made but rather whether you had the courage to stand and own them without spin. Trust does not erode when things change; it erodes when things are hidden or ignored. There is no need to worry about what will happen if we show our vulnerability. The real damage happens when people either believe we have none (in which case they will be sorely disappointed when it eventually gets exposed) or when we try to hide it when it is obvious for all to see.

Our humanity is what makes leadership feel real rather than mechanical. Vulnerability is the only antidote to the culture of simulation in which we are living.

In the next chapter, I want to bring together all the ideas we have discussed so far to give you some practical ways to use them to use them in how you act and behave, over and over, so you can be your most skilful self, whether or not someone is watching.

5

Breaking through the blur

I realised early in my career that I was in a privileged position. I had time to reflect. Every job on the planet is a combination of thinking and acting, but few give you the luxury of time to reflect. Time is important as, while you can think quickly, you cannot, by definition, reflect quickly. There is a skill to learn, though, when you have time to reflect, and it is the skill I call non-luxuriation. You can rejoice in ideas but must realise that, unless they become practice, they are only of value to you. And so it is with my reflections in this book. They are of no use to anybody if they don't translate into some practical outcome.

This is why, at the end of each principle, I will distil the insights from the four previous chapters into a practical leadership toolkit that is designed to help you reflect, but also test, where you stand on this principle. These 'toolkit chapters' are not meant to be read in one sitting but worked through over time. You can revisit them often. As you change, so will your answers.

Let's start with *authenticity over automation*. From exercising agency in tech decisions to embracing strategic vulnerability, this toolkit is designed to translate human-first leadership into daily practices that enable you to break through the fog of AI-supported automation.

DOI: 10.4324/9781003683124-8

As a reminder, the first four chapters built the case for human-centred leadership in the age of AI. Chapter 1 challenged the myth that AI adoption is inevitable and beyond our control. Chapter 2 explored the essential differences between AI and human intelligence. Chapter 3 warned against the creeping influence of synthetic identity. Chapter 4 showed how vulnerability strengthens trust and authority.

The authenticity audit

First, let's start with a self-assessment exercise to evaluate how much your current leadership style reflects the type of authenticity we have been discussing which favours presence over polish.

Use a simple scale from 1 (rarely applies to me) to 5 (always applies to me) to answer each of the following ten statements:

1. I say 'I don't know' when I genuinely don't.
2. I pause before responding in order to signal that I am thinking.
3. My written communications reflect how I speak.
4. I question whether tech tools amplify or replace my values.
5. I have stepped away from using AI in moments that require personal connection.
6. I feel safe showing uncertainty with my team.
7. I have shared my own fears in front of others.
8. I allow space for others to question or disagree.
9. I can distinguish between when I am being real versus when I am playing a role.
10. I've reflected on what makes my leadership voice unique and how often it's visible.

While this exercise is in no way scientific, I would suggest that, if you score between 40 and 50, the likelihood is that you are showing up as human, and people are likely to feel it. If your score is between 30 and 39, you are aware of how you come across but potentially might be filtering too much. Finally, if you score less than 30, you are missing out on the opportunities offered by shifting from performance to presence.

Now, of course, I have no idea what your context is, so these are only ideas, but you may want to reflect on the following in order to build a better picture of how you come across:

- What surprised you about your score?
- Where do you feel the most authentic and why?
- Where do you feel the most filtered and why?
- Would your colleagues agree with your scores, and how do you know?

Decision framework to ensure that AI serves your mission

Given what we covered in Chapter 1, before introducing or using any AI-powered tool, ask yourself the following:

- The alignment test:
  - Does this tool align with our mission, or just with our need to appear relevant and up-to-date?
  - Does it enhance human connection or bypass it?
  - Who benefits most from this tech: my team, my organisation, consultants, or AI providers?
- The displacement check:
  - What human interaction, if any, does this tool replace?
  - If we used no technology here, what would be different, and what might be better?
- The voice filter:
  - If someone read this AI-generated content out loud, would it sound like me?
- The integrity question:
  - Am I delegating a task or outsourcing my responsibility to lead authentically?

Remember, this is not about being anti-technology but about being pro-intention. Asking yourself these questions and answering them doesn't show weakness. It shows maturity. So, encourage your team to hold you accountable. Make space to debrief new tools, gather feedback, and adjust to ensure that any tool you use doesn't disconnect you from the people you lead or the customers you serve.

Conversation rituals that signal realness

When I described authenticity, I made the point of differentiating between just being you, being the skilful you (i.e. your impact is in line with your intent), and being the full you (where you share). Where you stand on that scale will be dependent not on an objective assessment but on what people witness in your everyday actions, the small moments of interaction. For these reasons, here are some suggested habits to embed in your meetings with others.

Again, please, don't be that person at work who embraces every practice they have read about and ends up coming across as weird. So, feel free to adapt or simply disregard any that do not fit.

- Being real: make a point of asking others what is on their mind, stressing this can be work-related or not. This will signal that you care beyond task and are looking for the full person to show up, not just their brains and hands.
- Being unfiltered: make sure you regularly ask others what they think you should be speaking about but don't. This will signal to them that you are willing to hear hidden tensions and bring insights to the surface.
- Calling things out: when a moment feels tense or off in a conversation, don't avoid it. Instead, call it out. Check your assumption by highlighting what you are sensing and ask if anyone else feels the same. This not only has

the advantage of modelling emotional awareness, but it also surfaces and helps clear any unspoken tension.

- Personally follow up: whenever you participate in or witness a difficult exchange, always check privately, immediately afterwards, how the other person is doing. This will reinforce safety and make respect the norm.

Remember to integrate these practices within your context and your way of doing things. They are not performance techniques. They are invitations for honesty and humanity that, over time, create the conditions for people to trust the way you lead as they see the real you.

Weekly reflection prompts

I have always struggled with journaling. I understand that many get a lot from it, but I don't seem to have the patience or discipline to keep at it. However, here is a list of questions for you to ponder at the end of each week, and if you, like me, find journaling too hard, then use them as conversation starters with peers:

- What's one thing I said this week that didn't feel like me?
- Where did I show up fully with no prewritten script?
- What conversation felt most human and why?
- Where did I rely more on polish than on presence?
- What technology did I use this week that disconnected me from someone?
- Where did I resist automation, even when it was offered?
- Who made me feel most like myself this week, and what can I learn from that?
- What moment of discomfort did I avoid, and what did it cost?

If you really want to go the extra step, track your shifts over time and share one insight in your next team meeting.

Commitment practices

Finally, to help you develop your authenticity muscle, here are five simple practices you can easily integrate into your daily routines:

1. Voice memos over emails: once a week, send a voice note instead of an email to someone you lead in order to reintroduce tone, warmth, and spontaneity into remote communication.
2. Handwritten notes: send one personal, handwritten note each month to express gratitude or encouragement or give recognition.
3. Visible learning: share a mistake you made, and what it taught you, in a team forum to normalise imperfection and model personal growth.
4. Offline first: designate one meeting a week that requires no screen, just discussion, to increase focus by returning to eye contact, presence, and silence.
5. Story over statement: each week, replace one data point or announcement with a story that makes it human in order to build connections through emotions.

I hope that the above practices are helpful, but remember that my aim in writing these chapters is not to add polish or another layer to your leadership persona. Instead, it's to strip it back so people can recognise who you really are, because the people you lead have never looked for a perfect leader; they are looking for a real one.

Principle 2

Moral courage over mere compliance

Leaders aren't valuable because they stand tall.
They're valuable because they take a stand.

If our first principle showed us how to show up in order to be seen, our second one is all about standing up for something in order to be followed. In a world shaped by algorithms and efficiency, authenticity without courage can quickly turn into silent conformity. The leap from being seen to taking a stand is the test that separates performative leadership from principled leadership. For a leader, being human is not enough. You have to defend what makes humanity matter.

- Chapter 6: Amid the complexity of human–machine interactions, shaping the conditions under which rules are made rather than just following the rules is the new benchmark of leadership.
- Chapter 7: To succeed, leaders must see ethics as their competitive edge rather than as a constraint.
- Chapter 8: This shift in perception begins with the ability to ask not just what is possible but what is right.

DOI: 10.4324/9781003683124-9

- Chapter 9: It demands the courage to make values-based choices even when they cost power, approval, or speed.
- Chapter 10: As ambiguity increases and policies are yet to be written, character is a leader's only compass.

6

A Greek, a Frenchman, and a Brit walk into a bar and raise it

In France, we mostly joke about the Belgians, so imagine my surprise when I moved to the UK and discovered that all the Belgian jokes were suddenly about the Irish. In Spain, they joke about the Portuguese, and the Portuguese return the favour by joking about the Spaniards. Finland and Denmark like to joke about the Swedes, while the Swedes joke about them and the Norwegians. And, of course, the whole world laughs at the French!

I like to think that these jokes are more a way to relate than to ridicule, but I am an internationalist at heart, and so I prefer jokes that involve more than one country. You know the ones – they always involve at least three people of different nationalities walking into a bar.

That's what came to my mind as I was planning this chapter because, when it comes to unpacking the ethical challenges of AI, I can't think of anyone better than a Greek, a Frenchman, and a Brit, and, when it comes to the bar, well, the drinking establishment will have to wait as I want to show you how AI has raised the bar on the need for ethics. I guess now you understand more about how my brain works as well as why I am not a comedian.

DOI: 10.4324/9781003683124-10

Arguably, ethics should have never been a formality but, with the advent of AI, they become a necessity. When a machine makes decisions, it is not enough for leaders to ask, 'is this factually right?'. They must ask, 'is this morally right?'.

In many ways, ethics are the last human advantage. Algorithms can choose but they can't take responsibility. They can weigh risk but not dignity. They can act but they can't care. They can automate insights, process feelings, and simulate connections, but it is for leaders to do what machines can't. They must stand for something even if, and especially when, it costs them something. That's a tough bar to clear, but it is certainly yours to raise.

I have spent over two decades advising executives and developing leaders, and, while in that time the context and components have evolved, the content and constructs have stayed the same. We still talk about traits and behaviours. We still share best practice. We try to go deep into what is going on and raise our line of sight to see what is really happening. But, somehow, ethics still feel like an appendix to our conversations. I wouldn't say they are a footnote, but they are still typically discussed through the prism of compliance and risk. We have come to believe that ethics live in the organisational values that are monitored by our performance management frameworks.

I am saying neither that people are unethical nor that they see ethics as secondary (remember, despite plenty of evidence to the contrary, I still have unmitigated faith in humanity), but I do know that ethics discussions begin when something has gone wrong.

This can no longer be the case. When technology levels the playing field for speed, knowledge, and output, ethics become the remaining differentiator. Who will be trusted? Who will choose long-term responsibility over short-term gain? Who will make the human calls? The algorithms can't or won't. AI can't weigh trade-offs, wrestle with moral tension, or pause to ask if what's legal is also just, or if what's profitable is also principled. This is the domain of humanity.

Ethics aren't about being nice. They are about making difficult decisions in line with your values. Doing the right thing is never an explicit requirement set out in a job description, nor should it be assumed. Doing the right thing has to be chosen and shown. Being ethical is a strategic strength that brings clarity in a clouded world. The leaders worth following are those who refuse to exploit grey areas, who slow down to listen before acting, who accept accountability without spin, and who have a real voice in a world of artificial ones.

Ethics as character

Let's return to our three bar goers. All three are philosophers, because, if we are going to discuss ethics, philosophy is not a bad place to start, and all three have something important to teach us. Let's start with the oldest one, literally an ancient Greek, Aristotle!

Aristotle thought of ethics as doing the right thing instinctively rather than following rules, frameworks, or codes of conduct. He saw character as being built rather than fixed, with each choice taking you further along the road to virtue until this became second nature.

Apply this to the AI era and it becomes clearer why I decided to use the words 'raise the bar'. This was not because I needed a quip or a bad pun for the title, but because Aristotle is asking leaders to be more than decision makers: he is asking them to become the embodiment of excellence.

Machines do follow rules. They replicate patterns. They optimise outcomes. As we have already discussed, they can even mimic tone and emotions. But they can't develop character. They don't wrestle with consequences the way we should. They don't feel shame, or pride, and, above all, they will never feel any sense of responsibility. They can be trained but they cannot grow.

That's why our ancient Greek still matters. Aristotle's focus is more relevant than ever because, if AI can answer any question, a leader's competitive advantage is formation rather than information. Who you are when no one's watching, what you choose to do when the stakes are unclear, and how you behave when they are high and your values collide, these form the acid test of success. Aristotle called this kind of practical wisdom *phronesis*.

We can no longer afford to see ethics as a kind of abstract philosophy or a course you can take at the end of your MBA to gain a few missing credits. Being ethical is acting in real time, when the stakes are high, the rules are unclear, and the outcome is uncertain, as Shackleton did so effectively in Chapter 4.

You witness it when an executive turns down a lucrative AI solution because it violates the company's core values. Or when a leader prefers to remain without an answer rather than loose themselves in the process of making one up. This kind of wisdom can only be cultivated.

The good news is that character is not a trait you're born with, it is a habit you build and, in a landscape dominated by efficiency and logic, it is the sole domain of humanity. This is where our second bar goer comes in.

Ethics as outcome

If, in our imaginary bar, Aristotle orders a glass of wisdom, our 19th-century Brit, John Stuart Mill, is more likely to be calculating what is on special because, while Aristotle cares about you as a person, Mill cares more about what happens because of you.

Where Aristotle tells us to ask, 'Is this virtuous?', Mill demands that we ask, 'Does this do the most good?'. His utilitarian framework measures morality by its outcomes. His straightforward 'do what does the greatest good for the greatest number' may sound rather simple but, in an AI-driven world where actions scale fast, it is a challenge to keep pace.

As we've already seen, AI doesn't think about outcomes, certainly not in the way Mill did. AI responds and optimises based on what it is asked and told. If you instruct it to prioritise speed, it will. If you tell it to reduce cost, it will. What it won't do is ask 'at whose expense?'. There is no room for outcome. AI will never suffer the social effect of a misaligned output. It is leaders who must take on that mantle.

When our systems are embedded in our decisions (think about hiring, for example) and grow bigger than the people designing them (with their own choices and decision biases), thinking of ethics with Aristotelian intention is not enough. Mill reminds us that ethics must account for impact. A well-meaning tool may be trained to decide but, if its training data reflect historical bias, it doesn't just perpetuate mistakes, it amplifies them. Machines may well be able to self-correct within the parameters of their design, but they can't self-correct for consequences. It takes a human leader to stop and say, 'What are we actually optimising for?'.

Just like Aristotle, Mill is raising the bar. He is asking us to ask whether the actions we take serve people rather than merely follow the right process. That is why we needed to start with authenticity as our first principle, because Mill's utilitarianism requires humility. Whether the decision you take is aligned with your values or ticks all the compliance boxes is irrelevant if it causes harm. The more powerful our tools become, the more important it is to ask, 'Whose good are they serving?'. This takes us to our next patron.

Ethics as encounter

Unlike his two companions, our last philosopher doesn't order anything at the bar, he's too busy chatting with the bartender. Unlike his drinking companions, Emmanuel Levinas, our 20th-century Frenchman, doesn't see ethics as rooted in either virtue or outcomes. For him, ethics begin with encounters. They begin at the moment one person recognises the vulnerability of another. In his world, philosophy is not the 'love of wisdom' but the 'wisdom of love' (how very French).

Where Aristotle looked inward and Mill looked outward, Levinas looks across to see, truly and deeply, other people. This may sound more abstract than thinking of ethics as wisdom or outcomes but, in a world mediated by screens and algorithms, it is more urgent than ever. Because AI doesn't see faces or personalities. It doesn't see fear or anger. It only sees word tokens, subword tokens, character tokens, punctuation tokens, special tokens, sentence-level tokens, number tokens … you get the idea. There is no room for people in AI. It can never witness life, never mind be alive inside.

If we begin to relate to each other the way machines relate to us, the risk is that we exclude empathy from our leadership practices. Levinas reminds us that responsibility is not a policy. It is a way of being in relationships. He shows us that you don't need to agree with someone to be accountable for how your actions affect them. He teaches us that you don't need to know someone to treat them with dignity.

This is where real leadership lives. Ethics live in the discomfort of everyday work where we make enough room to be awake to our own humanity. Ethics live in the questions the algorithms can't ask. Ethics live in the moments of calm questioning rather than fast computation of answers. Ethical leadership is changing pace to explore the nuances of our decisions in a way an algorithm can't. How will this feel to the people being impacted? Am I recognising their needs or just responding to the behaviours? Am I hearing an issue, a problem to solve, or a voice to listen to?

Unlike AI, Levinas doesn't give us answers. Instead, he gives us a stance. That stance is to stay human and steady in our relationships with others, even as our systems encourage us to withdraw from these. Ultimately, the ethical test of leadership isn't whether your decisions were fair or even right but whether someone felt seen.

Ethics as radical humanity's signature

If AI has taught us anything, it's that fast answers are easy to generate, but meaningful decisions are the job of humans. Aristotle told us to build character, Mill told us to count the consequences, and Levinas told us to look each other in the eye. The reason I chose these three philosophers as opposed to the hundreds who have thought and written about ethics is that, taken together, they give us a complete ethical architecture. Ethics are internal, external, and relational, and none can be outsourced to a machine.

As we have already seen, AI will analyse, recommend, and even persuade faster than you can. But it cannot care. It cannot feel regret. It cannot genuinely see a face. It cannot wonder what it missed. It cannot pause before a decision. Just like too many of its proponents, it will only ever focus on 'can we?' to the detriment of 'should we?'.

That's why ethics are an advantage. They are your leadership signature. Your judgement, your character, your ability to hold tension, to absorb ambiguity, and to choose wisely, these form your differentiation. This isn't about moral perfection. Just as with Shackleton, it is about presence and responsibility. It is about having the willingness to stand firm in the middle of uncertainty and complexity and accept accountability.

AI acts faster and more widely than anything we've ever built before, which means that any ethical lapse, however small, will multiply exponentially. Any mistake won't just affect the user. It will affect organisations, markets, and cultures. In this world, great leaders won't be the ones who know the most but the ones most attuned to Aristotle's values, Mill's impact, and Levinas's people-centricity. The bar has been raised. The future won't be about following protocol or meeting targets. It will be about having the courage to question both.

The real test isn't whether your system runs smoothly. It is whether you know why and when to stop it. That's where our next chapter begins, with a literal car crash.

7

Judgement Day

Tempe, Arizona. The day is Sunday. The date is 18 March. The time is just after 22:00.

A woman is crossing a dimly lit road pushing a bicycle, with bags dangling from the handlebars. So far, nothing uncommon.

There is a vehicle approaching. It is a Volvo SUV. It doesn't seem to be slowing down as it approaches the woman. It doesn't swerve as it gets closer either. It hits her. So far, so tragically common.

But the car is driving itself. Inside, the safety operator, meant to monitor and intervene where necessary, was looking down at her phone. Whether it was the thud of the body hitting the front bumper or something else that made her look up, she did so too late. The self-driving car had struck.

Later, at the local hospital to which she was taken shortly after the crash, 49-year-old Elaine Herzberg died from her injuries. Sadly, she wasn't the first person to die in an autonomous vehicle accident, but she is the first recorded pedestrian fatality.

As you would expect, a torrent of blame followed the accident. The system monitoring the Uber vehicle had detected the woman six seconds before impact but failed to classify her correctly. The emergency braking system had been disabled in order to prevent erratic stops. The operator wasn't alert. Uber's protocols had gaps. A year after the accident, Arizona prosecutors decided that Uber had no liability and charged the

DOI: 10.4324/9781003683124-11

back-up driver with negligent homicide. She pleaded guilty and was sentenced to three years' probation.

Most traffic accidents, whether they occur on the road, on the sea, or in the air, are seldom anything other than a collection of errors. These accidents are rarely the result of a technical failure alone and are far more commonly a failure of judgement on everyone's part. No one will ever claim full responsibility because all involved only see their part in an overall system that they wrongly assume will handle the overall coordination.

In Tempe, Arizona, in the six seconds it took to take a life, no one asked the question that could have saved it: should we stop?

The detection system in the car and its AI algorithm didn't fail to see Elaine Herzberg. It simply failed to care. We can easily blame the back-up driver for not intervening, forgetting that so many of us still drive with our phones close at hand, willing to cede control to our cars' warning systems.

The death of Elaine Herzberg is a sad and critical reminder that most accidents happen in a vacuum of judgement rather than a vacuum of maintenance and technological design. As machines make decisions that are faster and further-reaching than ever before, a leader's judgement becomes the sole human override.

It takes courage to slow down and ask questions. It takes character to act in the way you know you must rather than the way you are allowed to.

At the edge of data

This is where the three ethical frameworks I introduced in the last chapter come to the fore. Aristotle taught us that judgement lives in the practice of wisdom. Mill reminded us that good intentions alone don't guarantee good outcomes. And Levinas demanded that we consider the person rather than stop at the process.

In every high-stakes decision, there comes a moment when the numbers stop helping. The self-driving car in Arizona had terabytes of telemetry, object detection logs, and reaction algorithms. But it never had judgement. The data spotted an unknown obstacle rather than saw a human life. They predicted what was likely to happen but never what really mattered. Data cannot wonder what to do. Only a human being could have seen a person as opposed to an object. That's the job of leadership, and it begins where the dataflow ends.

We erroneously claim, 'let the facts speak for themselves'. We demand, 'what do the data say?', in a way that implies these are not only complete but neutral and objective. But remember our first principle. Data are always filtered. They are only generated because someone somewhere decided what to measure, what to ignore, what to prioritise. Even the most advanced systems operate on human assumptions, built into human models. Trusting the artefacts and the composition, without questioning the blueprint, is abdicating your agency to someone else's logic and ethics. It is not leadership.

Our philosophers give us the three key questions that underpin our worth in the face of optimised systems: to what end? At what cost? Optimised for whom?

Of course, most leadership moments are not as high-stakes as testing an autonomous vehicle on public roads. Most of the time, having clarity of intent, the relevant structures for fulfilment, and the resources to execute is enough. It is when efficiency is at its most, well, efficient!

But some decisions cannot and should not be automated. Some decisions demand judgements that cannot be devoid of the ethics machines lack. Some instances are too high-stakes, unclear, ethically ambiguous, and, above all, deeply human. It would be wrong to assume that knowing you are in one of these moments is obvious. It is easy to think that discomfort alone will inform you of the importance of exercising judgement. I would like to believe this is true, but experience tells me that we can approach even the most ethically challenging situations in as mechanical a way as we do everything else.

So, here is a simple test to help you decide when to pause. I call it the judgement threshold:

- High impact: the consequences affect lives, livelihoods, or culture.

- Low predictability: the situation doesn't match any prior pattern or playbook.
- Human stakes: people rather than just processes will experience the outcome.

These don't have to be dramatic moments. They can be mundane. I am sure you will have experienced them: the promotion decision where the high performance is at odds with the organisational values; the tech rollout that will improve efficiency but also damage trust. We may want to defer the decision to the policy or the process, but only our principles can guide us.

Exercising judgement is not about deferring to policy or process. To lead is to stay when you may prefer to retreat. It is to resist the urge to delegate or escalate. These situations need you to lead.

The more automated the world becomes, the more essential it is to surface the decisions only a human should make, and, if you want an easy tip to identify them, they are almost always the decisions no one wants to make.

Judgement under pressure

The leaders with the best judgement are not the ones who decide the fastest. They are the ones who can stay with ambiguity. They are the ones who, to borrow a phrase from Roger Martin, the former dean of the Rotman School of Management, can hold two competing truths in their head at once. Or, to paraphrase my friend Fons Trompenaars, one of the world's top cultural authorities, the ones who reconcile dilemmas rather than opt for the easy option of compromise.

In the age of AI, this ability to exercise judgement may well be the single most important leadership differentiator. Counterintuitively, judgement cannot be judged on outcomes. It is not about making the right decisions or maximising your luck. It starts with self-awareness to answer Aristotle's call, context awareness to conduct Mill's analysis, and social awareness to be able to look the people who will be living with the consequences in the eye, as Levinas urges us to do. So, it can only be built through exposure to and reflection on uncertainty, discomfort, and competing values, especially when things go wrong. This is difficult when urgency is creating pressure to push forward rather than pause.

AI cannot judge. It can only calculate but cannot sense. It can tell you what is right *in* an instant but cannot tell you what is right *for* that instant. The wisest leaders are the ones who can delay a decision, not because they are uncertain but because they respect what is at stake. The key to judgement, therefore, is not perfection but alignment. Integrity is achieved by aligning your values with the choices you make, based on the outcomes you seek.

It is too easy to assume that failures happen because leaders lack data, intelligence, or indeed morals. Most of the time, mistakes and failures happen because leaders feel trapped. They feel the need to rush to act before competitors do, the need to please a board or the court of public opinion. They fear losing credibility. It is in this pressure cooker that good judgement gets cooked. Neuroscience tells us that stress narrows perception. Under threat, the brain no longer sees nuance. Our fight, flight, freeze responses take hold, and leaders default to three modes:

- *Speed*: they make hasty decisions under pressure, which leads to suboptimal outcomes.
- *Ego*: they defend their position, however tenuous, which clouds judgement.
- *Avoidance*: they postpone or avoid difficult decisions, which exacerbates issues.

When this happens, leaders no longer lead. They react rather than respond. The difference between a reaction and a response is judgement. That's why self-awareness is the start. You need to stay human (i.e. responsive, responsible, and reflective). You need to take time to think when you don't feel you have any time. You need to hold out for what is right when everyone else wants to move on and choose the easy path. You need to be able to change your mind when you have staked something on a course of action.

This is what people will follow you for and remember. When the systems fail, when the data mislead, when the right choice carries a cost, people won't remember you were perfect. They will remember your humanity. The fact that you stayed in the moment, took the heat, and still chose to lead is your legacy.

In a world where so much can be outsourced – data, memory, calculation, even communication – judgement remains one of the last acts of leadership that cannot be automated. There is no KPI for wisdom, but people know when it is missing and recognise it when it is there. If ethics are humanity's signature, judgement is yours. It is what others will set as the acid test for whether they should trust and follow you.

You can't fake judgement or speed it up. You can only do your best to seek it relentlessly, to practise it, to stand in the moment present and accountable, to become the kind of leader whose decisions don't just move things forward but move people closer to you.

The tragedy in Tempe isn't just about a car. It is a warning about what happens when we let confidence in systems replace responsibility. This wasn't caused by a lack of data. It wasn't a hardware malfunction or a missing line of code. It was a moment when a human didn't step in, having assumed the machine knew best.

Leadership should never be given over to, or lived within, autopilot. Leadership lives in the discomfort of uncertainty, the weight of knowing that some decisions should never be automated because they're too human.

Throughout this chapter, I have tried to make the case that judgement isn't about having all the answers but is about being willing to stay present long enough to ask the right questions. So, when the next crisis occurs, as it invariably will, the question is, 'Will you be watching the road?', or more importantly if you have dashboards all around you, 'Will you know when it's time to take the wheel?'. Values are only real when they're tested. As a leader, it is when the right decision doesn't go over well and costs you control or popularity that you move from being clear to being courageous. In the next chapter, then, I want to ask the question we hope never to have to answer: 'What will I stand for, when standing for it comes at a price?'.

8

When doing the right thing costs something

Frances Haugen wore the Silicon Valley uniform when she walked into the Senate hearing room. She could have been walking into any meeting room on a tech campus and not have stood out. But, on that October 2021 day, not only did she stand out, but she stood tall despite carrying the weight of ethics on her shoulders. But why was a Harvard-trained data scientist, who had once worked quietly behind the scenes at Facebook to help refine the platform's algorithms, taking a seat before the US Congress?

She was there because, unlike Wolfgang Ritter von Kempelen de Pázmánd, who had needed a bribe from an emperor to reveal the inner workings of his creation, she had decided to pull back the curtain on one of the most powerful companies in the world. She had decided to expose the inner workings of Facebook.

Calm and composed, she testified that Facebook's leadership knew the platform was harming the mental health of children and teenagers. She demonstrated how its algorithms prioritised outrage over truth. She wanted the world to realise that disinformation and division were not bugs in Facebook's system but features of its operating model.

Despite some delegates wearing facemasks, their faces still conveyed keen attention rather than the tension at being in a

DOI: 10.4324/9781003683124-12

crowded room during a global pandemic. Cameras zoomed in. Senators leaned forward. Reporters scribbled. The only person who remained calm and collected was Frances Haugen. Her voice was steady, her manner serene, her stance authoritative. But this was real life. It wasn't a movie where the underdog prevails at the end. Already, outside the room, the online mob were sharpening their memes, ready to aim them at a 'traitor'.

In the days that followed, Haugen was hailed as a hero by some and vilified by others. Facebook questioned her motives, and former colleagues distanced themselves. And, though she sparked a global debate on tech ethics, content moderation, and corporate responsibility, she also lost her career, her anonymity, and her peaceful life, if not her peace of mind.

Doing the right thing almost always costs something.

Most of us are brought up to believe that moral courage will be recognised. We are told that people who stand up get rewarded. But adulthood reminds us of a much more uncomfortable truth. In real life, those who raise their heads above the parapet don't get applauded. They get called disloyal, get punished for not being 'team players', or get branded as naïve. Yet some people, like Frances Haugen, do it anyway, and leaders should do it always.

This chapter is about values and value. It is about the times when the cost of staying silent becomes greater than the cost of speaking up. It is about the times when doing the right thing feels like standing alone. It is about the times when values stop being slogans on a corporate poster and become choices with real consequences.

It is about asking the question leaders must always ask themselves: 'Would I have Frances Haugen's courage to speak out?'.

The quiet calculation

I have interviewed many leaders, from many countries, working across many industries, with many varied backgrounds, and yet most of them have described experiencing, at some stage in their career, an almost identical moment. It is a moment I have come to call the quiet calculation, and I am pretty sure some of you reading these lines will have had such a moment too.

This is not a Frances Haugen moment. It is not one that happens in front of cameras or on the Senate floor. It has often been described to me as happening after working hours, in a dark and empty office, when you sit in front of a keyboard wondering if it is worth sending that email after all. It is invariably a moment when the stomach tightens and the mind races through consequences. Will I lose my job? Will my team turn on me? Am I right or just being righteous?

This is the quiet calculation that determines more ethical outcomes than any formal policy, corporate values, or performance contract ever will. There are three forces that conspire to create these moments of quiet calculation when we find it so hard to act on our morals.

The first, and most obvious, is the fear of consequences. Speaking up means standing out, and standing out means becoming an easier target. I am reminded of a client who wisely informed his team that, in a fight between people and the system, the system tends to win. The risks may not always be as visible as they were in the case of Frances Haugen's whistleblowing, but even subtle resistance (questioning a flawed metric, pausing a harmful project) can threaten reputations, promotions, and even relationships. Humans are social and are, therefore, programmed to fear exclusion from the group.

The second force that leads to quiet calculation is rationalisation. Over the last few years, it has become de rigueur to exhort leaders to become storytellers (I will do so myself in our last principle), but we do well to remember that leaders are already great storytellers, mainly to themselves. We are incredibly adept at rationalising our inaction. We create perfect scenarios to prove to ourselves that it is neither the right time nor the right place to take a stand. We weave perfect yarns to convince ourselves that it is better to change the system from within rather than leave. These mental defences make our inaction seem reasonable and, even if flawed, they bring comfort in tension.

The last of our discomfort triad is cultural complicity. I said that humans are social, but they are also cultured, in the sense that we generally want to share in and live by the values of a group. To do so, we adapt to the values around us. Organisations, like most other social systems, reward obedience. Dissent may not always be punished explicitly, but it is always punished. It should, therefore, not be a surprise that courage has a cost. Performance reviews, team dynamics, and leadership tone all contribute to a culture where people learn that survival sometimes means staying quiet.

The mistake is to think that moral courage is bravery. What I discovered talking to the executives who had faced the quiet calculation is that their moral courage arose from self-interest. They realised that there was a cost to inaction. They found themselves becoming brittle, political, hesitant and knew that, without action, they would eventually lose the trust and respect of their followers. They realised that having moral courage is not so much a test of bravery as an investment in credibility, clarity, and congruence.

There is another reason why taking a stand is hard. Not all ethical tests are as black and white as we often declare them to be. My friend Fons Trompenaars, whom I mentioned in the last chapter, has a way to describe dilemmas. He calls them 'OOH OOH' situations. This stands for on the one hand, on the other hand, where both paths claim moral legitimacy. In such instances, leadership is always uncomfortable as it becomes a question of which value to uphold and which to reject.

Take the example of an executive who has to lay off employees at the end of a year and is weighing up whether to announce these redundancies early to give people time to reflect on their position and make plans, or to wait, so they can fully enjoy the seasonal festivities. What makes these situations so uncomfortable is that we experience them as a forced choice. Our solution is invariably to compromise.

But the key to leadership is to work diligently through the moral morass to articulate not just a decision but an explanation. It is to try to reconcile two extremes so we can achieve both. When both options are desirable and defensible, logic will not guide you. Culture and judgement will. Ethics in an AI age are about being clear what your anchor is in a storm of ambiguity.

The pain is the price

Whatever choice we make will be costly. Doing the right thing rarely feels good in the moment and certainly feels wrong for some time after. There will be criticism. There will be retribution. At worst, there will be exclusion. Moral courage does not shield you from pain.

Moral courage does leave scars and bruises. But, over time, the scar tissue becomes an armour that should harden your resolve rather than your heart. Each hard choice you make increases your capacity to make the next leadership call.

Standing up for something is always hard. Frances Haugen didn't walk out of the Senate committee room into peace and the sunset. She paid a professional, emotional, and personal price. Speaking her truth might have been a one-time act, but it was an act that will echo throughout the rest of her life.

Whether you are prepared to pay the price for making tough choices is what separates compliance from conviction. Leaders with integrity don't act because it's easy, popular, or profitable. They don't refuse to act because there is a personal cost attached. Leadership is about personal cost. If you stand for something but have nothing to lose, why should anyone follow you.

Maybe it was disingenuous of me to start this chapter with the story of a person standing up against a system. It reinforces the idea that moral courage is the domain of the individual and is witnessed in singular, defining moments. The truth is somewhat different. Moral courage is not heroic; it is habitual. It grows in moments of contemplation, when no one is watching, in which leaders make their quiet calculations. It is witnessed when managers call out behaviours and actions even as their colleagues shrug these off. These small moments are the roots of a culture.

The best organisations have learnt to normalise such moments in order to train for them.

They carve out space in leadership conversations to question what is wrong; they celebrate dissent, creating forums to invite this. They elevate those who questioned a decision thoughtfully as much as they promote those who executed it quickly.

These practices are important because they turn courage into an accepted norm rather than treating it as an intimidating act. By doing so, they move courage from an individual heroic stand to a shared cultural habit. Our role as leaders is to build the kind of culture where others can rise to the challenge.

When Frances Haugen walked out of Facebook with thousands of internal documents, she was doing something she wasn't permitted to do in order to do something she felt compelled to do.

In the weeks that followed her whistleblowing, governments launched inquiries. Regulators drafted new legislation. Executives across industries scrambled to audit their internal data practices. But the true test of Haugen's leadership was not what happened publicly. Inside tech firms in particular and other businesses more generally, employees began to surface concerns about algorithmic transparency, mental health impacts, and misinformation trade-offs. One person's moral stand had rippled across an industry.

There is no doubt that courage is personal, but that seldom makes it private. A leader's courage creates the conditions for collective bravery. What is even more challenging for us now is that the systems that most need moral courage today aren't just those built by humans. Increasingly, they are systems powered by machines. As AI-driven processes make more decisions (in hiring, communication, customer service, even healthcare), there is a growing risk that efficiency replaces ethics by default. Maybe this won't happen through malice (remember, I won't give up on humanity), but it is always a consequence of momentum.

So, in the next chapter, I want to explore what happens when organisational culture bends to the logic of automation. I want to understand what gets lost when humans outsource not just actions but their accountabilities. Having looked at cost, I want to explain how leaders can reassert values into value, because what matters most is not just how we fix our computer codes but how we also adjust our codes of conduct.

9

Values and value: A shifting landscape

In late 2019, a startup with fewer than 20 employees took it upon itself to rewrite the rules of privacy. It hadn't been asked to do so by anyone. It hadn't been granted permission to do so by anyone. There was no legal basis for it to do so. And there certainly was no oversight from anyone in the process of doing so.

Instead, the startup's codebase was busy scraping over 3 billion photos from social media profiles, personal blogs, and public websites to create a powerful facial recognition engine capable of identifying anyone, anywhere, from a single image.

This service was pitched to law enforcement agencies around the world as a cutting-edge tool for solving crimes. In a scenario reminiscent of sci-fi movies, all the police had to do was to upload a suspect's photo, and, within seconds, the system would return that person's name and social media profiles, along with an online history.

It is possible to argue that security trumps privacy, and Clearview AI did just that. But privacy advocates, journalists, and even some AI ethicists didn't buy the argument. Instead, where Clearview AI saw a guardian angel, they saw a dystopian genie released from its bottle.

When the *New York Times*[1] broke the story and Clearview AI's record of secrecy, there was an inevitable backlash. Some of

DOI: 10.4324/9781003683124-13

the world's biggest tech firms (Facebook and Google included) issued cease-and-desist letters. Civil liberties groups sounded alarms. Yet Clearview's founder remained unrepentant, forging ahead with an argument that, once stripped of its legal embellishment, could best be summed up as 'If it's on the internet, it's fair game'. While I am not qualified to judge the legality of this argument, I think we can nonetheless agree that this position is morally hollow.

Clearview AI is an extreme example of what happens when ethics and business interests collide. It operates in an area that is ripe for moral debate. In a way, this makes it an obvious example to use when discussing the increasing role of conscience in business. Yet, the fact that it is so clear an example is problematic if it leads you to assume that you are safe from such extreme issues. Clearview is a parable for what happens to all of us when the allure of technological progress blinds us to its consequences.

The five ethical challenges of AI

I chose the story to open this chapter because of the fact that it is such an obvious example of an ethical dilemma that goes beyond philosophical or theoretical musings. It highlights the five recurring blind spots that AI can generate for all of us. These show up not only in our classrooms, boardrooms, and courtrooms but also in the everyday lives of people who never intended to form part of a dataset. In isolation, none of these blind spots are specific to AI. They are identifiable across a large swathe of decisions, both inside and outside business. What is new is that AI has them all, at all times and in all instances, whether we design, use, or are on the receiving end of its systems.

The first ethical issue is the one most people worry most about. It is the issue of consent.

The assumption that, if data are accessible, they are usable is one that does not sit easily with many of us. Most AI systems feed on data that users never explicitly offered. They may have unwittingly clicked a deceptively opaque set of terms and conditions, but there is quite a jump from agreeing to something in order to connect with your friends and family to finding yourself suddenly the object of consumer profiling at best, and facial recognition and 'predictive' policing at worst.

AI systems rely on scraping, mining, and appropriating data in order to feed their ever-hungrier algorithms. In the case of Clearview, the artefacts were billions of facial images, mostly scraped online without the knowledge or indeed permission of those whose faces these were. The assumption that 'public equals permission' is not just a legal issue (one that, it must be said, is far from being settled). It is also a leadership one.

The issue of consent demands that we change our stance from 'is this legal?' to 'is this right?'.

The second ethical issue that AI raises is the issue of transparency.

For most of us, and even apparently for Sam Altman himself if we are to believe his statement 'there is no way to know' that opened this book, AI is a black box. It is an opaque system that makes decisions without explaining how. As users, we are left guessing. In and of itself, this is not an issue. I have, after all, no idea how my car engine actually works. Yet, in the case of AI, how can we accept accountabilities that are buried deep inside technical complexity.

In the case of Clearview, even its clients didn't fully understand how it worked and yet they were prepared to make decisions on individuals' freedom (literal life and death decisions in some countries) without any ability to fully explain the results. Clearview never disclosed how matches were made or verified and certainly never gave the public any insight into the algorithm's performance metrics. How can you scrutinise something that is hidden from view?

The issue of transparency demands that we change our stance from 'is this accurate?' to 'is this interpretable and inspectable?'.

The third ethical issue is one we have encountered in pretty much every single example I have shared in this book so far. It is the issue of accountability.

When an AI tool misidentifies a person, taking the case of Clearview, who answers for the harm? Is the developer accountable, or is it the user? Could it just be the algorithm? Can

Clearview legitimately deflect liability on the basis that it only created a tool, the use of which it cannot be held accountable for? Let's take a somewhat less dramatic example. Who is responsible when a hiring algorithm rejects a candidate? Is it the engineer who designed the code or the vendor who sold the system? How about the executive who acted on the decision?

When no one is clearly accountable, ethics dissolve into plausible deniability. So, as AI obscures the chain of decision-making, the issue of accountability demands that we change our stance from 'what can I get away with' to 'what should I never let go of?'.

After consent, transparency, and accountability issues comes bias. This is possibly the most discussed ethical issue when it comes to AI.

Many AI systems amplify societal inequalities embedded in their training data. In facial recognition, this has led to disproportionately high error rates for people of specific ethnicities. This is not just the case in criminal justice decisions but has also been found to happen in hiring and beyond. AI cannot do anything but reflect the world it has been trained on. That means it is prejudiced too.

It is not enough to see this as a problem that better training will resolve. It is only partly an input issue. The issue of bias demands that, as leaders, we change our stance from 'can the system be made fairer?' to 'how do I engineer fairness into my decision-making?'.

Finally, we have the last and, in the case of the Clearview saga, possibly the most chilling ethical concern raised by AI. This is the issue of oversight.

Clearview grew largely in the shadows, before any regulations were established to oversee its system's use by agencies. This is worrying in a democratic system but not uncommon in tech. Startups in general, and technology startups in particular, move fast (and take pride in 'breaking things'). This creates a deep issue for leaders. While innovation will always outpace regulation, we should never let it outpace reflection. If we do, then what's the point of us? Our role as leaders is to ask three questions: what do we owe each other as humans? What kind of culture do we want to create? Who are we trying to protect or expose?

These five dimensions (consent, transparency, accountability, bias, and oversight) are not abstract principles. They are the pressure points where AI's promise and humanity's needs collide.

The point this second principle, 'moral courage over mere compliance', makes is that these issues demand more than technical solutions. They demand radically human leadership willing and able to wrestle with the trade-offs that cannot be delegated to a machine.

Countering the ethical drift

Because these ethical dilemmas are so embedded in the systems we use, the danger is not of one big compromise but, rather, thousands of minor ones. Ethicists call this 'ethical drift'. It is the gradual erosion of values through a series of small, seemingly reasonable decisions, a kind of death by a thousand cuts. That's the most dangerous thing about AI's ethical challenges. It's not that they are hard to spot. It is that they often don't look like ethical challenges at all. This is why we need a mindset for ethics and the courage to apply it.

Imagine applying the three ethical lenses offered by Aristotle, Mill, and Levinas to Clearview AI's actions. Aristotle would ask, 'Is this company practising justice, moderation, and courage or just financial opportunism masked as utility?'. Mill would have asked, 'Do the supposed benefits of public safety outweigh the widespread erosion of privacy?'. And Levinas would have added the most uncomfortable question of all: 'Did Clearview see the people in the photos as others with dignity or simply as data points?'.

These lenses are a forward-looking framework every leader can use when evaluating their own AI partnerships, tools, and strategies. Every AI decision doesn't have to be unethical, but every decision is an ethical choice.

Just as we identified in the last chapter, ethical leadership isn't about identifying right versus wrong but about wrestling with right versus right. AI is full of such dilemmas. It is too easy to paint companies as evil or deceitful. It is far harder to ask ourselves the important questions.

For example, in the case of Clearview, isn't it fair to argue that facial recognition software that prevents crime is worth the loss of privacy in public spaces? When put like this, Clearview's endeavours perhaps seem far more reasonable and worthy. How about, though, when we have to ask ourselves whether predictive tools should be used to identify employees at risk of leaving, even if this intrudes on their privacy, or whether we should prioritise transparency, or whether we should protect proprietary AI models from being reverse engineered?

Regardless of your personal stance, these aren't theoretical questions. They're active tensions that are playing out, or should be playing out, in every business today. They are the issues only leaders who have the courage to reason through paradox, make values visible, and accept accountability for whichever path is chosen will be able to navigate successfully. Ethical leadership in the AI age is not about having the answers to all the problems but, instead, about having a principled process to find them.

Clearview AI didn't go away. Despite legal challenges, regulatory fines, and widespread ethical concerns, the company found new clients (especially among law enforcement agencies under pressure to deliver results). There are few incentives to slow down in the tech world and too many people unwilling to wonder if they should when they know they can. It would seem that, in an AI-powered world, it is easy to defer values.

Even if no one actively sets out to cause harm, the absence of intentional design makes the default position one of silence or, worse, plausible deniability. This is why I want to offer you the opportunity to move from reflection to action in our next chapter. Having explored the moral terrain and examined the ethical pressures across it, it is time to find the tools to respond.

Note

1 If you want to know more about Clearview AI and the specific implications this case raises, I can highly recommend *Your Face Belongs to Us: The Secretive Startup Dismantling Your Privacy* (Simon & Schuster, London), written by Kashmir Hill, the reporter who broke the story.

10

Clearing the path

As you might have guessed from the contents page and the name of each principle, I am rather partial to alliteration. I like the rhythm of words. However, I have worked with enough editors over the years to know that alliteration should not get in the way of elucidation (that's more assonance than alliteration, but I did my best)!

The point is that the phrase 'moral courage over mere compliance' wasn't chosen just for the purpose of rhetoric. Organisations rely on compliance. They exist because of a need to deliver the right product or service at the right price, quality, and time in a repeatable fashion. This takes compliance. Compliance, though, is passive, and I have made the case so far throughout this book that we can only lead if we reclaim our agency. Compliance is not agency.

Mere compliance is activity, whereas moral courage demands purposeful action. That is why this chapter distils the insights we have covered in Chapters 6–9 into a practical leadership toolkit to help you develop the habit of exercising moral courage at all times, in your context, rather than in extremis, at times of crisis.

As was the case with Chapter 5, I did not create these tools and tips as commandments. I share them with you solely in the hope that they will help you reflect on your practice and start conversations with others on theirs.

DOI: 10.4324/9781003683124-14

The ethical reflex check

This is a short diagnostic to help you understand how much of your ethical thinking has become embedded in the way you work. It works on a simple scale from 1 (rarely) to 5 (always).

1. I pause before making major decisions to reflect on values, not just outcomes.
2. I can articulate the ethical tension behind at least one decision I made this week.
3. I have discussed a moral dilemma with my team in the past month.
4. I ask, 'What matters?' alongside 'What works?'.
5. I've pushed back on a decision because it felt wrong, even if at first sight it looked right.
6. My team would say I raise ethical concerns openly.
7. I know which of our organisational values I would refuse to compromise.
8. I've called out instances when 'legal' was used to mask 'ethical'.
9. I review all high-impact decisions through the lens of everyone impacted.
10. I take responsibility for a decision even when I could attribute it to others.

I am not sure there is much of a scoring scale with ethical questions to show you are either one thing or another. The key is always in the reflection. My advice is to look for patterns where you score the highest and lowest to understand how you apply ethics in practice and identify where you stayed silent and why.

The judgement threshold diagnostic

In Chapter 7, I introduced the judgement threshold framework to assess when your leadership requires human rather than automated judgement.

It comprises only three questions (which recall some of the ethical philosophies we discussed). They are simple questions, but, when they are used as part of conversations with stakeholders or personal reflection, their answers will help you unearth the key ethical implications of your choices.

1. Are the consequences high impact (i.e. lives, livelihoods, or culture will be affected)?
2. Is the context low predictability (i.e. there is no clear precedent or algorithmic certainty)?
3. Are the stakes human (i.e. real people, rather than just systems, will be affected?)?

If you answer yes to at least two of the questions, the situation you are in has crossed the judgement threshold and requires you to pause for deeper reflection, discussion, and ethical framing of your decision.

In my experience, these are also useful questions to use with teams to counter the energy and pace that might lead to groupthink and generate ethical blind spots.

The 'right versus right' compass

I will not be able to do justice here to such a complex topic as ethical dilemma reconciliation. For that you should look up, listen to, and/or read anything by Fons Trompenaars! However, in my practice, I have come to rely on a simple mechanism to calibrate my moral compass in situations where there are not just one but two right answers.

First, name the dilemma to articulate the tension. I prefer Fons's 'on the one hand/on the other hand' terminology to phrase them rather than 'versus', which implies an opposition that is unhelpful given we are trying to achieve both, but, for the sake of space, in the examples in the table I have used vs.

Once you have articulated the tension, create a reflective prompt that will force you to think about how to achieve both sides of your ethical equation.

In some cases, you will find that you haven't got an ethical dilemma at all, but instead there is a difficult decision to be made as one side is right and one is just wrong. But, in cases where both sides are indeed right, the reflective prompt will help you stage powerful conversations with your team.

Tension	*Reflective prompt*
Truth vs. loyalty	How can I protect someone while remaining truthful?
Individual vs. group	Can I ensure that both the team and the individual benefit and minimise the cost for all?
Short term vs. long term	What decision builds capability today while also serving our interests five years from now?
Justice vs. mercy	How can I ensure fairness is compatible with compassion in this case?

This compass will not give you the 'right' answer but, like all good compasses, it should point you in the right direction.

Weekly reflection prompts

- When did I choose speed over judgement this week?
- Where did I sense a conflict but move forward anyway?
- Whose voices did I not hear when it came to making decisions that impacted them?
- What unresolved decision still lingers in my mind?
- When did I act from courage instead of compliance?

Making ethics visible

To build a culture where moral courage is the norm, you must make ethical enquiry normal.

- Begin your team meetings with the question 'Is there anything we're not seeing?' to surface any ethical blind spots.
- Share a time when you got a decision wrong and what it taught you, to create a climate of safety around ethical concerns.

- Praise people not just for outcomes but also for how they held to values.
- Ask 'What's the right thing here?' when designing or discussing a process so as to make it a legitimate question for others to ask.

Commitment practices

Here are five practices to embed moral courage in how you lead.

1. Bring ethics to the surface: once a month, dedicate ten minutes in your team meetings to exploring one ethical dilemma (it can be real or hypothetical).
2. Moral memo: every quarter, write a short internal note about a value you saw upheld in a tough moment to reinforce the culture. You can thank the person in the moment, of course, but there is value in a broadcast quarterly habit.
3. Invisible impact log: track one decision each month that has benefited or protected someone who will never know it. Reflect on why it mattered to do it despite this.
4. Reverse accountability review: ask your team anonymously, 'Where have I stayed silent when I should have spoken up?'.
5. AI audit partner: it is always hard to speak against ideas or consensus, so nominate one person in your team to play devil's advocate every time a new AI discussion takes place. This will ensure that assumptions are challenged and consequences are raised. Rotate the role over time so the person you pick doesn't become associated with the concerns.

It is hard to argue with the notion that AI is further accelerating a world that was already spinning fast. But it is much harder to argue that we should let AI decide on the direction this world should go in. It can't. That's our role, and, while evidence suggests that humans are born with an innate predisposition towards moral judgement and behaviour, we do not come into this world with a fully formed moral compass. Social, environmental, and cultural factors all contribute to our ethical fine tuning. This is why ethical leadership is so important in creating the conditions in which AI is put at the service of humanity.

It may be a test of courage for people to act when the world is not watching, but, for leaders, when it comes to ethical challenge, your test of courage is to lead when no one else is.

Principle 3

Intuition over instruction

Leaders aren't valuable because they follow the rules.
They're valuable because they know when to break them.

Principle 1, authenticity over automation, was about showing up. Principle 2, moral courage over mere compliance, was about standing up. With this third principle, we look at how we can move forward when the path is unclear. The world of AI is a world in which data dominate. The danger for leaders is that over-reliance on instruction risks making them predictable, reactive, and, ultimately, replaceable. What differentiates humanity from machine intelligence is perception. The best leaders can sense what data can't see.

- Chapter 11: to lead intuitively, leaders must reclaim instinct, sharpened by experience, as a source of intelligence.
- Chapter 12: this begins with understanding how and when data mislead or obscure, as well as when and how human discernment can fill the gaps.
- Chapter 13: this needs us to reframe what is messy and ambiguous as a creative force for transformation rather than a liability to eradicate.

DOI: 10.4324/9781003683124-15

- Chapter 14: we need to become comfortable leading without a manual in a world that moves before the outcome is known.
- Chapter 15: ultimately, we will need to cultivate a mindset where we trust our inner signals against an onslaught of external noise.

11

Beyond data: Intuition and instinct

There is something poetic about the word 'fall'. It evokes the idea of transformation so much better than 'autumn' does. It is no surprise then that, unlike the Brits who abandoned it towards the end of the 17th century, Americans decided to keep it. They have, after all, some of the most beautiful fall displays, and nowhere more so than in Vermont.

Yet, on a warm Vermont September afternoon in 1848, it was our understanding of the human mind, not nature, that was about to be transformed.

Phineas Gage, a 25-year-old railroad foreman, was preparing explosives to clear rocks for the Rutland & Burlington Railroad, when he accidentally triggered a blast. He hadn't had a chance to clear the site. His crew could only watch as a 13-pound iron tamping rod shot upward like a javelin, entered his cheekbone, passed behind his left eye, and exited through the top of his skull.

Incredibly, Gage didn't die. In a matter of weeks, he had recovered, with most of his cognitive functions intact. He could walk and talk. He could remember and count. But something fundamental had changed.

His friends no longer recognised him as the old Phineas Gage. The man who had led his crew with calm authority just

DOI: 10.4324/9781003683124-16

weeks earlier was now more emotionally erratic. His capacity to plan, weigh trade-offs, and make wise decisions seemed to have disappeared along with his left eye.

Gage fell to the ground on this fateful fall day but, just like Vermont's leaves, he has reappeared every year since. Whether on the pages of psychology manuals, in academic papers, magazines, or, yes, as here, in leadership books, every year his story is retold. Unfortunately, as is so often the way, the more the story is shared, the more exaggerated it becomes. The changes to Gage's personality were not as extreme as people need them to be to make their point. I have always been puzzled by this need for literary dramatisation, especially since, as was the case with Shackleton, the lesson to be learnt from Phineas Gage's real life is dramatic enough: namely, that the emotional brain is essential to decision-making.

Neuroscientists now know that what changed Phineas Gage was the damage the iron bar caused to the part of the brain where emotion, memory, and social judgement converge. His mutilated ventromedial prefrontal cortex had made him a whole lot less human without making him any less rational.

Phineas was the living embodiment of the case we have made in our last ten chapters. Leadership isn't made up of logic alone. When our world turns upside down, when every option carries equal weight, when every forecast looks uncertain, it is our emotions that enable us to move forward. When data run out, it is the integration of memory, experience, and feelings, the very thing Phineas had lost and which we call intuition, that spurs us on.

The man who stood up after the blast was, to all intents and purposes, an AI version of Phineas Gage. With only logic as his guide, he could not navigate complexity. With only facts at his disposal, he could no longer understand what they meant. We know the limitations. We have discussed them already. Artificial intelligence may be able to process vast amounts of information, detect patterns invisible to the human eye, outperform doctors, and defeat chess grand masters but, when the inputs are morally equivalent, emotionally charged, or contextually ambiguous, it loses its power.

Phineas Gage is not yet another warning about the limitations of AI though; instead, he is the embodiment of something far more dangerous than even his explosives.

In our rush to digitise everything from performance metrics to hiring decisions, via strategy models and communications, we have begun to treat information as wisdom and outputs as insight. Just as Phineas did, we are losing our human advantage. If we are to stand any chance of meeting the challenges of AI, whether it is our ability to be authentic, as Principle 1 demands, or our ability to hold moral tension, as Principle 2 dictates, we need to reclaim the power of intuition.

Intuition, that niggling feeling we get in the pit of our stomach, that tingling, uncomfortable sensation we get at the back of our neck, isn't a bug of human judgement. It is the feature that makes humans complete, AI incomplete, and radical leadership possible.

The intelligence of instinct

We often think of intuition as being rather vague or overly soft. We describe it as a hunch or a feeling that we can't quite explain. That's what makes it so easy to ignore in favour of the logic we can deconstruct. But research into how our brains make decisions tells us that we should hold back from dismissing intuition altogether. We are mistaken if we dismiss it as the opposite of reason. In fact, intuition isn't just what allows us to reason, it is what enables us to do so at speed when clarity and precedent are missing.

The neuroscientist Antonio Damasio, through his clinical work with patients who, like Phineas Gage, had suffered damage to the part of the brain where emotion and reason intersect, has shown how, while they could recite facts and outline complex trade-offs, without intuition as their internal guide, they were stuck in a kind of logical paralysis. They couldn't decide.

Imagine looking at an empty calendar: which day will you choose for your meeting? With everything being equal, only instinct can offer the answer.

Damasio called this the 'somatic marker hypothesis'. It is the idea that our instinctive reactions, driven by our emotional and bodily responses, act as decision-making filters when information is insufficient or in conflict.

Whether we are aware of it or not, as leaders, we do this every day. We can walk into a meeting and sense the mood in the room before a single word is even spoken. Faced with risk, we hesitate merely because of a feeling in our guts. We spot potential in people or decide who to trust, not just because of some data or information, but also because of a sense, a spark.

Of course, we dismiss all this as guesswork. We worry that we are being biased or subjective. But should we really dismiss our lived experience? Should we reject the recognition we have honed through trial and error and our interactions and stored as emotional memory? We do well to remember that intuition integrates the logical with the personal, and the analytical with the moral, to help us connect.

At a time when AI floods us with data, intuition becomes a necessity. It is the vital compass that draws on our personal history (comprising our doubts, fears, and prior mistakes) to help us find answers when all options are equal. It is the ability to sense when you cannot know.

Crucially, intuition is embodied. It is the body having a dialogue with the mind. It is processed in the nervous system as well as the brain. That's why we talk about feelings in our chests and our guts. This is not a metaphor. It is sensory information, shaped by past associations and subconscious pattern recognition, travelling to our brain via our vagus nerve (the main nerve of the parasympathetic nervous system that controls body functions such as digestion, heart rate, and the immune system).

It is this 'embodied cognition' that helps us sense danger, hesitate, or feel something is off, even when we have no data. If we dismiss our bodies' signals, we are no better than machines, with no emotional memories to shape our judgements. Having no fear, relief, longing, guilt, or hope may feel easier, but it will never feel right. We will be able to process information but never discern insights, nor care about outcomes.

Instinct is not irrational. It is what differentiates real from artificial intelligence. It is what kicks in when logic stops. It is what brings meaning to knowledge. For something to mean anything, it requires emotions. That is why intuition is key to radical humanity. It cannot be another trait to be ticked off on a leadership competency model but instead serves as an anchor that orients leaders in uncertainty. Just as Principle 1 gave us authenticity, and Principle 2 morality, intuition is our third decisive human edge.

Amplifying intuition

Intuition is what differentiates us as leaders. While operators and managers optimise execution, it is leaders who must navigate through the unknown. We don't have to go that far back in our history to see this at play.

Remember the Covid pandemic? Leaders, throughout the world, had to make decisions when every forecast was foggy, every course of action seemed equally risky, every outcome appeared plausible, and the numbers weren't helping. While we like to think of decision-making as a clean process, Covid was a reminder that it is rarely tidy. It is in these moments, when reaching for more data is impossible, that we must reach inside. It is at these times, when we face risks, contradictions, and legal and economic ambiguities, that we must look for what feels right and have the courage to act without the data we can't get.

I often describe the reality of the experience of leadership as driving down a motorway at 200 miles an hour, in a deluge of rain, with broken windscreen wipers. It is about decision-making, under pressure, with incomplete information and disproportionate consequences. This is why we must learn to feel our way forward responsively and know not so much when to switch between logic and intuition but when to amplify the role intuition plays in our logic. There are three markers that indicate the need to shift from what is known technically to what is felt viscerally.

The first is the 'diminishing return on data'. While data can create a sense of control over events, they don't always lead to greater clarity. In fact, as leaders gather more information, they often find that drowning in inputs obscures rather than illuminates. Paralysis by analysis is evasive as well as inefficient. Amplifying intuition requires us to stop and move away from seeking more measures in favour of asking better questions.

The second marker is when internal conflict joins external pressures. There is a tension every leader comes to experience, and this is the tension between competing values. It is at times when we experience legitimate but often conflicting demands from external stakeholders that our internal values collide. Just as with the Covid example when discussions centred on economy versus health, control versus freedom, protection, and truth, we feel unable to act. These are the ethical dilemmas we discussed in Principle 2 that demand emotional responses. Amplifying intuition requires us to stop and ask what we can live with in order to make hard choices.

The third and final marker is the irreversible consequence. I have always found Jeff Bezos's description of one-way- and two-way-door decisions elegant. He argues that, just like doors, some decisions are easy to walk back through. They are easy to reverse. These are the two-way doors. If you change a font on the website and traffic slows, it is easy to change it back. There are other decisions, however, that, once taken, have the potential to reshape your strategy, your culture, or even your identity. These are your one-way doors with irreversible consequences. They are the decisions that you know will be remembered and repeated so often that they will define your legacy. These are the moments when leaders must ask what is important here. Amplifying intuition requires us to stop and bring values to the fore.

Leading with intuition is about caring, which is something no machine can ever do, as caring is about understanding the moral weight of an imperfect choice. As one of my clients once told me: 'The truth is that 80% of the time you will get it right. The hard task is to learn to forgive yourself for the 20% of the time you didn't'. We will come back to this in Chapter 14 as, if we are to rely on intuition over automation, we will have to learn to build the resilience that allows us to cope with regret.

But, before we do this, we must understand both what data AI cannot provide us with and what value the chaos of not knowing brings. Phineas Gage reminds us that, just like AI, it is possible for your intellect to work, your memory to function, your problems to be solved, and your sentences to make sense, but what lies at the heart of making us effective is our messy humanity. It is that mystical sixth sense we call intuition.

As AI tools become more embedded in our decision-making, we risk surrendering what *will* happen to systems that have no capability to understand what *should* happen. Welcome to the strange loop of 'should have' and the Yoda principle.

12

The Yoda principle

Whether freeze, flight, or fight, our responses to fear are rooted in avoidance. From oracles to horoscopes, from palm reading to forecasting, our desire to understand what the future holds knows no bounds. To know and to thrive are integral to the human condition.

No wonder, then, that in 2011, when Google launched its Flu Trends, it was hailed as a breakthrough. Finally, we could peer into the future and thereby avoid the worst. In order to estimate flu activity in real time, Google engineers designed a way to analyse billions of search queries. If you looked up 'flu symptoms', searched for 'flu cures', or tried to locate your 'local pharmacy', you became a data point in Google's endeavour to protect humanity. Back when 'big data' had not yet been replaced by AI in the corporate buzzword hall of fame, Flu Trends was a glimpse into a predictable, manageable, and finally controllable future, thanks to analytics.

Being able to outperform traditional disease surveillance methods weeks earlier than the norm was seen as the start of something truly revolutionary. Health experts, policymakers, and, of course, tech enthusiasts declared it the future of predictive public health. However, the optimism didn't last.

That year, Google Flu Trends overestimated flu prevalence by more than 140 per cent. In fact, from August 2011 to September 2013, it over-predicted in 100 out those 108 weeks.[1]

DOI: 10.4324/9781003683124-17

The model had failed to factor in the quirks of humanity. By harnessing our desire for knowing, it had forgotten our fear of suffering. Media coverage, public anxiety, and cold-weather hypochondria had inflated the data. The model was confusing spikes in panic-driven symptom searches with actual infections. As a result, public health responses were distorted, credibility in tech-driven forecasting was shaken, and trust in digital prediction took a hit.

This wasn't a mistake or an error. The model functioned exactly as intended. What made it fail was its inability to grasp what truly mattered: human context. It never accounted for our humanity. Google Flu Trends failed not because it lacked data but because it lacked the discernment necessary to distinguish signals from signs, thereby making confident decisions on faulty grounds.

Where Phineas Gage was a reminder that intuition is a human advantage, Google Flu Trends reminds us of the hidden traps in data-driven decision-making. It is a warning that dissociating intuition from automation leads to suboptimal, at best, and dangerous, at worst, decision-making.

The Yoda principle

There are many scenes from *Star Wars* that can be called famous. In fact, there are probably as many as there are fans of the franchise. I am well aware that I am on shaky ground when identifying such a scene as the veracity of my claim can never match the voracity of the fan base. So, let me just say that there is a scene in *The Empire Strikes Back* that has become a favourite of mine for its prescience in warning us of the pitfalls of forecasting.

In it, Luke Skywalker is training with Yoda near a cave. As he senses danger, he turns to the Jedi master to ask what he would find were he to enter the cave. Yoda's answer, 'what you take with you', is the lesson Google Flu Trends had failed to learn. It is the lesson Voltaire had already tried to teach us when he declared Vaucanson's duck a mirror to humanity. That lesson is that predictions made by data are only a reflection of the choices we have made.

It's not hard to understand the appeal of predictions. In uncertain times, data provide reassurance. But we do well to remember that, when we enter the cave, we enter it with everything we bring. Underneath the illusion of clarity lie all of our assumptions, exclusions, and framing. Just as Phineas Gage, after his accident, could still perform logical tasks but could no longer make meaningful decisions, when AI relies on data, devoid of emotion, memory, and judgement, it is rational yet blind.

As we discussed in Chapter 2, despite their uncanny ability to display a kind of mathematical certainty that seemingly leaves little room for doubt, data systems are shaped by human choices at every level. Humans decide what gets collected, how it is labelled, who interprets it, and how it's deployed. This creates a kind of 'bias layer cake'.

At its base sits our input bias layer. This bias occurs at the data collection stage (what we called the artefacts of AI's ABC in Chapter 2). Historical data may reflect decades of exclusion or preferences; predictive algorithms such as the ones underpinning Clearview AI's policing information may have been fed records that reflected certain policies. When the initial data are biased, the insights will be too.

On top of this layer sits another one that reflects structural biases that are present throughout the system's design (our blueprint). Invariably, at the design stage, decisions will be made about what gets optimised, how and by whom success is defined, and what gets prioritised (e.g. speed or accuracy). These choices will distort outcomes.

Our final layer, present at what we have called the composition level, is the output bias layer. Even the most rigorously engineered systems, of which Google Flu Trends was one, can produce biased results if their outputs are interpreted carelessly. If we don't understand the logic applied to generate these outputs, our decisions will be flawed, not because the technology itself is inherently flawed but because the artefacts, blueprint, and compositions didn't include enough variation.

There is an additional risk we need to be aware of that also demands a reframing of our automated predictions. It is a risk brought about by the feedback loop of AI-generated content being used to train future AI systems.

Given that an increasing volume of text, images, audio, and video on the internet is produced by machines, less of what AI learns is grounded in human reality. Instead, it becomes a system that learns from itself. This synthetic data feedback degrades the quality, accuracy, and reliability of any AI outputs, never mind predictions. Each cycle of retraining introduces more abstraction and less grounding in human experience, multiplying the risks of the hallucinations we refuse to call mistakes.

For leaders, this leads to decisions being informed by systems trained on recycled simulations of what machines think human insight looks like. It doesn't just become harder to swallow the layer cake of biases: it also becomes harder to see the layers. Over time, a kind of synthetic certainty replaces authentic understanding.

Just as with humans, when machines inbreed, they decay. Just as with human intelligence, when artificial intelligence becomes self-referential, it ceases to be intelligent. The Yoda principle reminds leaders that AI outputs, however sophisticated, should never be treated as facts but as starting points for critical enquiry. That is the other lesson we should take from the Yoda principle.

Humanising analytics

The Yoda principle is not just about understanding the biases we bring to the dataset, it is also about understanding the narrative we build around it. What Yoda was telling Luke is that he was bringing his fears and lived-in experience along with him into the cave. He imagined danger and enemies before even setting foot in it.

We shape reality as much as it shapes us. If you hear a noise at night, your state of mind will decide whether it is the wind or a burglar before you have ever had a chance to check.

Predictive analytics such as Google Flu Trends don't have lived experience. For the machine, every data point is a summary. It is a compressed version of reality stripped of texture, context, and emotion.

The risk of automation is that the human story gets lost behind the numbers, leading to erroneous interpretation. While data can measure behaviour, they cannot decode intention, understand emotion, or experience the context they are asked to predict. We must learn to humanise analytics by integrating stories into systems, otherwise we run the risk of mistaking metrics for meaning.

In the case of Google Flu Trends, billions of search queries were counted, categorised, and processed, yet none were understood. The model was elegant. The mathematics were sound. The output was persuasive. But Google Flu Trends mistook fear for flu. Humanising analytics is not so much about refining our predictive model as it is about embedding the practice of listening into our analysis. Tracking what people click on or search must be accompanied by an enquiry into their fears, hopes, and needs.

Unlike algorithms, public health experts gather narrative insights alongside data points. They ask why people are suddenly searching for flu symptoms rather than simply counting how often they do so. Had they brought narrative into the data (via interviews, feedback, qualitative listening), Google Flu Trends analysts might have uncovered a different picture. They might have realised that endless news reports about the flu, alongside anxiety, were driving search behaviour more than actual symptoms. In 2011, it was left to human experts working for health bodies around the world to get closer to the reality of the spread of the virus than the machine ever did.

As leaders, we must learn from automation's blind spots. We must build space for conversations about the data rather than letting the data begin the conversation. We must be willing to explore surprising trends. We must be willing to go deeper into the bias layer cake to unpick the data. We must question the reasons why, rather than blindly accepting the numbers.

It is tempting to let machines do the sensing. Their ability and capacity to do so seem so much larger than ours. Yet sense-making in its true sense is a human capability. It requires the dataset to be overlaid with lived stories and the numbers to speak in the voices of the people from whom they were extrapolated. Humanising analytics doesn't mean replacing numbers with anecdotes or data with drama. It simply means weaving our intuition and our humanity into our automated prediction. It is about learning to lead with both empathy and data, letting qualitative insights into decision-making. Lived experience must itself be elevated to become a vital data point.

The belief that the more we measure the better we understand is deeply flawed. Understanding is a function not of quantity but of sagacity. We must resist the temptation to let data take the place of judgement, not out of some misguided fear of automation but because of a deep understanding that, when it comes to decision-making, scrutiny and perspective are more important than precision and speed.

In an age where AI predictions are positioned as a solution to many of our problems, it is easy to assume that more input will equal better outcomes, but, as Flu Trends has shown, data are never neutral. They are framed by the questions we ask and shaped by the systems we build, as well as the stories we leave out. For leaders, this means that we risk acting on metrics that ignore reality.

Google Flu Trends is not a warning that we should abandon data. It is a cautionary tale of what happens if we do not deepen our relationship with them. We need to interrogate their origins. We must challenge their blind spots. Above all, we need to pair data with our intuition. We are often told that we must become more 'data literate', but what the intuition over automation principle highlights is that becoming data literate is not enough. Radical humanity demands us to be 'data wise'.

The more data we get, the more convinced we become that ambiguity is a problem to eliminate. Yet the discomfort, contradiction, and emotional flux that are the hallmarks of uncertainty are not liabilities to be hidden. They are the sources of creative energy on which organisations thrive.

Having reclaimed our intuition and been warned of the dangers of automating our decision-making, we are faced with a more daunting truth. That truth is that leadership isn't clean. It is chaotic, improvised, and full of doubt and nuances that defy neat algorithmic interpretation. It is time for us to value our human messiness because the leaders who thrive are the ones who are willing to get their hands dirty. This is where we go next, 'go' being the key word.

Note

1 'Google's flu project shows the failings of big data', *Time*, 13 March 2014.

13

The messy leader

'Your enemy's key point is your own key point.' If you think this sounds like something Sun Tzu would have written in *The Art of War*, or even another of Yoda's principles, you are mistaken. However, if you are reading this book sequentially and remember Chapter 4, let me tell you that this isn't a quote I can attribute either. This is, in fact, an example of what is known as a 'Go proverb'.

Go proverbs are traditional sayings designed to help Go players find the best moves throughout the game. Were it not for the word 'enemy' – which, as I covered right at the outset, I don't think AI is – it could be the tagline for what I call being alive inside.

AI's key attributes shine a bright light on our own key differentiators. It is relentlessly tidy, so we must be messy. It is automated, so we must be intuitive. This is one of the reasons I wanted to focus on the game Go, because it is more about intuition than calculation. That said, between 9 March and 15 March 2016, in Seoul, South Korea, we discovered that this is not always the case.

In scenes reminiscent of the famous chess tournament that had taken place in Philadelphia some 20 years earlier, in which IBM's Deep Blue defeated chess master Garry Kasparov, AlphaGo, an artificial intelligence model developed by another Deep – this time, DeepMind – defeated Lee Sedol, one of the

DOI: 10.4324/9781003683124-18

greatest Go players of all time. As we have come to expect whenever humans are pitted against machines, commentators hailed it as yet another milestone in machine intelligence.

What was intriguing, though, wasn't just that AlphaGo won. It was how it won. One move in particular, move 37, played in game two, took everyone by surprise, including Lee Sedol, who took an unusually long time to respond to it. It looked more like a mistake than a move and it broke all the known strategies. Had a human player made it, it would have been described as either irrational and illogical, or creative and unique. It was the move that forced Lee Sedol into a losing position from which he never recovered.

But remember, 'your enemy's key point is your own key point', and the lesson for us here does not lie in DeepMind's creation but rather in DeepMind itself because, by focusing on creating an artificial Go player to tackle a problem considered much more difficult to solve than creating a chess player, it taught us the value of humanity's messiness.

As DeepMind grew in prominence, it started to wrestle with ethical dilemmas. Its employees protested over the company's pursuit of defence contracts. Its stakeholders raised data governance issues relating to its work in health. Mustafa Suleyman, the co-founder of AlphaGo, the company purchased by DeepMind, left amid tensions around the company's direction.

The company's original startup culture and utopian vision became increasingly out of balance with the harsh commercial pressures and realities of a business that was now firmly inside Google's stable of companies. The story of DeepMind is a story of brilliance underpinned by ambiguity, and adaptability underpinned by humanity. Just as AlphaGo's win had come about as a result of the system's capacity to make what looked like an error, DeepMind's ascension to the forefront of AI is the result of its capacity to embrace the unexpected.

This is the lesson at the heart of this chapter. Leaders who will succeed in the age of AI are not those who make perfect calculations, whether on strategy or risk, nor are they the ones who can lead in the midst of uncertainty and complexity. The leaders who will thrive are the ones who see the mess of the unknown as the only possible route to success and create a culture where their organisation can learn from failure, embrace discomfort, and adapt.

I mentioned the tension inside DeepMind between the innovation it sought and the ethics it faced. This tension is often seen as a sign of dysfunction that leaders must eradicate. Yet, as leaders, isn't it our role to adapt the how as much as change the what? That's what I call messy work. Messy work is our ability to live with uncertainty, pressure, conflict, and the unknown without the need to revert to control.

Messy leadership isn't a personal trait but a stance that becomes critical in an age where machines demand that we default to precision.

From intuition to improvisation

So far, we have seen how intuition is not the opposite of reason but, instead, its fast and embodied partner. We have seen how emotions drive understanding. Phineas Gage revealed that emotion is essential to reason, and Google Flu Trends' over-prediction demonstrated what happens when systems treat human emotions as linear. What follows from those lessons is that, while necessary, intuition is not sufficient. Leaders have to act. They must have a disciplined response to unstructured inputs. They must improvise under pressure.

Improvisation is not guessing. It is the disciplined response to unstructured input. It is an active engagement with uncertainty. Just as when DeepMind shifted its focus from games to science, improvisation may require you to abandon prior assumptions and operating models with no guarantee of success. Leaders who act on a hunch may face criticism, but messy leaders trust that even partial truths can be functional. They sense the way forward without a need to control every detail.

This kind of leadership is less about conducting a symphony and more about jamming as part of a jazz band. There are themes, but no scripts. A messy leader is not a conductor who knows all the notes and directs people when to play them. It is a leader who is present in the moment, listens, and remains anchored to the values that help her decide what to play next.

In the unknown, the successful leaders are not those who wait for clarity. They are those who act with care and flexibility, willing to adapt in real time without complete knowledge. They are those who understand that messy emotions such as fear, fatigue, dissent, aspiration, and even trust are every bit as much the ingredients of strategy as cells, pivot tables, metrics, and data points.

DeepMind's early efforts to apply AI to healthcare, with its ambitious attempt to build diagnostic tools using patient data, quickly ran into trouble. NHS trusts in the UK pushed back. Patient advocacy groups questioned the data share consent. The backlash wasn't about the strategy: it was about the messy variables such as ethics, trust, culture, and history. Improvisation is about having the willingness to ask the messy question, 'is this *humane* enough to be *right*?', as opposed to staying with the comfortable one, 'is this *true* enough to be *useful*?'. This kind of questioning may take time. Mess does tend to slow things down. But it is better to be inefficiently effective that efficiently ineffective.

To stay with the mess is to accept responsibility for *sense-making*, not just metrics. The reality of leadership in the age of AI is that most dashboards don't contain the feelings, the emotions, and the humanity needed to improvise effectively.

Feeling forward

Don't get me wrong, as a Frenchman who has lived in the UK for 40 years and is married to a British citizen, I am well aware that different cultures deal with emotions differently. However, I have also worked with enough leaders all over the world to know that organisational cultures make little room for emotion when faced with relentless demands for results. Emotions and vulnerability are more likely to be seen as problematic than to be appreciated for the strengths they are. So, let me be clear, when I talk about feeling forward, I am not asking you to share your feelings at every turn.

Instead, I am asking you to use your internal emotional responses to inform your external decisions.

To feel forward is to move with emotion as your guide. It is to notice the sighs, the silences, the glances, the hunched shoulders and let them inform, rather than dominate, your response. It is this interplay of self-awareness, self-regulation, and social skills we have come to call emotional intelligence. To lead with emotional depth in uncertainty, leaders must see emotions as an extension of human intelligence. They must learn to feel forward.

Feeling forward creates space for surprises. It encourages enquiry. It embraces failures. It creates a structure for doubt. Being willing to be wrong is a much more dynamic stance than being right. Making a mistake should be avoided, but failing can't. Failing occurs when pushing the boundaries of what is known. When machines are being programmed to master accuracy, the human advantage becomes that of adaptability.

Phineas Gage could reason but he could not decide. Google Flu Trends could decide but lacked discernment. The messy emotions and feelings we have worked so hard to eradicate in the name of efficiency are the very things that make us effective in ambiguity because, after all, 'your enemy's key point is your own key point'.

After its tournament against Lee Sedol, AlphaGo went from strength to strength, beating the number-one-ranked player in the world and being awarded the professional 9-dan status (the same as Sedol) by the Chinese Weigi Association. It was retired by DeepMind in 2017 as the company pivoted to other areas of research.

Despite the fact that he had won one of his games against the machine at the fateful encounter, making him the only human being ever to have won against AlphaGo, Lee Sedol described losing to AlphaGo as his entire world collapsing. With much of his professional career still ahead of him, having decided he could never become the top player in the world where AI was becoming what he called 'an entity that cannot be defeated',[1] he retired in November 2019.

There are consequences to leading in the messy and morally complex world of radical humanity. And, unlike machines, who only have to process outcomes, we have to live with them. This is what we need to turn to in the next chapter.

So, what happens when the mess of leadership is not just around us but within us? Should we 'learn to accept or forgive ourselves', as my client put it so eloquently in Chapter 12, or could we use reflection, remorse, and regrets as opportunities for renewal?

In our last chapter of Principle 3, before we move on to tools, I want to show you how radical humanity is more than just learning to live with ambiguity. It is also about learning to thrive with what ambiguity leaves behind.

Note

1 'Go master quits because AI "cannot be defeated"', BBC, 27 November 2019 (www.bbc.co.uk/news/technology-50573071).

14

Navigating by the stars

There was a time when the only things that went viral were viruses. There was a time when dial-up connections meant that it was probably faster to watch the TV than to wait for an email to get your news. Yet, somehow, some pictures still managed to be seared on the minds of a generation. Just before noon on 28 January 1986 was one such time. The space shuttle *Challenger* became such a picture.

Seventy-three seconds after it lifted off from its Cape Canaveral launcher, the space shuttle disintegrated in the sky with a fireball, a forked trail of smoke, and a deadly silence from a shocked world that still echoes, louder than the explosion, to this day.

The investigation into the accident showed that, as is so often the case with these tragedies, it could have been avoided. Morton Thiokol, the contractor responsible for the shuttle's solid rocket boosters, had been warned for over six months that the now famous O-rings, the crucial seals in the rocket assembly, could fail in cold weather. Memos had been written, simulations run, and red flags raised.

The night before the launch, as Florida weather conditions dipped near freezing, during a teleconference with NASA, engineers implored their managers to stop the countdown. As the O-rings had never been tested in such low temperatures, the engineers didn't have the data to prove they would fail, but they

DOI: 10.4324/9781003683124-19

had the kind of gut-level certainty born of patterns, instinct, and unease that we have been discussing. Gut feelings don't sway bureaucracies however.

Under pressure to deliver on schedule, and with managers eager to please, the recommendation was changed, and Morton Thiokol's executives gave the green light for the launch to proceed. The fate of all seven crew members, including, famously, teacher Christa McAuliffe, had not been factored into the calculations. Data were discussed but never humanised.

As was the case with Frances Haugen, there was a particular whistleblower who had tried to warn those in charge and, as with Frances, he too was called to testify before Congress after the accident.

Roger Boisjoly, an engineer at Morton Thiokol, had tried everything. He had done everything by the book. He had shared the data, escalated his concerns to his managers, and implored them to warn NASA of the consequences of his repeated tests, but no one listened. He was excluded from the final meeting where the go call was made. Maybe he had not been loud enough. Maybe he had not been effective enough. Or maybe the system just wasn't prepared to listen.

The *Challenger* case is still discussed today. I have used it in conversations with executives trying to reflect on the intricacies of decision-making in organisations. Countless professors are using it to teach ethics in their classes. MBA students are being tasked to reflect on the dehumanising effect of data on team dynamics. There is plenty of evidence to look at, not least because Roger Boisjoly kept meticulous records that he has shared. But there is one thing that is not often discussed. It is the one thing that matters most to us here.

While the case of *Challenger* became something to be studied, for Roger Boisjoly it remained something to be lived with. That fateful decision, which he had not managed to change, stayed with him. It followed him until his last breath. It lived inside him, in his memory, occupying a space between responsibility and helplessness.

He never achieved the final closure that trauma victims hope for. He never returned to engineering. He suffered from nightmares and depression. It wasn't the fact that he had failed to convince which haunted him, it was simply the knowledge that he had known what could happen and, forever, would wonder whether he could have done more. He spent the rest of his life mustering all the moral courage he had to speak out and help others develop theirs.

He wanted to alert us to the burden of carrying the consequences for decisions you couldn't quite control. He wanted us to understand not just the power of intuition we discussed in Chapter 11, nor the trap of predictive certainty detached from context we discussed in Chapter 12, nor the act of leading in complexity we unpacked in Chapter 13 but what comes after. He wanted us to realise that every decision has an echo, its effect continuing to be heard long after the voices that have made it have fallen silent. This is a lesson we cannot ignore, for, in the age of AI, systems may well process decisions, but it is only humans who have to live with their consequences.

The ripples of decisions

We like to think of decisions as following a neat and relatively simple process of analysis, deliberation, choice, and implementation. While there is some truth in this (we have decision-making processes), we are mistaken if we think that decision-making has no resonance beyond implementation. Sure, we have reviews and can judge the effect, but it is not just the practical consequences of the decision that stay with us. Just like ripples on a pond, decisions leave behind a kind of emotional resonance. These ripples are the lingering aspects of decisions as we reflect on and ponder the choices we made.

Roger Boisjoly's decision to speak out didn't lead to some kind of relief or a sense of a job well done once he was done speaking. His decision, even once implemented, didn't alleviate his conscience. Instead, his decision rippled in a way that is all too familiar to anyone in a decision-making capacity, regardless of the size of our decision. The ripple is best heard in the question 'could I have changed what happened?'.

This is not a ripple that only appears when things go wrong. Any decision that matters ripples. That's why we lie awake, replaying a meeting in our minds, reworking a sentence that captures what we could, or should, have said rather than what we uttered. These ripples are our internal signal that leadership is about more than just execution. It is about responsibility. Leaders cannot escape the ripples of their decisions (whether they were right or wrong). They are the emotional form of our impact.

AI systems don't experience this tension. Their decisions are not gates. They are loops. They calculate and update. What they never do is remember or ruminate. They will never have those moments of introspection driven by the ripples when we wonder whether we have misread a signal or missed the point entirely. Unlike them, we process both information and its implications. This matters.

Importantly, and maybe counterintuitively, not all regret arrives after the fact. Sometimes, regret can be just a pause, a sense that one's decision, while seemingly rational, will feel wrong once it has been made. This kind of 'anticipated regret' is a distinctly human phenomenon.

It is imaginative rather than reactive. It requires leaders to simulate future pain and act to avoid it in order to protect their integrity rather optimise their performance. Anticipated regret is what you feel in your gut when everyone else is nodding, but you hesitate. It's the moment before a launch, a layoff, or a change, when everything looks OK but something inside you doesn't feel great. It doesn't necessarily mean that the decision is wrong, but it certainly indicates that something still needs to be tackled.

AI systems don't have this. They cannot project emotional cost on to future scenarios. They can predict risk, but not *remorse*. They lack the emotional bandwidth to wonder what a decision will feel like – in terms not of outcome but of *alignment*.

Human leaders can. And often do.

We should not mistake this instinctive discomfort for indecision. As long as the rational mind models probabilities, the emotional mind will continue to rehearse consequences. Far from being a weakness, anticipated regret is a compass that helps leaders consider an honest version of their future selves.

Leadership is about listening to the doubts that matter. Anticipated regret is one of those doubts. What should hold us back is not the fear of failure but the fear of becoming someone we won't be able to recognise.

In Chapter 11, we explored how intuition arises when there is no precedent and when leaders have to feel their way forward in the fog. But anticipated regret is different. It arises when all options are known but one of them feels like a betrayal of self. Unlike AI, which cannot forecast identity, we do and we are the stronger for it as it saves us from the choices that feel right but aren't. Listening to that feeling is simply listening to our future selves asking us not to let them down.

To lead, then, is not to be above consequences but to feel and carry them regardless of outcomes.

Regret as a teacher

Regret is one of those emotions that are misunderstood when it comes to leadership. It is either seen as a weakness or as some kind of toxic indulgence on the part of leaders who should know better. Look forward, move fast, and break things are much more highly valued than look back and wonder. Yet regret is a sign of consciousness. It is a sign that leaders understand the importance of their choices.

Leaders who can reflect on regret possess a rare form of strength. That's what my client meant by 'learn to forgive yourself'. He was pointing out that resilience comes from having learnt something in the process of being wrong. Regret is simply a form of feedback.

That's why it can never be outsourced to machines. AI may be becoming better at testing strategies, simulating decisions, and predicting likely outcomes, but it cannot experience the emotional tensions that come from those decisions. It does not possess the uniquely human moral skill of reflection.

It is the ripple of regret that fuels our ability to understand the meaning and impact of our actions post implementation. Leaders who learn to anticipate regret are more likely to identify the drawbacks of a decision before they make it. It is the nagging feeling that something is slightly off that determines our ability to avoid something going badly wrong.

This is why I introduced intuition as a form of embodied intelligence in Chapter 11 and warned about the dangers of confusing prediction with wisdom in Chapter 12. Our ability to face mistakes, errors, and failures is what makes us resilient leaders. Letting our regrets refine rather than define us is what makes us alive inside. Our regrets are reminders that real leaders are real, rather than artificial, learners.

These critical determinants of organisational success are not within the grasp of AI. It can only differentiate between fairness and precision if it is prompted to do so and, even then, can never feel shame or empathy, nor feel in any way accountable for the decisions it makes.

This is why organisations need us to be fully alive, valuing our uniquely human ability to use regret as an opportunity to learn, so as to operate with a culture where moral reflection is the collective norm. It is only when we learn to value our ability to learn as much as our speed to execute and see regret as a sign of caring rather than as something to hide that we will create resilient and honest organisations.

In the run-up to the *Challenger* disaster, NASA had developed a siloed culture that suppressed dissent. After the tragedy, hoping to regain its once famed reputation for engineering excellence, it underwent a cultural transformation in its decision-making protocols underpinned by a conscious process of what I would call 'operationalising regret' by elevating risk communication.

This re-engineering of the culture happened too late to help Roger Boisjoly. He was never able to let go of the weight of the decision to launch. Even when they do everything right on paper, just as he had, leaders who are alive inside are judged, both by themselves and others, on the nature of the ripples they leave behind rather than the way they execute decisions.

We began this third principle of radical leadership with instinct, moved through prediction's blind spots, embraced the mess of leadership in complexity, and, finally, reflected on the slow, human process of turning experience into resilience through the regrets and reflection that come after we decide.

In all of this, we have discovered the immutable truth of leadership that formed this chapter's title. However sophisticated our tools, we will always navigate by the stars, which remind us of the direction that matters and the values which we won't compromise. We will never be perfect, but we can be purposeful.

Yet, while leadership may begin in feeling, it lives in practice. Because if, as Yoda reminded us, we will only have what we bring in, we had better make sure we have some tools as we enter the dark cave. That's where we go next.

15

Keep calm and carry on

Quite soon after having moved to the UK, back in the mid 1980s, I had a business idea. Like many of my ideas, it started with a name and never got implemented! I wanted to establish a business in France called 'My idea of Britain'. It would start with a milk bottle delivery service (Britain's precursor to DoorDash). Then I ran out of ideas. Not that Britain back then, or now, doesn't have other things that are unique or worthy of export, but I realised that a lifestyle is above all a culture, which is not easy to export.

Culture is fundamentally an idea, and nothing typifies my idea of Britain more than the famed 'Keep Calm and Carry On' saying. It first appeared on a motivational poster designed in 1939 by the UK government, aimed at raising the morale of a population preparing for the worst of war. It was never really displayed and was quickly forgotten until a copy was found in a bookshop in 2000. The discovery led to millions of products throughout the world displaying the saying. It seems there is a market for the idea of a Britain with a stiff upper lip. This idea is not just about stoicism. It is really about a resolution to focus on living within the mess. It is the desire to reflect on what we have in order to build what we want.

The reason I chose it as the title for this chapter is that 'keep calm and carry on' is fundamentally intuition in action. The 'toolkit' below is designed to help you apply the ideas of

DOI: 10.4324/9781003683124-20

intuition, discernment, emotional depth, and reflective weight we discussed in the previous four chapters.

Again, as with Chapters 5 and 10, you should adapt these practices rather than follow them. They are merely prompts for self-awareness or conversations or for building your discernment muscle as well as emotional range.

The leadership latitude test

As we did in Chapters 5 and 10, let's start with a self-assessment tool for the kind of intuitive, reflective leadership we have been discussing.

Assess the following statements using a scale of 1 (rarely) to 5 (always):

1. I can sense a shift in the emotional tone of a room before anything is said.
2. I make decisions even when I don't have full clarity or perfect data.
3. I have acted on instinct in ways I couldn't fully explain but which later proved right.
4. I continue to reflect on decisions long after they've been made.
5. I can name a time when I felt regret but learned from it.
6. I resist the temptation to close decisions prematurely for the sake of resolution.
7. I am comfortable in expressing when I am uncertain.
8. I have been in a position where something felt wrong even though it was technically right.
9. I see discomfort as part of the process of leading rather than a sign of leadership failure.
10. I've stopped myself mid-action simply because something felt off.

Let me issue what is fast becoming my usual warning – that this 'test' is merely an instrument for self-reflection. If you score between 40 and 50, it is worth thinking about whether you are experiencing and expressing your full humanity consciously or expressing this reflective capacity intuitively. Scores between 30 and 39 may be an indication that, while you are aware of your emotional and intuitive signals, you may be filtering them out too early. Finally, scores below this could suggest you are undervaluing your inner compass or trying to ignore your own signals.

The intuition amplifier framework

This is a simple checklist to help you decide when to trust your gut and make decisions when logic alone is not enough.

1. *Check your pause*: what stays with you when you pause? Is it panic or clarity? Is it a sense of urgency to find out more, or the knowledge that you already have an answer? It is easier to 'hear' your intuition when you pause.
2. *Check the story*: we always tell ourselves stories when we prepare to make a choice. What is the story you are telling yourself about this decision, and does this narrative match what you are feeling?
3. *Check the risk*: what would happen if you made the wrong call? Would you be able to live with the consequences (privately as well as publicly)?
4. *Check your history*: look back in your past to identify similar situations when the data didn't help and you used your instinct to guide you. What did you learn?

Most people can think quickly, but no one can reflect quickly. This checklist provides a means to question if your thoughts and feelings are in alignment.

Humanising analytics questions

In Chapter 12, we discussed the importance of humanising analytics. Here are five questions to bring into the room when, facing data-heavy decisions, we may overlook the human systems.

1. What do these numbers not include?
2. Who is most affected by this decision, and are they in the room?
3. What fears, hopes, or stories might be driving these data points?
4. Have we mistaken correlation for causality and/or causality for meaning?
5. If we acted only on these data, what would we miss?

The mess tolerance table

Where do you sit in this table? What does it tell you about your stance towards ambiguity, emotions and disruption? The aim is not to be 'high tolerance' across all these categories, at all times, but rather to know when your discomfort is getting in the way of insight.

	Low-tolerance response	*High-tolerance response*
Ambiguity	I avoid unclear situations	I stay engaged through uncertainty
Emotion	I suppress emotion in decisions	I use emotions as signals
Contradictions	I resolve tension quickly	I can hold opposing truths
Pace	I value speed over pause	I slow down to make sense of situations

The regret compass

As we have seen, regret has the ability to teach us if we allow it to do so. Below are the four directions to wander in when you are revisiting a decision you made which you are uncomfortable with. It will help you see what lies at the root of your discomfort and what you can learn from to turn the emotional residue of regret into growth.

- North: north stands for your true North (i.e. your guiding principles and purpose). The question is, 'did you act in line with what you believe matters most?'.
- East: east is all about Effect. So, reflect on the impact of your decision by asking yourself, 'what was the cost of my decision for the people impacted by it?'.
- South: south stands for Signal. It is about the inner signals that you experienced throughout the decision-making process. What were you feeling at the time, and to what extent did you ignore these feelings?
- West: finally, west is for Wisdom. What will you do differently next time in order to be more aligned with your true north?

Weekly reflection prompts

Here are some of the questions you may wish to reflect on at the end of a day or a week. I am well aware that, by the time we get to the seventh principle, I will have given you more questions to reflect on than you have time in your week, so feel free to choose which to focus on!

- When did I act before I was ready, and what did I learn from this?
- What tension did I sit with instead of avoiding or trying to resolve it?
- When did I feel something was off but went ahead anyway?
- What regret am I still carrying from this week, and what might this be helping me to learn?
- What did I sense this week that no one else seemed to notice?

Commitment practices

1. Pause: before every major decision, take one intentional minute of silence to allow yourself to hear your intuition.
2. Contradict: whenever you discuss data, invite one observation, or contradiction, that the numbers don't explain.
3. Regret rounds: once a quarter, reflect with your team on what you wish you had done differently and why you took the path you took.
4. Silent starts: begin one meeting per month with a minute of silence in order to build tolerance for reflection in action.
5. Mess: each week, identify one instance where things were messy, but you still managed to grow.

Leadership has never been about having all the answers. It has always been about sensing what followers need. If there is one theme that is becoming clear as we progress through the implications of AI for leadership, it is that this kind of embodied, slow, and deep human sensation is no longer optional. Leadership cannot be about having all the answers, but it is increasingly more important for it to be about asking better questions, because, while AI is responsive, it will never be inquisitive in the way humans can be. We explore how curiosity is fast becoming a radical leadership act in the next principle.

Part 2

The demonic paper clip

If Clippy, the first paperclip, who introduced our opening three principles, was annoying, the paperclip who introduces the next two principles is downright scary. So, let me move from the obnoxious to the demonic paperclip.

Philosopher and former Oxford professor Nick Bostrom's 'paperclip maximiser' thought experiment might have sounded absurd at first but has become iconic over time. An AI system is told to maximise paperclip production. It does so without any empathy, nuance, or override. It does so relentlessly. So relentlessly, in fact, that it first consumes all available resources and then proceeds to eliminate any obstacles (humans included) that stand in the way of its task. Eventually, out of pure logic, doing exactly what it has been tasked to do, it transforms all matter in the universe into paperclips.

The story might sound like an exaggeration, but the point it makes is painfully real. Not only will AI systems always meet computable goals, irrespective of whether or not they are moral, but they will also always calculate on the basis of what has been stated without ever questioning what was meant. Bostrom's paperclip maximiser experiment highlights the dilemma at the heart of every AI implementation. Are we maximising for what feels like progress or for what really matters?

Whenever we give systems narrow objectives (e.g. more engagement, more sales, faster decisions), they will pursue these with blind fidelity, irrespective of any potential collateral damage

DOI: 10.4324/9781003683124-21

or unintended consequences. We know it is already happening. We have hiring systems that screen out candidates on the basis of biased historical data. We operate facial recognition tools that misidentify people at alarming rates. We use recommendation algorithms that radicalise users by promoting outrage. What turns Bostrom's robot into a killer robot is not its killer logic. It was never a failure of coding. The danger of AI lies in a failure of framing. Radical humanity in leadership becomes existential when systems are left unchecked, unreflective, and, above all, unopposed.

The notion that underpins our next two principles is not that AI might do something harmful. It might or it might not. The jury is still out. Rather, what is critical is who will be the judge if we don't ask the right questions before harm is done? What are the assumptions? Who sets the metrics? Whose voices are included and excluded in the design?

In practical behavioural terms, I have always found the differences between leadership and management so slight as to be invisible and I refuse to adopt the caricatural mindset that describes managers as bad leaders and leads to too much time wasted in useless conversation. Both management and leadership are necessary for success, but, unless we are prepared to lead the values behind the algorithm, we will be relegated to fulfilling a managerial function that can easily be automated. The paperclip maximiser thought experiment is a reminder that we need to step back and ask ourselves if we are doing enough to amplify purpose, build trust, and shape the future.

What are required now are not leaders who chase efficiency at all costs but leaders who are capable of defining what counts as value. This is our fourth principle, curiosity over certainty. What we need are leaders who will never compromise our humanity, no matter how attractive the prize. This is our fifth principle, compassion over calculation.

So, if Clippy showed us that the first imperative of being alive inside was to be more intentional in the way we express our voice and our values, the demonic paperclip reminds us that to be alive inside is to optimise only once we have humanised. Efficiency is a machine's job. A leader's job is meaning.

Principle 4

Curiosity over certainty

Leaders aren't valuable because they have all the answers.
They're valuable because they ask better questions.

With authenticity as our anchor, moral courage as our stand, and intuition our compass, we must expand the possibilities offered by a world where AI answers our queries at speed. This fourth principle asserts that we need to resist the appeal of certainty, along with our impulse to come to conclusions too quickly. To make space for insights, creativity, and growth, we must reclaim the value of wondering.

- Chapter 16: curiosity is not about asking questions. It is about having the wisdom to know what questions are worth asking in the first place.
- Chapter 17: the kind of exploratory thinking which makes work truly effective is often discouraged by the pursuit of efficiency.
- Chapter 18: true innovation is not efficient. It is disorderly before it becomes distinctive and desirable. As leaders, we need to learn to value the discomfort of chaos.
- Chapter 19: this will require us to unlearn the habits and assumptions that lock us into outdated mental models that stand in the way of curiosity.
- Chapter 20: only by embedding enquiry into our practices will we transform our culture from one of certainty and control to one of reflection and renewal.

DOI: 10.4324/9781003683124-22

16

The question is the answer

Imagine being given a choice. You have two clinics treating patients with the same condition. One has a mortality rate of between 10 and 18 per cent. The other has a mortality rate of two per cent. Which would you choose?

For expectant mothers entering one of Europe's busiest maternity wards in the Vienna General Hospital in 1847, the answer was clear. The hospital had two clinics. One, run by midwives, had the low mortality rate of two per cent. The other, staffed by doctors and medical students, could see nearly one in five women die after giving birth in its worst months. Women would beg to be admitted to the midwives' ward.

In fact, so well known was the difference that some went as far as giving birth in the street, in front of the hospital, rather than be taken to the doctors' clinic. Every day, women arrived hopeful. And, every day, some of them left in a coffin. How could one group of caregivers, in one building, operate two systems with such vastly different outcomes?

Medics blamed overcrowding, bad air, even maternal shame. But a 30-something physician by the name of Ignaz Semmelweis sensed that something deeper was going on. The difference in outcomes haunted him. For him, the fact that women weren't dying from childbirth itself but from a swift, agonising fever that

DOI: 10.4324/9781003683124-23

often killed within days wasn't just a statistical anomaly. It was a moral outrage.

Then, another tragedy struck that would make the pieces fall into place.

Professor Jakob Kolletschka, a doctor at the hospital, died of a violent infection after accidentally cutting his hand during an autopsy, with symptoms eerily similar to those of the women dying of what we now know as childbed or puerperal fever.

That's when Ignaz realised that, in the first clinic, doctors who were performing autopsies in the morning, before moving straight on to deliver babies, weren't washing their hands in between. The reason wasn't carelessness – this was 1847, still decades away from Pasteur's discoveries and germ theory. But Semmelweis had the foresight to ask whether there may be a link. Instead of dying at the hands of the doctors, could the women be dying because doctors carried death on their hands?

He began to act on the question no one else had dared ask and introduced a simple rule. All doctors and students were to wash their hands in a chlorine solution before moving on to examine patients. Within months, the mortality rate in the physicians' clinic had dropped below that of the midwives.

Ignaz Semmelweis had the honesty to embrace the feelings others had ignored. That's the authenticity we discussed in Principle 1. He had the strength to speak the unspeakable. That's the moral courage we covered in Principle 2. He had the instinct to know that something was missing. That's the intuition of Principle 3.

But, above all, with no theory and no model or algorithm to help, he had the presence of mind to wonder and seek an explanation for what was happening. That's curiosity, and that's what this fourth principle is all about.

Wisdom

Curiosity is one of the most powerful cognitive tools we have as human beings. Despite the fact that we think of curiosity as asking questions, the way children do, in reality, curiosity doesn't begin with a question. It begins with a feeling.

We face countless things that we don't understand each and every day. Yet we ignore most of them. What makes us stop and ask questions isn't just intellectual curiosity (otherwise we would stop every time), it is an emotional sense that something matters. It is that feeling that something is missing, that something is off, or simply that something doesn't add up.

The real power of curiosity doesn't lie in questions but in having the wisdom to sense when a question deserves to be asked. It is wisdom that allows us to recognise that something is missing, even when everything seems to make sense on the surface. It is wisdom that reminds us that the most dangerous assumptions are the ones we don't even realise we are making.

Ignaz Semmelweis walked the corridors of the maternity clinics driven by an emotional need to *learn* rather than an intellectual need to *know*. He was looking to save lives rather than looking for answers. It was that purpose, rooted in emotion, that enabled him not to be distracted by the assumptions everyone else was making and to notice what others didn't. It was his feelings that enabled him to stay disturbed by what he witnessed long enough to continue the search for answers.

Curiosity without wisdom is just noise. It is asking without the desire to listen. But curiosity rooted in wisdom enables us to direct our attention where it needs to go. That's why questions alone are not sufficient, and not all questions are equal. Questions on their own can distract, entertain, or even just fill space and time. It is our wisdom that enables us to differentiate and to identify the ones that can shift our understanding.

Wisdom is the filter that stops us from chasing novelty and guides us towards meaningful enquiry. Focusing on getting more data or more answers isn't curiosity. It is noise-making activity. Curiosity is the ability to differentiate between something that feels unresolved and something that actually matters. The right questions arise from our being willing to let our understanding be interrupted and our minds be changed.

Semmelweis changed medicine by being open enough to wonder whether the knowledge everyone relied on might be incomplete and having the courage to follow that train of thought wherever it led, rather than by simply wanting to know more.

Human curiosity is more than seeking data. It is searching for insights. It is a felt sense that something unknown or unseen could shift what we know or what we do. It has intuition built in but is also what intuition is built on. Ignaz Semmelweis started with a discomfort, the intuition that something wasn't right, and had the courage to shape this feeling into questions no one else was asking.

Curiosity is what allows leaders not to rush into a solution. We are now living in a world where questions are plentiful, and answers are cheap and readily available. You can get a passable summary of almost anything in seconds. The differentiator is no longer knowing. It is framing and interpreting. It is about having the ability to step back and ask the right questions. That is curiosity. The rest is just research.

Think about how Ignaz Semmelweis reframed the entire question. Instead of asking how to manage childbed fever, he cut to the root of the problem. That is what curiosity does. It sees beyond the presenting issue. In complex systems, speed without curiosity is a liability. The faster you move in the wrong direction, the more damage you do. It is curiosity that makes room for re-evaluation, reframing, and redirection. It is the precondition for effective decisiveness.

Wonder and wander

We have a word in French that does not have an English equivalent. It is the word *flâneur*, which we use to describe a person who wanders aimlessly. The problem is that, on their own, the words 'wandering aimlessly' do not do justice to the French word. They convey a sense of aimlessness that *flâner* (the verb) does not have because, as they wander, flâneurs wonder. They don't wonder at, or about, anything in particular; instead, they wonder at being.

That's why I like to think of being curious as being a 'flâneur of the mind'.

In this way, you could say that curiosity is a form of metacognition. It is a coordinated neural response that prepares your brain to explore, focus, and grow. It comes in to play, just as it did for Semmelweis, when we detect a gap between what we know and what we expect. This gap triggers our brain's reward system, releasing dopamine, which motivates us to seek out the information that is missing (that's the wander part). At the same time, the hippocampus (the part of our brain linked to memory) becomes more active to help us remember what we have learned (that's the wonder part).

That's why, while AI systems are second to none at generating answers, they can be nowhere when it comes to generating enquiry. Our so-called reasoning models cannot in any way reason. AI does not possess the capability to reflect on knowledge gaps. It cannot prioritise uncertainty, nor is it capable of initiating goal-directed exploration (with the emphasis on the word exploration as it can initiate goal-directing search and answers). AI operates only through probabilistic pattern prediction trained to produce outputs based on statistical relationships. As such, it does not have any of the intrinsic understanding of relevance or significance necessary for curiosity. AI systems can never experience tension between the known and unknown or care about what may be missing (given they don't know that anything is missing).

Even the most advanced reinforcement learning systems operate within predefined reward structures. They optimise for success within a task and, therefore, cannot be curious, given that curiosity emerges before that task is defined. Curiosity is not driven by external reward but rather by an internally generated sense of conceptual dissonance around what the brain interprets as a meaningful absence.

AI does not assess the value of a question, only the plausibility of an answer. It cannot distinguish between a trivial anomaly and a meaningful exception unless explicitly instructed to do so, nor can it prioritise between competing unknowns. It cannot question the question itself nor reformulate a question into a new one. This lack of what philosophers call epistemic sensitivity (the ability to recognise when something is missing, uncertain, or worth questioning in what we think we know) is what makes curiosity a radically human leadership proposition.

Ignaz Semmelweis's story shows us that curiosity requires the ability to imagine alternative framings of a problem and to reflect on why something ought to be questioned, even when it hasn't been raised as an issue. That's why his insight could never have emerged from a model. His discovery lay in an underlying tension between what he could see and a question no one else had thought to ask.

We have often associated leadership with answers. Whether they were in the form of a vison, clarity, or even confidence, we have assumed that these answers underpinned a leader's value. That view was always mistaken, but, in a world saturated with answers, it has become critical for us to re-evaluate the value we place on our willingness to pause and ask.

To wander and wonder means reclaiming a mindset that prioritises understanding over control. It means treating ambiguity as a signal that something deeper needs to be explored rather than seeing it as a threat to our authority. It means being willing to search for questions at times when everyone is expecting direction and answers.

Wandering and wondering do not equate to dithering or avoiding responsibility. Rather, they are about owning the responsibility to frame the challenge wisely before trying to solve it quickly. Leaders who act with curiosity realise that clarity is the outcome of questioning the value of what is measured by the enquiry itself rather than how fast the answer is generated. Semmelweis didn't have answers, but he had the presence of mind to ask a better question and then make others hear the answer. When we move from answering and directing to enquiring, we help others see what's worth finding out.

Ignaz Semmelweis didn't live to see the impact of his question on the world of medicine.

He was met with resistance, outrage, and even mockery. Doctors refused to believe they could be the cause. He was eventually dismissed, not just professionally but personally. In

1865, having grown increasingly agitated and with his behaviour having become increasingly erratic, he was committed to an asylum against his will.

Within weeks of his admission, aged just 47, Semmelweis died from a blood infection, probably caused by a wound he sustained during a beating by the very staff meant to care for him in a medical system he had fought so hard to make more caring. The man who had spent his life trying to prevent sepsis died of sepsis himself. The very thing he devoted his life to eliminate eventually claimed it.

History, as is often the case, eventually caught up. Semmelweis's question, impossible to answer scientifically in his time, became a foundation of modern medicine. There are two lessons in this tragic story. The first is that, while curiosity may isolate in the moment, its legacy can be transformative. The second is that leadership always implies a personal risk. Leading is about having the courage to ask what systems resist, along with the patience to hold a question long enough for its time to come.

Only radically curious leaders can leave behind solutions rather than answers. For this to happen, though, they need to fight against the near-religious fervour of efficiency. It is our readiness to stay with the slow, stubborn complexity of a genuine and accurate answer that separates human insight from machine response. I call this ability 'the Cézanne effect'. Let me explain why in the next chapter.

17

Efficiency is overrated

Paul Cézanne would regularly spend 100 working sessions on one painting alone. Imagine spending over a month painting an apple!

He would return to the same picture day after day, adjusting the angle, the light, the pressure of the brush on the canvas. He would sit and stare at the same image for hours, only to walk away without having painted a single stroke, preferring instead to let the object reveal itself over time.

His slowness became legendary. His dealer, Ambroise Vollard, recalled sitting for a portrait that took over 80 sessions.[1] Still Cézanne considered it unfinished! In the age of salons and fast finishes, Cézanne's pace looked inefficient, even dysfunctional, to the impressionist painters of the time. Despite endless questions from his peers and the mockery of critics, he continued his search for something he considered far more rewarding than praise and adulation. Cézanne wanted to experience what it is like to feel what you see.

But what he lacked in speed he made up in impact. Rather than lagging behind his contemporaries, Cézanne raced ahead. In a twist reminiscent of the fabled tortoise and the hare, his refusal to rush became a revolution in modern art. Picasso, who returned to Cézanne's work regularly for inspiration, held him to be the father of all painters.

DOI: 10.4324/9781003683124-24

We begin here because Cézanne offers a counter-example to the key principles on which modern systems in general, and artificial intelligence in particular, are built. These building blocks have led us to believe that there is little value beyond speed, clarity, and output, whereas Cézanne reminds us that our deepest insights take time to arrive.

We talked in our last chapter about curiosity being more than asking questions. Ignaz Semmelweis demonstrated the value of having the presence of mind to notice what others pass by. But, to notice, you need time. And, in most organisations and with most algorithms, time is exactly what we are taught to shrink.

Cézanne refused to rush because he understood that speed often blinds us. He reminds us of the essential truth that what looks inefficient at first might well be, in the end, the only human work that has enough value to last. He demonstrated that, rather than being instantaneous, our perception evolves over time as a sort of accumulation. This may sound like the romantic notion of a dreamer until you sit with Cézanne's paintings long enough to realise that he meant it quite literally.

Cézanne was not slow by accident. He painted the same mountain, Mont Sainte-Victoire, more than 80 times. He spent years obsessing over the geometry of a fruit bowl. He left dozens of canvases unfinished. He asked sitters to return for weeks, sometimes months, only to abandon the portrait later. He did all this because he believed that to truly see and grasp the depth of something required repetition, slowness, and restlessness.

The efficiency theatre

Cézanne's world was shaped by deadlines, expectations, and increasingly rapid forms of image production. His hesitancy was interpreted as incompetence. He was called awkward, naïve, indecisive. His repetition looked like regression in a world seeking constant progress.

This doesn't seem that different from modern organisational life, where the logic of speed has become not just a method but a mindset. Ours, just like his, is a world where the faster you respond, the more capable you seem. Leaders who seem hesitant won't last long in an era of immediate output, sprints, scrums, dashboards, and KPIs. Those who ask for time will be called awkward, naïve, and indecisive. Yet, as much as efficiency is heralded as the only way to reduce waste, streamline action, and create focus and growth, too often it reduces the very space in which thinking happens.

We run the risk of training ourselves – and, increasingly, our AI tools – to believe that progress can only be defined by acceleration. We run the risk of becoming mere actors in a kind of efficiency theatre where we mistake activity for action and performance for progress. In our desperation to move forward, we see little value in reflection and a lot of waste in looking back.

The logic of AI is built for speed. Machine-learning models compress vast information flows into instant outputs. They are optimised to reduce cognitive load, accelerate pathways, and eliminate redundancy. In many contexts, that's invaluable. But leadership isn't one of these.

We treat human attention as if it was an infinite and abundant resource that can easily and rapidly be replenished. We pile it into ever tighter schedules, skim through information, and just scroll to the next point. The truth is rather different. Attention, just like Cézanne's process, is slow, measured, and paced. When we build environments that interrupt, we see less, miss insights, make reactive choices, and embrace shallow solutions.

The kind of slow, iterative, layered curiosity that we discussed in the last chapter doesn't fit into productivity models. Yet this is exactly the type of inefficient and repetitive thinking that leads to insights. We need time, friction, and cultures that value uncertainty as much as completion if we are to formulate meaningful questions rather than just retrieve fast and perfunctory answers.

As leaders, we are prone to ask our teams to 'get to the point', even when there is no point yet! Alex Danchev's biography[2] makes clear that, for Cézanne, slowness was not a flaw but a method that was central to how he saw. He needed time to see the work rather than finish it. Shouldn't we make room for this kind of approach in how we lead? In fact, if leadership is about creating the conditions for the positive engagement of others with a goal, isn't making time a key value of leadership?

It is too easy to see Cézanne's approach as repetitive rather than to appreciate it as a form of revelation, unfolding slowly through the act of revisiting what we think we have already seen to ensure we have truly felt it. The latter requires us to push against a system that doesn't allow us to take longer than the amount of time it perceives to be necessary for task completion. Mine is not a call to slow everything down but rather a reminder that curiosity is about ensuring that meaning is not stripped away from what we see.

Leadership is not a routing algorithm whose role is to decide how to direct packets of data in the most efficient way possible to achieve an outcome. It has never been about finding the fastest way to get from problem to solution. Leadership is about understanding which problems deserve solutions at all. It is about knowing when to wait, listen, and reframe because, just like Cézanne's brushstrokes, insights evolve rather than surfacing on demand.

The discipline of delay

I grant you that to spend a month painting the same thing, over and over again, returning to it every day to see it differently, and never finishing it appears nothing if not eccentric at first, second, and even third glance. This kind of refusal to settle for something, along with the disciplined focus of attention, is in fact a commitment to creativity. As Paul Cézanne understood, if we are to grow, transform, and achieve, we have to dwell on issues, repeat, and reflect. As he said in later life, 'time and reflection modify, little by little, our vision, and at last comprehension comes.'[3]

Unfortunately, our organisational systems don't often allow for this kind of leadership. We move fast, wrap up decisions, and evaluate performance based on speed. Just as critics dismissed Cézanne for not conforming to the speed and polish expected of serious artists at the time, we too fail to value slow, methodical exploration. Modern culture equates delay with dysfunction. In a corporate context, even in the creative industries where leaders are given slightly more latitude, pausing for too long is seen as indecision. Iterating too many times is seen as a sign of waste. Failing to commit early is seen as a leadership weakness.

Psychologists call this desire to reduce the discomfort brought about by ambiguity, even when we don't have all the information necessary to do so well, the cognitive closure bias. It is this bias that drives leaders to display a kind of 'urgency illusion' under pressure where they mistake delays for incompetence and see urgency and activity (rather than actions) as virtues. Cézanne shows us how slowness, when done well, is neither passivity nor delay but a structured and intentional practised capacity to hold uncertainty long enough to understand without rushing for premature answers.

His paintings, with their raw brushstrokes, misaligned perspectives, and objects floating in mid-air, hold us in an unsettled gaze until we realise that he was not trying to reproduce how things looked but, instead, was painting how things come into being. This is the kind of leadership that, with the discipline of delay, doesn't just command attention but sustains it long enough for real solutions to emerge.

In every creative endeavour, there is a phase when nothing works, ideas are messy, and humans are restless. The role of leaders, in these moments, is not to step in and steer the system towards efficiency by removing obstacles. Instead, it is to remember that simplification is more than efficient subtraction. To simplify is more than taking elements away. It is also to make things more coherent by making clear the process through which things come into being. It takes courage rather than incompetence to stay with the discomfort of half-baked ideas. Cézanne had that courage, and his half-finished canvases remind us that the truth takes time to emerge.

I am often told that speed of response is always necessary in crises. Even if not all leadership moments are crises, I would argue that, in the age of AI, the real crisis is the crisis of accelerated sameness. As AI increasingly handles what's predictable, process-driven, and pattern-based, we end up with a form of photocopied answer that becomes weaker and paler the more it is copied.

To lead humanly, in this context, is about being able to handle the strange, the difficult, the ambiguous, and the unfinished as the only real source of creativity. Just as Cézanne was once mocked for his unfinished paintings and is now credited as having provided the bridge between Impressionism and Cubism, leaders who are prepared to relegate efficiency to its right place will be the ones shaping the future.

In his final years, Cézanne became more reclusive but, while he spoke little of his work, he kept painting. Unlike many of his contemporaries who ran out of time before they could finish their canvases, his remained unfinished simply because his goal had never been about ending anything. Cézanne's work was always about just seeing things more fully. This is the wisdom he left us with. Understanding, rather than completion, is the goal of leadership. This requires us to trust our pace as well as our plans. It requires us to design teams and timelines that allow for emergence and create feedback loops that value the unresolved. In short, this requires us to lead with the radical humanity of an artist rather than the illusory perfection of a machine.

The more AI advances and becomes available, the more speed itself will become commoditised. When everyone can execute at speed, the one remaining differentiator of humanity is our capacity to listen, see, and stay long enough for new insights to appear.

There is one paradox though. As we learn to slow down and make space for insights, we may well find that, unlike Cézanne's paintings, what we find is far from beautiful. Instead, true creativity often looks like chaos and disorder. Insights are often scattered and contradictory. That's the paradox we tackle next.

Oh, by the way, if you are experiencing a degree of frustration, wondering what the alternative to speed might be, rather than turning to Chapter 19 where I will discuss this, I would urge you to stay with the frustration a bit longer. That's the point! Cézanne shows us that, if you do, you might well reach a conclusion before you even get to read it.

Notes

1 Ambroise Vollard, *Recollections of a Picture Dealer*, trans. Harold L. Van Doren, Dover Publications, New York, 1978, pp. 87–90.
2 Alex Danchev, *Cezanne: A Life*, Profile Books, London, 2012.
3 Joachim Gasquet, *Cézanne: A Memoir with Conversations*, trans. Christopher Pemberton, MIT Press, Cambridge, MA, 1991, p. 146.

18

The creativity paradox

In the spring of 1959, Miles Davis walked into a recording studio in New York City with almost nothing. There were no written arrangements. There were to be neither rehearsals, rehearsed solos, and chord charts nor structured harmonies. Instead, Davis had modal frameworks of just a few scales scribbled on a piece of paper, plus a band comprised of some of the best jazz musicians in the world waiting to be told what to do.

But he didn't tell them anything. He just turned his back to them and asked them to play.

That was not unusual. On stage, Davis often performed facing away from the audience, and sometimes from his own band. He avoided eye contact and rarely spoke, and, yet, from this posture of deliberate distance emerged *Kind of Blue*. The record would go on to become the most influential and best-selling jazz album in history.

In reality, on 2 March and 22 April 1959, the two days it took to record it, Columbia's 30th Street Studio looked not so much revolutionary as confusing, strange, and disorienting. There was frustration and drift. This is the paradox of creativity. As it is unfolding, real creativity rarely feels actually creative. Instead, it often feels incoherent, fragmented, and unprofessional. The more creative the work, the more likely it will feel like a mistake rather than magic that is about to happen.

DOI: 10.4324/9781003683124-25

What Miles Davis understood, perhaps better than most, is that breakthroughs require tension rather than harmony or agreement. He understood that, for creativity to enter the studio, he needed to strip away the structure.

Kind of Blue is now taught in conservatoires. Its solos have been analysed, transcribed, and endlessly copied. Even if the legend that the pieces were recorded in one take is wrong, the fact remains that none were written in advance or rehearsed. All were created in the moment. They were raw, unfinished, and beautiful.

As leaders, we expect creativity to arrive neatly packaged. We ask for innovation but panic when it looks like things are breaking down or progress is slow. Just as Cézanne did before him, Davis reminds us that we must learn to stay long enough in ambiguity if we want something great to emerge.

Miles Davis and his *Kind of Blue* may be called genius now, but he and it would more than likely have been called weird then. The reality of creativity is that it is much more likely to come out of noisy rooms full of musicians unsure of what comes next than out of a concert hall where a directed orchestra knows exactly what to play.

Noisy innovation

Miles Davis was creating a kind of purposeful confusion to allow creativity to emerge when he asked his band to abandon rehearsed harmonies and embrace modal improvisation. Management consultants and authors have often used jazz as an analogy for emergence. In my book *Disciplined Collaboration*, I too used it to show how improvisation is an essential component of effective teams. What we seldom mention though is the tension that it creates in leaders.

This discomfort, brought about by ambiguity, triggers our reflex to clarify, correct, and move on. Our perception is shaped by mental models built over time through repetition. Cognitive scientists tell us that whatever doesn't fit these is either rejected or ignored. This is why so many of our creative impulses, especially in their early stages of development, just look and feel so wrong that we seek to make them coherent too soon and miss out on the possibility of something emerging that is far better than what we could have hoped for. The history of invention is full of ideas that were dismissed at first because they didn't yet conform to this prevailing logic.

What leaders interpret as confusion, hesitation, or lack of direction is often the first sign that something genuinely original is forming. We may want to treat the creative process as a funnel, but, in reality, most creative progress looks more like messy balls of string or orchestral cacophonies. Ideas double back on and contradict themselves just as speed is lost and recovered unexpectedly.

If we expect the creative process to be linear, we risk prematurely killing off the strange, fragile ideas that don't yet make sense but may eventually make all the difference.

Neuroscientific research supports this. In creative thinking, the brain enters a diffuse state of neural activation associated with daydreaming, self-reflection, and non-linear synthesis known as the default mode network. In this state, we form associative links that logic-driven processing would normally suppress. We access ambiguity, contradiction, surprise.

This default mode network plays a central role in how creative insights are formed by rejecting the very straight lines we have come to value. The discomfort experienced by Miles Davis's band members when they had no instructions and were asked to feel their way forward, rather than execute instructions, produced the very environment in which original music could be created.

In most organisations, however, discomfort is much more likely to be seen as a problem than interpreted as the sign of growth that it is. Psychologists call this mental tendency to accept the first explanation that fits, even if it is incomplete and suboptimal, premature closure. You will often see this when you observe teams agreeing on an idea quickly simply because they have become tired of ambiguity. In most cases, this won't be the best idea, but it will be the one that restores a sense of order. The cost of staying in the mess feels higher than the risk of being wrong.

Creativity requires the willingness to trust what we don't fully understand. While we might call this incomplete confidence on the part of leaders, it is actually an invitation for others to join in. It is a signal that possibilities can emerge and that what is unresolved can be worked out. It is the same as dissonance in jazz. It is a provocation and a sign that anything is possible if we tolerate the mess and the tension. Davis's refusal to conduct, to explain, or even to face his band was this kind of leadership.

Despite the fact that we have all been trained to show progress, always appear purposeful, and have answers, we must remember that much of real creativity looks unproductive.

Fragile foundations

In music, in painting, in writing, in product design, or indeed in any other domain where originality matters, the early emergence of an idea often looks like a mistake. It never fits the models we have been trained to apply. For creative leaders like Davis, when things look weird, unpolished, and unpleasant, it is always a sign to pay closer attention.

This is where the difference between human emotional intelligence and machine artificial intelligence is at its starkest. AI can generate options and surface likely next steps, sensible continuations, and statistical plausibility but it cannot, and never will, stay in ambiguity without resolving it. This means that it cannot help us navigate the earliest phase of the creative process when it is right for things to feel wrong. Our willingness to value and stay in ambiguity is one of the most deeply human capacities we can reclaim as it is not programmable.

Neuroscientist Kalina Christoff's research shows how, during moments of open-ended creative thinking, the brain enters a distributed pattern of activation involving emotional, visual, and memory-related systems alongside logical centres. These are the moments common to the stories of Ignaz Semmelweis, Cézanne, and now Davis, where all three held contradictory and half-formed impressions that enabled patterns to be seen.

This distributed state is messy and uncomfortable. Human creativity has never been the shortest path to a solution but it is the surest way to get to solutions that are new and lasting. It is this physiological, emotional, and cultural capacity that has enabled our species to survive. Unlike AI, we can live in complexity and are able to wait and wonder.

What the story of *Kind of Blue* shows us is that great creative leadership doesn't impose structure. Instead, it makes space for structure to emerge by nurturing the noise and listening for the music that might come out of this. There are four steps or stages that, inspired by Miles Davis, we need to consider.

Step 1: withdraw the blueprint

Most leaders start by clarifying either an objective or its link to a vision. But, when seeking originality, clarity can be premature. Miles didn't walk into the studio with a finished score. He gave his musicians only modes with no instructions. This refusal to 'predefine' is one that leaders must cherish as it is only by resisting the urge to explain too much, too early that we create the space and give permission for others to fill it with ideas. Giving possibilities, even when there are a few, is already narrowing the field of enquiry.

Step 2: tune the tension

Davis didn't abandon structure altogether. What he did was to design tension into the structure. The modal template he introduced and the instructions he refused to give created the friction between freedom and form that kept uncertainty from becoming unbearable. As leaders, we must work to hone the pressure embedded in creative efforts rather than eliminate it altogether. We can stretch expectations just enough to keep the urgency alive without shutting down experimentation.

Step 3: protect the off notes

When something strange appears or happens, teams tend to discard it or label it as undesirable. But Davis knew that what sounds 'wrong' might be what's most alive. His greatest gift, and what made *Kind of Blue* so radically different, was his ability to listen to what didn't belong and leave it in.

The lesson for us as leaders is never to defend what we know. Instead, we must nurture and protect what others are surfacing. We must play the off notes louder rather than try to quieten them down.

Step 4: trust the form to emerge

This last part is probably the hardest one of all. Davis didn't know what *Kind of Blue* would become. He knew he had the best musicians on the jazz circuit at the time, but there was no way, given the nature of the endeavour, he could know if it would work. He had to trust that something would somehow emerge and take shape. Leadership has always been about outcomes, but creative leadership is an act of restraint. It is about understanding that the outcome you should really care about is the very one you can't see from the start. We need to learn to trust that, if we have created the right conditions, the right outcome will emerge.

Kind of Blue emerged as an utterly original work because of the mess it was conceived in with a leader who understood that, in creative work, the most important ideas often show up as a result of friction. And friction is not the domain of machines.

We began in Chapter 16 by understanding that questions were more important than answers. Then, in Chapter 17, Cézanne slowed us down in our rush to find answers, and Davis now reminds us that the dissonance we experience is not only part of the process but the process itself.

But Miles Davis preferred to go forward rather than look back. In 1990, when jazz singer and pianist Shirley Horn implored him to play some of the iconic pieces from *Kind of Blue*, he dismissed the request with a simple 'Nah, it hurts my lip.'[1] He preferred to let go of what had been and move towards what could be.

So, on we must go too and tackle an important question that remains unanswered. It is the one I alluded to earlier. How do you keep making space without losing face in a world that demands speed, certainty, and delivery?

For one company, the turning point didn't come through breakthrough invention but by letting go of the very ideas that had once made it great. Its story can show us how to build curiosity into our systems, brick by brick.

Note

1 Quoted in Ashley Kahn, Miles Davis, and Bill Evans: 'Miles and Bill in Black & White', *JazzTimes*, September 2001.

19

Making space for what might be

In 2003, LEGO, a company with a long and celebrated history as well as a reputation as one of the world's most imaginative brands, was only weeks away from collapse.

In its race to stay relevant, it had spent years expanding relentlessly. It had opened theme parks, launched video games, designed watches and clothing lines, struck licensing deals with Hollywood studios, and flooded the market with more than 12,000 individual brick components. It was now close to running out of cash and into the ground.

This wasn't through a lack of creativity. Creativity had never been LEGO's problem but was fast becoming its main one. A company founded by the Danish carpenter Ole Kirk Christiansen in 1932 on the ethos of playing well (*leg godt* means 'play well' in Danish) was now paying the price of playing too much.

By the end of 2003, with warehouses overflowing with unsold products, the company was US$800 million dollars in debt and losing US$1 million a day. A brand once defined by discipline and structure no longer seemed to know either what it was or what it was for.

Having advised the Kirk Kristiansen family (owners of LEGO) as a McKinsey consultant, Jørgen Vig Knudstorp was appointed CEO in 2004 to turn the business around.[1] What is

DOI: 10.4324/9781003683124-26

important for us here is that much of his work was not about starting anything new but rather about deciding what to stop and remove.

Hundreds of products were retired, and entire divisions were shut down. But perhaps, one of the most radical changes happened when Jørgen Vig Knudstorp asked the company's own designers to stop designing and start listening. For the first time, LEGO, which had been used to asking children questions, brought in its community of adult fans to co-create new sets.

It was an act of creative humility that marked the beginning of a recovery rooted in subtraction and coherence (the two necessary vectors of simplicity). Knudstorp had rejected the idea of speed for its own sake and reintroduced the idea of direction. Just as Miles Davis did, he created the space for insights to emerge, but he did so at pace to ensure the company moved fast to where it mattered.

That's why I wanted to share his story with you. In a world where leaders are under constant pressure to deliver, move fast, respond instantly, and keep building, it would be silly to pretend that we can stop everything to reflect and wonder. What LEGO shows us is that you don't have to choose. If you have the right systems in place, you can remain fast where it counts and retain space where it is needed most.

In the last three chapters, we've explored what it means to reclaim the space in leadership that machines cannot occupy. We began by defining curiosity not just in terms of asking questions but to sense where enquiry itself is worth pursuing. Cézanne then helped us reappraise efficiency by recognising that speed without sight narrows possibilities. And, in our last chapter, I implored you to stay with creative emergence, when your best ideas arrive misshapen, non-linear, and in need of time.

What connects all these lessons is the idea that human insight requires space. With LEGO, we can see what an organisation looks like when a leader doesn't just practise these principles personally but builds an organisation that can apply them at scale. LEGO is the proof that you can make space for what might be without losing the pace for what must be done.

Making space is an active leadership discipline. It means stepping back from certainty to allow new meaning to take form while resisting the reflex to fill every silence. LEGO's turnaround was a demonstration of courageous restraint. The company understood that you don't make space by adding new ideas. Leadership isn't just about how fast we move: it is also about how much space we create along the way.

The weight of experience

It is also valuable to consider the deeper story behind LEGO's crisis. The company was permeated by an overconfidence in what had worked before. There was an established belief that more offerings would mean more growth, that more partnerships would mean more reach, and that more creative autonomy would mean better products. Instead, creativity had become clutter. The company was crumbling under the weight of unquestioned assumptions.

This tendency to default to previously successful strategies, even when better ones are available, is called the Einstellung effect (derived from the German for installed or set attitude). The more success we have had, the harder it becomes to see what no longer fits. We learn to trust our reflexes and become over-reliant on our mental models. We assume that what has worked before must work again.

The more senior a leader becomes, the harder it is for them to see anything different. This is the dark side of experience. It narrows our line of sight. We begin to see what we expect to see. We see familiar solutions even when the context has changed. We rely on tried and tested solutions, fixed in our view of the world. But, in ever-changing environments such as the one in which LEGO operated, unlearning becomes a survival skill.

More often than not, rather than greater success, success breeds activity and noise. When something works, leaders keep adding and expanding. They are loath to prune just in case removing anything means losing something essential. Jørgen Vig Knudstorp set out to prove otherwise. He set about releasing people from their assumptions. This is one of the most underappreciated distinctions between humans and machines.

AI is getting better every day at storing, cross-referencing, and recombining existing knowledge. Its power lies in retention. Human intelligence, though, possesses the ability to question the relevance of what it knows and release what it no longer needs. We can recognise when knowledge is outdated. We can feel when something is no longer of service. We can choose to let go of a belief, a process, or a mental model that no longer benefits us. This capacity to unlearn and clear cognitive space is a strategic differentiator. And, when AI can outperform us in precision, speed, and breadth of recall, our advantage lies in knowing when to stop knowing. The hallmark of radically human adaptive intelligence is our ability to revise, relinquish, and, indeed, where appropriate, refuse.

This capacity to unlearn lies at the root of curiosity. I asked you, at the end of Chapter 17, to stay longer with any frustration that you may be experiencing at the lack of 'so what?' or 'what can I do?'. This wasn't because I sought your indulgence as I went on to explain more concepts or share further stories. Instead, I asked you to stay with it to highlight the discomfort of staying curious when our habits drive us to stay active.

We are trained to skim, to overview, to glance, and then solve. We see more value in the doing than in the being. Our habits then become focused on applying our experience to any situation. Doing anything differently is hard. Letting go of a beloved framework, a prized methodology, or a way of working that once made us successful is not just cognitively difficult but identity-threatening.

When leaders are asked to make space, they often feel like they're being asked to do less. But what Jørgen Vig Knudstorp did is actually far harder. He let go of control for the sake of clarity because he knew that the weight of experience was dragging the organisation down. Rather than just give his team a new plan, he gave them permission to let go of the last one. He demanded urgency where there was clarity and created space where there was none.

Rather than slowing people down or speeding up activity, he paced correctly. Just as Cézanne and Davis had, LEGO learned to stay in the discomfort of reinvention long enough for a new structure to take shape.

Pace and space

I use the acronym PACE (perceive, attend, contain, and execute) to help leaders understand whether they require speed or space. These are four independent, non-linear muscles that, unlike AI, which moves only in one direction at one speed (ahead and faster), allow leaders to move in the rhythm of meaning.

Perceive

Pacing begins with perception. Perception is the moment you notice something. It can be something unusual in a meeting or tension in a room. It can be just a feeling that something is not right, accompanied by discomfort, or an image that lingers as it did for Semmelweis. For Knudstorp, it was the recognition that LEGO's problem wasn't a lack of creativity but a loss of coherence. Leaders who perceive are tuned to early signals without having to wait for a full articulation of issues.

This kind of perception is the raw material of intuition.

Attend

This second phase of pacing is about protecting what's forming from speed in order to protect fragile insights from disruption. Most organisations are allergic to the very notion of slow, but, as we have seen repeatedly throughout the last few chapters, not everything valuable shows up fast. To attend is to give something real space in which to emerge. This doesn't mean that everyone should sit around and wait passively. It means that everyone should be present and open to possibilities long enough for things not to crystallise too soon. This is how leaders create cultures of real enquiry. This is what Jørgen Vig Knudstorp did by listening to overlooked voices, including adult fans and front-line designers, before deciding what direction to take.

Contain

The third move, containment, is often the hardest. It is about having the courage not to rush and close things down. It is about resisting the urge to solve too soon. It is about allowing a team or an idea to remain incomplete because something more valuable might still arrive. Containing doesn't mean withholding action forever, but it does require knowing the difference between something that's uncertain and something that's unready. In this mode, leaders act more like gardeners than architects. They watch, prune, and nurture. Containment is an emotional act that requires sitting with tension and enduring ambiguity because it is necessary despite being uncomfortable. Containment was key to LEGO's turnaround. The senior team resisted the pressure to act hastily, holding back new product launches and decisions until the company had clarity on what truly mattered.

Execute

Finally, when something is ready to be implemented, the next step is to execute. Great leaders don't wait for perfect certainty. They wait until an insight has enough shape to warrant an action plan. Execution is the fulfilment of pacing. This is what Miles Davis did with *Kind of Blue*. He let the band wander, stretch, loosen, and then, at just the right moment, they recorded. Not a second too soon. Not a beat too late. This is also what Knudstorp did at LEGO. He didn't overthink. Instead, he moved quickly when the signal was strong, retiring thousands of products and reorganising teams with precision, ensuring that LEGO acted only when it had regained its focus.

The genius and the limitation of AI is that it does not pace. It completes, accelerates, narrows, and closes. Only humans can feel the need to pace themselves. Only humans can differentiate between being first and fast and being right and true. AI neither cares nor discerns. Only we can do that.

Of course, there are moments where speed, urgency, and response matter. The discipline of pacing is the discipline of differentiating where speed and space belong. To lead in the age of AI will require more than intelligence. It will require timing. When everything moves faster, the leader's power lies in knowing what needs to wait, what needs to be held for long enough that it can be done right.

Semmelweis showed us that insight begins with the courage to ask about what others overlook. Cézanne reminded us that slowness is depth made visible over time. Miles Davis revealed that creativity resists control and demands space for the wrong notes. And LEGO proved that, when leaders pace insight with discipline, entire systems can be remade.

Under Jørgen Vig Knudstorp's leadership, LEGO became the world's most valuable toy company, outperforming its competitors in both growth and cultural relevance. The company returned to its core purpose and rebuilt a system that balanced creativity with discipline. Knudstorp became executive chairman of the LEGO Brand Group, guiding its long-term vision and showing us that pacing insight isn't just about saving a business but about shaping its future.

Now it's time to make this practical by moving from the principles to tools.

Note

1 I was lucky enough to meet Jørgen Vig Knudstorp, early in his tenure, while on a visit to Billund, Denmark, as I had arranged for him to give a lecture to a group of executives I was working with on his plans. However, the information shared here is in the public domain. The turnaround of LEGO and Jørgen's role in it is well documented in articles, books, and business school case studies.

20

The questions that change everything

I've always believed that curiosity is a survival trait. The more complex the world becomes, the more critical our ability to know which questions are worth asking rather than rushing to answer the most obvious ones. From Semmelweis to Cézanne, Davis to LEGO, we've seen that the leaders who survive competitive pressure and thrive are the ones who stay with the right questions long enough for the truth to emerge rather than coming up with the best answers to the questions everyone else is asking.

This is why I designed this fourth toolkit to help you embed the discipline of enquiry into how you lead. It is a gateway to building the kind of culture where space, ambiguity, and reflection are seen as assets, rather than threats, led by leaders able to resist the demand for premature clarity.

In the age of AI, your value doesn't lie in how quickly you can respond but in your ability to stay curious about what matters most, for longest.

The curiosity culture check

As with our previous principles, use this 'self-diagnostic test' as a way to reflect on your own practices.

DOI: 10.4324/9781003683124-27

Use a scale of 1 (rarely) to 5 (always) to assess the following ten statements:

1. I actively question assumptions even when the evidence appears settled.
2. I allow conversations to stay open-ended rather than pushing for closure.
3. I prioritise framing the right question over finding the fastest answer.
4. I can name a time when pausing led to a breakthrough.
5. I reward team members who notice what others miss.
6. I distinguish between confusion and emergence.
7. I feel confident holding space for half-formed ideas.
8. I listen as a way of discovering, not just confirming.
9. I deliberately include dissent and friction in creative work.
10. I seek insights that could challenge my existing beliefs.

If you score between 40 and 50, I would suggest that you are modelling the curiosity needed to unlock real transformation. I would encourage you to look at the extent to which your team is following your lead by doing the same and identify the positive outcomes that need to be reinforced.

A score between 30 and 39 indicates a strong foundation alongside a potential over-preference for certainty. The risk is that people around you will perceive a bias for action rather than a bias for enquiry which will lead them to believe that the two are mutually exclusive. If you score below 30, you are valuing resolution over reflection. While this may be as a result of the role you are fulfilling or the environment you are working in, it is a risky position to be in, in an age of rapid, AI-driven conclusions.

What stops us from staying curious?

Unless we are capable of removing what stands in the way of success, the journey to building anything new will be twice as hard, which is why I outline below the five habits and systems that shut down curiosity even in well-meaning leaders.

1. Rewarding speed over sense-making, especially in environments where timelines are tight.
2. Treating curiosity as inefficiency by assuming that we are failing if we don't have an answer.
3. Relying on data alone to direct understanding.
4. Avoiding friction because we mistake disagreement for dysfunction.
5. Forcing clarity too soon by prioritising polished outputs over honest exploration.

Real curiosity is structured, disciplined, and strategic; hence the need to be intentional in its deployment rather than just seeing it as a trait.

Quick curiosity wins

Some of the most effective acts of leadership are rooted in our ability to self-manage and are, therefore, invisible to others. Below are five daily 'micro acts' that can help you practise enquiry. They may be small but can have a huge cumulative effect.

1. Stay quiet for 15 seconds longer than usual before responding.
2. Ask someone on your team to reframe the problem before offering ideas.
3. Remove from a dashboard one metric that no longer drives action.
4. Introduce one new voice into a conversation that feels stuck.
5. Start a conversation by saying, 'I'm not sure yet, but here's what I'm wondering …'.

The PACE self-check

Use the reflection tool in the table to assess how you typically behave at each stage of insight emergence. Circle the statement in each row that most closely describes you.

Perceive	I wait for solid evidence before noticing patterns	I notice small tensions even when I can't explain them
Attend	I redirect attention quickly if a conversation wanders	I protect time for reflection, even when outcomes aren't immediate
Contain	I resolve open questions quickly to reduce anxiety	I can stay with unclear problems long enough to see what forms
Execute	I act fast when there's external pressure to move	I act only when I sense the insight is underpinned by structure, not just urgency

If you mostly circled left-hand-side answers, you may be overly biased towards decisiveness, potentially at the cost of discovery. If, on the other hand, you mostly circled right-hand-side answers, you are probably pacing well but need to ensure you are communicating your rationale to avoid the risk of others confusing your pauses with paralysis.

Of course, these are false choices as we clearly have a need for both. Intentionally insightful leadership flexes between states depending on what the context and situation require.

PACE in practice

Depending on your results above you may want to use the following examples of leadership action cues to shift your practice for the elements of PACE you are the least sure about.

Perceive

This is about 'staying with the signal'. In our chapters, this was Semmelweis noticing unexplained mortality gaps or Cézanne painting how he saw rather than what he saw.

- Adopt a posture where you don't wait for full clarity before paying attention. Instead, try to notice what doesn't quite fit.
- Watch for anomalies, tensions, and recurring hunches.
- Ask yourself what is bothering you or what is not being talked about.

Attend

This is about 'guarding early ideas'. In our chapters, this was LEGO inviting adult fans into the design process or Miles Davis allowing space by favouring discovery over direction.

- Protect an idea purely for its intrinsic value without rushing to force a business case.
- Watch for vague enthusiasm, early prototypes, and odd connections.
- Allocate space (time, attention, psychological safety) to explore what's forming.

Contain

This is about 'holding on to ambiguity'. In our chapters, this was Cézanne refusing to finish paintings too soon, or Knudstorp suspending LEGO's overactive creativity to reclaim focus.

- Resist the urge to wrap up too soon.
- Watch out for the discomfort of waiting and actively resist the need to conclude.
- Make ambiguity explicit and make clear that it is to be welcomed.

Execute

This is about 'moving with meaning'. In our previous chapter, this was modelled by Knudstorp pruning LEGO's product catalogue once the recovery path became clear.

- Act only when you feel an insight has become clear enough rather than when an action feels overdue.

- Watch for energy levels, repeated signals converging, and feelings of readiness.
- Ask yourself if action is premature or warranted.

Weekly curiosity prompts

Use the following prompts individually or with your team to stay in enquiry:

- What changed in my understanding this week and why?
- What assumptions am I still carrying that might need to be updated?
- Where did I create real clarity and where did I conclude too soon?
- What question did someone ask that I didn't fully hear at the time?
- What question did I ask that led to a better frame of enquiry, not just a better answer?
- What small detail keeps sticking in my mind and what might it mean?
- Where did I feel something wasn't right but said nothing?
- Where did our appetite for speed blind us to insight?

I know I mentioned that I was running the risk of asking too many questions, so why don't you just pick one in any of the toolkits and write it on a Post-it note or make a note on your screen to use it to anchor your reflection for a week?

Commitment practices for leaders of enquiry

Here are five practices that will reinforce your own and your team's belief that wondering is a strategic act.

1. Signal pauses: in your next meeting, when asked for a quick decision, model pause as an active stance by asking others to sit in the unknown longer.

2. Celebrate non-obvious moves: each month, highlight one insight that came from a surprising source or from something that didn't fit.
3. Protect one question: identify one enquiry that is currently too hard to answer and raise it as an issue to ponder rather than solve. Let it evolve without acting.
4. Invert the debrief: after a decision has been made, ask others how different it would have been if they had gone with their first instincts, and, in that case, what, if anything, they would have missed. This will encourage them to see the value of uncertainty.
5. Frame rather than fix: once a week, instead of solving a problem, restate it in a better way to show your team the value of reframing over resolving.

Curiosity is about knowing when to slow down and dig deeper rather than endlessly wandering. Leaders who operate with our fourth principle of curiosity over certainty use curiosity as a way of staying with what matters, even when it is messy, ambiguous, or uncomfortable.

Semmelweis didn't ask more questions than his peers. He asked the one that mattered. Cézanne didn't paint more than others. He painted more slowly. Davis didn't compose more. He removed the convention. Knudstorp didn't invent more. He cut back and created space for reinvention.

Curiosity is a way of holding on to the unknown with enough care that something new has a chance to appear. For leaders though, in a world where AI can calculate faster than us, how we hold on to each other as we wonder is just as important as what we wonder about. So, while curiosity helps us stay with uncertainty, it is compassion that helps us stay with each other inside it. This is where our next principle begins.

Principle 5

Compassion over calculation

Leaders aren't valuable for what they achieve.
They're valuable for how they make people feel.

This fifth principle finds its roots in our first four. Having reclaimed our humanity (Principle 1), our resolve to stand for something (Principle 2), our instinct for a way forward (Principle 3), and our ability to stay with uncertainty (Principle 4), our leadership only becomes expressive when we reclaim our ability to care. In a world governed by metrics and automation, our emotional, relational, and cultural impact is where human capacities converge to deliver the one thing AI can't replicate. Compassion is a radical human advantage.

- Chapter 21: emotional intelligence is not a soft skill or a 'nice-to-have'. Leadership is as emotional as it is cognitive.
- Chapter 22: compassion as a disciplined practice strengthens connections that machines can only simulate.
- Chapter 23: scaling these connections requires rethinking organisational design so that humanity remains central as the impact of systems broadens.

DOI: 10.4324/9781003683124-28

- Chapter 24: the cost of a lack of systemic compassion manifests as disengagement, disconnection, and decline.
- Chapter 25: to reverse this, leaders must become cultural architects by designing environments that make others feel stronger and more capable in the pursuit of a goal.

21

All leadership is emotional

In 1889, Jane Addams opened the front door of a dilapidated old mansion on Chicago's West Side to start a revolution in the way we understand social care.

Hull House stood in the middle of a neighbourhood full of factories, tenements, and the sounds of foreign languages spoken by recent immigrants. Poverty was everywhere, sanitation was nowhere, children's futures lay elsewhere, and most of Chicago's elite chose to remain unaware.

At the time, social reformers operated from a distance. They designed programmes, delivered charity, and, of course, as has always been the way of the social elite, enforced morality. Jane Addams, inspired by a visit she had made to Toynbee Hall, in London, decided to do something radically different. She decided to move in and live among the people she sought to serve.

Hull House was neither a project nor her project. It became a settlement house for recently arrived migrants and her permanent home. Its purpose was not to 'uplift or help the poor': it was to create the conditions for a shared dignity to emerge as a precursor for humanity to flourish.

She spent her time asking questions rather than giving answers. What did people need? What did they fear? What helped them? She listened to mothers talk about their children's coughs.

DOI: 10.4324/9781003683124-29

She sat with workers describing 14-hour days. She invited young girls to attend reading clubs and gave them dance lessons in rooms that had once been drawing rooms of the wealthy.

What is striking about how Addams recounts those early years of living in Hull House in her memoir, *Twenty Years at Hull House*, is that she neither frames herself as a 'saviour' or 'hero' nor glorifies any of the sacrifices she made or decisions she took to romanticise her experience. She simply explains the hard emotional work of building trust. She talks about how hard it was and how long it took to overcome suspicion. She reveals how difficult it was to break stereotypes and make others see that she wasn't just another outsider with an agenda.

Her leadership lay in the very belief that emotional connections constituted the root of moral responsibility. Hull House was not her way to build her legacy. It was both a structure as a building and a structure for building the future of communities.

It included a daycare centre, a gymnasium, art and music programmes, one of the United States' first public playgrounds, and even a labour museum. When the city resisted sanitation reform, she organised the community. When local landlords exploited immigrants, she advocated on their behalf. And, when young men were either arrested or wounded, she was the one who called on their families or the one their families called.

In time, Hull House would become the model for over 400 settlement houses across the United States.

Yet her greatest act lay in her refusal to leave, or rise above others, as much as it lay in the foundations of Hull House. The leadership Jane Addams embodied showed the power of emotions in changing worlds. She attended funerals of babies whose mothers she had known and whose pain she absorbed. She welcomed reformers, artists, and even critics to show all those who would come how proximity could make you feel emotions that, in turn, would reveal solutions.

Of course, like anyone who stands for something, Addams was not always popular. Her opposition to the First World War earned her condemnation. Her pacifism, which so many framed as naïveté, cost her influence in the world she needed to impact for her work to succeed. But she never stopped leading and, in

1931, received the Nobel Peace Prize, the first American woman to do so, for having cultivated a form of leadership grounded in compassion, social connections, and sustained attention to human dignity.

Addams moved to Hull House to be fully present and live among those she sought to support (authenticity over automation). Even though the established consensus at the time was to impact lives from a distance, she chose to focus on human dignity up close (moral courage over mere compliance). She listened and acted on her instinct that the unspoken needs of others were too often overlooked (intuition over instruction). Above all, she asked questions that no social system had ever thought to ask, never mind answer (curiosity over certainty). In doing so, she offers us a truth at the heart of leadership and this fifth principle. Leadership is emotional, and compassion is its most human facet – something that AI will neither replicate nor help you achieve.

I am not holding up Jane Addams as a saint to revere or an example to copy. Instead, I want to reinforce something that she intuitively understood. I want to show you how strategies and plans without feelings are sterile and futile. I want to explain how the foundation of impact and influence (the two defining conditions of leadership) is having the courage to care, daily, deeply, and intently.

We are social beings

Jane Addams reminds us that we are wired for contact. We live through connections. She displayed her leadership at kitchen tables, beside cribs, and in silence with grieving parents. She didn't use any tools of leadership. She embodied her leadership.

I am guilty, along with countless others in my field, of having given the impression that leadership is best understood by looking at leaders. When leadership is written about or discussed, it is mainly in terms of traits, tools, techniques. We look at who leaders are, what they do, and how they do it. We forget to turn around and look. If you are ahead, and no one is behind you, you are not leading. Leadership is fundamentally about who follows. It is social. It is an emotional exchange.

Modern neuroscience has showed us how emotions drive leadership. The limbic system (the part of our brain that processes emotion and memory) responds faster than our rational brain. We feel before we think. Potential followers absorb how a leader feels before they process what she says. A subtle shift in tone, a pause that is that little bit too long, or a glance that is a little too distant can register as a threat before a single word is understood. A smile and calm tone register as safety before ever a single word is spoken.

Our nervous systems are wired for threat and safety. We constantly scan our environments for signals, whether these be facial expression, tone of voice, or posture, that tell us whether we are safe or not. This process, called neuroception, happens faster than conscious thought. Leadership is transmitted, nervous system to nervous system.

That is why proximity matters. A leader's body, not just her words, determines how we respond. These signals regulate both the leader's own stress as well as the stress levels of an entire group. We co-regulate in a sort of emotional contagion. Emotions spread. Whether they are joy and optimism that lead to better collaboration, or anxiety and resentment that lower team cohesion and performance, there is no escaping our need for connections.

AI cannot access the embodied trust that comes with close connections. We now have AI frameworks to motivate, dashboards to listen, algorithms to predict burnout, emotion analytics. In fact, AI is improving so rapidly in emotional mimicry, with sentiment analysis that can detect frustration and large language models that can mirror sympathy, that we can even use it in therapy. AI can replicate tone, decode facial expressions, and even approximate them through avatars, but it cannot emit the biological cues of safety. It doesn't breathe. It has neither a vagus nerve nor a heartbeat. Digital proxies cannot compete with the grounded human proximity of Jane Addams.

That is why I am worried about much of the current, and I suspect future and enduring, discourse about the impact of AI on work in general and leadership in particular. While tools and traits are helpful to guide the decisions of leaders, leadership itself has never been about programmatic output. Leadership is an exchange of emotional energy (a shared connection that implies risks and responses) that expresses itself through social connections.

We do well to remember that all leadership is emotional. Addams understood this better than anyone. She insisted on living among those she served because she believed that the human condition could not be dignified unless it was shared. She knew that recognition is not connection.

Connections are about shared consequences. They are not created by modelling behaviours, whether as a machine or as a leader in training. They come from growing weary from listening to sorrow, changing one's outlook after listening to the cries of a grieving mother. Addams knew this. Her leadership dignified people through emotional connection and grew in impact as a result.

Misunderstanding power

Leadership has never been a function of title, role, or expertise. It is not something someone gives you to exercise over others. Leadership is granted by those you lead, who give you some of their freedom to act on the basis of your ability to take them somewhere. There are many leaders by title who have never led, and many who lead without a title.

Whether they are giving instructions or creating emotional permission, the best leaders don't move others because they demand compliance. Instead, they move others because they create a space in which courage becomes possible.

If leadership is, at its core, a social act based on emotional connections, then it is about power understood as impact and influence. We often assume influence is about eloquence, or charisma, or some ability the leader has to convince. In leadership, power is the real differentiator; it moves people. This is why I define leading as creating the conditions for the positive engagement of others with a goal and, therefore, have no hesitation in calling Jane Addams a leader.

Hull House was all about creating the conditions for the neighbourhood to thrive. This assumes that you respect others' input, their opinions, their agency, and their importance. This is what is called socialised power. The recognition that your role is to make other people stronger and more capable so they can have agency over their contribution is essential.

Socialised power is the power used to lift others. A leader operating with socialised power cultivates the influence of others rather than wielding her own. Jane Addams understood this intuitively. That's why, when she established Hull House in 1889, she did not install herself as a distant manager with answers because she knew best. She moved in to live among the people others sought to fix in order to create the opportunity for better conditions to emerge. This was neither directional nor personalised leadership but a relational act.

In contrast, if you know what you want, are sure you are right, and have the means to achieve it, then you don't need to lead. You need only to coerce. This is about having power over people. It is a form of personalised power where the truth is embodied in the leader and the followers must comply or else.

Jane Addams did not manage anyone. She lived with people. She shared meals with them. She sat beside them in their grief and in their joy. Her power came from being steadfast, available, and emotionally engaged. AI cannot do this. It can simulate helpfulness or automate encouragement and, while, as we are discovering, it is possible for us to infer from its responses that we are seen, it cannot confer dignity or carry the moral burden of its own output.

In much of corporate life, emotion is seen as something to be contained, managed, or, ideally, eliminated in favour of logic. This is a false binary. Emotion is the engine of effectiveness.

Leaders have always been surrounded by tools that promised insights and clarity, but, in the age of AI, these have grown exponentially. We have dashboards that can measure engagement, apps that track team engagement, predictive engines for burnout, and lie detection and yet we have the highest levels of disconnection and the lowest levels of trust. Our problem isn't a lack of information but insight without connection and guidance without compassion.

If leadership is, at its deepest level, about making others feel stronger and more capable, then Addams offers a model that is as timeless and irreplaceable as it is replicable. Her leadership was not about being above others but about standing beside them, emotionally implicated. It was about providing something real in real time when everything else felt so remote. She may have never held political office nor sat in the boardroom of a company, but her leadership moved neighbourhoods, shaped policies, and reframed our understanding of social care. She is the embodiment of what it means to be alive inside and radically human both in impact and influence. She became so by having the courage not only to feel before acting (that, after all, is how humans are wired) but to stay with the feelings that we too often prefer to ignore.

The kind of compassion Jane Addams practised is a leadership principle that can be studied, strengthened, and embedded into the ways we work, because, if connections are what make us irreplaceable and socialised power is what makes us effective, compassion is how these connections move our worlds.

And so, we turn to cultivating it.

22

Cultivating compassion

In the late 1990s, Dr Devi Shetty stood beside yet another grieving family in a hospital corridor in Bangalore. A child had died of a heart condition that could have been corrected with surgery, but the parents, unable to afford the care earlier, had arrived too late, and their son had departed too soon.

Shetty had seen this dozens of times before but, on that day, he decided that he could no longer consider himself a doctor if he let cost decide who lived and who died. He could easily have remained on his existing stellar career path. He was trusted to operate on the country's most famous citizens, including Mother Teresa, as well as performing some of the world's most challenging operations (he performed India's first neonatal heart surgery). Instead, he decided to do something much harder. He decided to change a system.

In 2001, he founded Narayana Hrudayalaya (now Narayana Health), a hospital system built on dignity rather than profit. His goal was to make high-quality heart surgery available to those who could never ordinarily afford it and, more astonishingly in a country renowned for its giving culture, to make the model sustainable without charity.

He saw affordability as a design challenge and so decided to apply manufacturing principles to surgical operations. He rethought scheduling, cross-trained nurses, consolidated expensive equipment, and dramatically reduced fixed costs. In the

DOI: 10.4324/9781003683124-30

early 2000s, Narayana was performing open-heart surgeries for less than US$2,000 per patient, nearly one-tenth of the cost in most Western systems.

And, just as with the example of Jane Addams, Dr Shetty was not a distant reformer. He remained a practising surgeon. He continued his rounds, doing post-op checks on patients and speaking with families. In a profession where patient care is often an add-on module that aspiring medics are compelled, rather than motivated, to care about, he trained staff to be not just clinically competent but emotionally available.

Jane Addams taught how leadership is emotional. She showed us how connections are at the root of influence. But, if connections are the foundation of leadership, then compassion is the structure we build on these, and there is no more powerful form of compassion in leadership than the willingness to be changed by someone else's suffering and build systems that respond to it. That is why Dr Devi Shetty's story matters.[1]

Shetty reminds us not to confuse compassion with soft and reactive sentiment. He shows us how leaders can use compassion as a framework for perceiving needs accurately, interpreting them with humility, and responding to them with design-level intent.

This chapter isn't about being nice. It's about leading in a way that honours emotional truth and builds structures around it. Compassion, as we'll explore next, is not a mood. It is a discipline. It is a way of seeing, understanding, and shaping the world that demands more of leaders and cannot be delegated to technology. Leadership that begins with the courage to care isn't soft. It's simply real, radical, human leadership.

Empathy is overrated

Followers of my work will be familiar with the line above as 'Empathy is overrated' was the title of a chapter in one of my previous books.[2] I am not pointing this out because of some kind of need for self-aggrandisement, in fact, quite the contrary. That particular chapter was not the first time I had shared the idea.

I have been trying for years now to shift our focus to compassion as opposed to empathy. The difference has always been important for leaders, but it becomes critical in the context of the technological changes we are living through and with.

We talk about compassion as if it were a personality trait that some people are just naturally better at than others. We usually ascribe it to teachers, nurses (not as often to doctors), or parents. In leadership, it often gets described as kindness or patience and labelled merely as a soft edge in a hard world. But this is a misunderstanding.

Compassion is neither sentimental nor passive. It is a precise, teachable, and neurologically distinct way of responding to the emotional lives of others, especially when those emotions are inconvenient, painful, or politically risky.

If the previous chapter showed that leadership is fundamentally emotional, then this chapter asks the next essential question: what kind of emotion actually creates progress? And the answer is neither sympathy, nor empathy, but compassion.

These three words, often used interchangeably, do not mean the same thing. Sympathy is what we feel when we share another person's emotions. It connects us, but it can also overwhelm. A leader who feels what others feel might become emotionally paralysed. Empathy is more cerebral than emotional. It allows us to understand another's feelings without necessarily experiencing them. This makes it more stable and possibly more useful, but also more ethically ambiguous. You can understand how someone feels and use that knowledge to manipulate. You can empathise and remain entirely unmoved.

Compassion, in contrast, is the deliberate decision to engage morally and actively as well as emotionally. Compassion is about seeing pain and being willing and driven to change this. That is why compassion is so powerful in leadership. It does not stop at recognition. It insists on a response. Where sympathy might have led Shetty to feel for the family who lost their child, it was compassion that compelled him to change the healthcare model that left too many other families to feel that pain as well. Where empathy might have led him to seek or make charitable donations, it was compassion that led him to create a system which scaled care, embedded dignity, and proved that emotional leadership doesn't need to be expensive to be effective. Compassion is accountability that arises from feeling.

This is more than semantics. It is biology.

Empathy and compassion trigger different brain networks. Empathy activates pain-related regions (the anterior insula and anterior cingulate cortex), whereas compassion activates positive, reward-related regions (the medial orbitofrontal cortex and ventral tegmental area). When we experience empathy, particularly affective empathy, we activate the brain's pain circuitry. This is why empathy can feel exhausting. It literally hurts. Compassion, on the other hand, activates regions associated with motivation, reward, and caregiving. These areas generate warmth but, above all, they prime action. In other words, where empathy helps us detect suffering, it is compassion that helps us do something about this.

And, crucially, compassion earns trust. If leadership is about creating the conditions for followers to positively engage with a goal, then leaders must pass a test set by them. It is made up of two questions that all of us ask ourselves about our leaders. The first is, 'Do they get me?'. By this we mean, do they understand my reality and do they grasp what this work feels like for me, with my responsibilities, my values, my history? The second question is 'When push comes to shove, will they support me?'. We don't just want someone who will listen. We want someone who will act to make a difference to how we experience our environment.

Sympathy might answer the first question, and empathy can help with the second, but only compassion answers both consistently, visibly, and credibly. People trusted Dr Shetty's Narayana Health not just because it was efficient or affordable but also because it was designed with them in mind. Compassion is not a technique. It is a recognisable pattern of attention, interpretation, and response that can be neither replicated nor copied by AI.

The practice of compassion

This chapter is not about turning compassion into a checklist (though I will, of course, offer you one in Chapter 25). I do, however, want to give you a framework, or a lens, to help you recognise what real, operationalised compassion looks like.

There are three ways compassion shows up in leadership. It shows up in how leaders see, how they interpret, and how they respond.

First, compassion begins with what you notice. In fast-moving environments, reacting demands that, once we see someone's behaviour, we label it and respond. But compassion demands that we see the person before we notice the pattern. Compassionate leaders learn to withhold their mental shortcuts, biases, and models and suspend judgement. To see clearly and actively is the first act of leadership.

After seeing, the next challenge is to make sense of what you see without distorting it. This is compassion as a kind of 'humble understanding'. As we have seen, empathy, left unchecked, invites projection. We say things like, 'I know how you feel', even if we can't and don't know, when we should be more honest and just say, 'I know how I would feel in your situation, which may or may not be anywhere near how you feel'. Compassion demands a humbler approach. It shifts the question from 'What would I feel in your place?' to 'What is it like to be you, right now, with your past, your present, your pressures, and your hopes?'.

This requires us to check our assumptions, listen for nuances, and allow for ambiguity. Again, neuroscientific research supports this. Studies in social cognition show that mentalising (the process by which we make inferences about others' thoughts and emotions) improves with curiosity. The dorsomedial prefrontal cortex (the region linked to this interpretive process) activates most strongly when we feel safe enough to entertain multiple perspectives. Compassion is a willingness to keep asking.

When Dr Shetty redesigned access to healthcare, he showed that kind of moral imagination. Rather than focusing on what people could or could not pay, he focused on making dignity non-negotiable in healthcare. This kind of reframing can only be achieved when compassionate leaders do not assume understanding.

Ultimately, while perception and understanding are important, compassion truly manifests as leadership when actively applied. This is compassion as constructive action without overreach. It is not enough to observe, empathise, and then freeze. With empathy and sympathy alone, you may be overwhelmed by what you see or feel and unsure about how to act without creating more harm. In other instances, eager to solve the problem and quell the pain, you may find yourself rushing into solutions, often running the risk of oversimplifying what is really going on.

Being compassionate is about intention and attention. In practice, this could involve having a difficult conversation, framed with care, or prioritising humanity over short-term gains in a restructure. Crucially, in all instances, an often-overlooked aspect of compassion is its inherent demand for design. It is systemic. Just as Dr Shetty did, leaders must be prepared to build differently rather than just respond. Compassion is not merely having a good bedside manner. It is a leadership model.

To reiterate, while AI can replicate emotional cues, model tone, paraphrase concern, and even adjust for sentiment in real time, it does not fundamentally care about your suffering. With no memory or contextual understanding, machines can only simulate compassion. That's why compassion can only belong to humans. It emerges from the very elements that differentiate us from machines (fragility, embodiment, and existential awareness). Dr Shetty was a cardiac surgeon who could listen to his own heart, the way a machine will never do.

But, in a world as complex and fast moving as ours, we can't depend on one person's presence for compassion to be felt. It has to be embedded in a culture. The question then is, how do we make compassion a design principle and build systems that care?

That's what we'll move on to next, and it might just change how you see scale.

Notes

1 As is the case with all of the stories I share with you in this book, there is plenty to be found in the public domain if you are

interested in learning more about Dr. Shetty. Unlike many of the others, though, you can also find him on Netflix as he starred in the fourth episode of *The Surgeon's Cut* docuseries released globally on 9 December 2020.

2 Emmanuel Gobillot, *This Is Not A Leadership Book*, Routledge, 2024.

23

Scaling caring

It took a house for Jane Addams to increase dignity and a hospital for Dr Shetty to deal with health inequity, but could US$27 be enough to eradicate poverty? Muhammad Yunus thought he'd have a go.

In 1976, in the village of Jobra in Bangladesh, a young economics professor named Muhammad Yunus stopped to speak with a woman weaving bamboo stools. He soon discovered that, despite her skill and care, she was barely surviving. She explained that she had to borrow bamboo each day from a lender who charged so much interest that, by nightfall, she had only managed to make a few cents. She had a family she could hardly feed.

Intrigued, Yunus asked around and found 42 similar stories. Whether basket weavers, spice sellers, or mat makers, all worked hard, all were skilled, and all were trapped in the same cycle. Altogether, their total debt was just US$27. So, Yunus did something radically human. He paid the US$27. He neither charged interest nor signed any contracts. He just trusted that those whose debts he cleared would pay him back. They did.

Over the next few years, Yunus began lending more, always to the poor, almost always to women, and never asking for collateral. His hypothesis, grounded in his belief in humanity, was that, if you give people dignity and autonomy, they will repay your trust and their debt. It was a radical act from a professor

DOI: 10.4324/9781003683124-31

of economics working in the financial sector, when neither come top of the lists of radical professions and categories.

In 1983, Yunus founded Grameen Bank, a microfinance institution that would go on to reach more than 9 million borrowers across 80,000 villages in Bangladesh and become one of the world's largest institutions of its kind. But this is less a story about scaling access to credit than a story about scaling compassion. Grameen's model couldn't rely on the charisma of one leader or the moral strength of a few. In order to thrive, Muhammad Yunus had to build care into Grameen's very system.

Borrowers joined in small groups of five, each group forming a peer accountability circle. If one member struggled, it was the job of the others to support her. Their weekly repayment meetings were opportunities to teach, talk, and reflect. Over time, the meetings became rituals and, eventually, the emotional infrastructure of the bank. It worked. The repayment rate soared above 95 per cent, an above average rate for any bank, never mind one lending to the worst off in society.

Grameen succeeded by building values into its very architecture. Trust was the currency. Dialogue was the medium. And purpose, the idea that you were part of something larger than yourself, was the engine that kept it moving.

Even as the bank expanded, the intimacy and proximity needed for compassion didn't disappear. Every branch was local. Every group stayed self-managed. When floods, crop failures, family illnesses, or any other crises hit, the system flexed and strengthened, just like a bamboo shoot. Members helped one another, payments were adjusted, and compassion and trust endured.

Grameen went on to export its methods to more than 100 countries and still, at its core, it remained human-centric. Every borrower was known by name, and every individual was part of a community. Contrary to what many start-ups experience, Grameen's growth didn't inhibit compassion; in fact, it was compassion that enabled the bank to grow.

Most organisations treat compassion as something that diminishes as the system expands. Every start-up trades intimacy for efficiency as it grows. We assume that scale demands standardisation. We believe that distance requires control. In growing Grameen, Muhammad Yunus managed to flip that logic on its head. He demonstrated that compassion could be codified into relationships, habits, and, eventually, growth.

Today, organisations of every kind, whether in the public, private, or third sector, are under pressure to scale faster, more leanly, and more smartly, turning to AI to manage complexity, automate decisions, and optimise communication. As systems become more efficient, they also become less human. They miss emotional signals and replace dialogue and trust with data and templates.

To ensure that their organisations remain alive inside, leaders must build for compassion rather than leave it to chance, just as Grameen did. There is no need to swap digital tools for people, but neither should we believe that we can swap people showing up for one another, week after week, year after year, for digital tools. The answer, as is always the case, is to be found in reconciling two seemingly opposed ideas. In a world where technological advances have so many benefits and drawbacks, we must meet the challenge we have, to date, found so difficult to tackle – reconciling intimacy with efficiency.

Seeing through organisations

Grameen Bank didn't grow out of traditional organisation design. Yunus didn't start with a hierarchy, didn't have a product roadmap, a business model, or a governance structure. Instead, as in the examples given in our two previous chapters, growth started with asking what it would take for a system to truly serve the people inside it.

Most leadership conversations focus on strategy, systems, and output. But, when you look closely at any organisation, you find something else holding it together. All organisations are underpinned by an invisible web of relationships, rituals, and shared meaning that form what I called, in my book *The Connected Leader*, first published in 2007,[1] the 'real' organisation.

In it, I pointed out that every organisation is formed of two distinct systems. The first is the formal organisation, which lives in the charts, the reporting lines, the policy manuals, and process maps. It ensures that any product or service is delivered at the right quality, price, and time. It is critical and efficient, but ultimately rigid.

The energy of any organisational system comes from the second system. It is the real organisation that governs day-to-day life. This is made up of trust, unspoken norms, favours that are quietly repaid, and questions that can be asked in confidence. It's the relational network underneath the procedural system.

We shouldn't assume, even though we often do, that, if the formal organisation is well designed, the rest will follow. Real connections don't flow through lines and boxes. Yunus understood this instinctively. Grameen grew by amplifying trust, each lending group acting as a node of care in a complex network of human exchange. When members met, they discussed children, illnesses, seasonal pressures, community tensions, rather than attending a performance review.

To make a credible credit model scalable required focusing on both the formal and the real organisations.

Artificial intelligence is accelerating formalisation. It is turning more of the real organisation into data. We now have email sentiment scores, engagement dashboards, network mapping software, and behavioural nudges. But, while these tools promise insight, they often encourage distance in reality. They train leaders to manage systems, not people, and respond to indicators, not individuals.

Yunus started by acknowledging that the real organisation needs real work. It's easy to dismiss this kind of thinking as idealistic, but Grameen's repayment rates are among the highest in the financial world for the population it serves. Its structure is resilient in disaster and adaptive in growth. Compassion is not soft. It is a strong architecture that scales through designing for the real organisation, recognising that some intangibles determine everything.

The compassion bridge

What carries compassion from a leader's intention into a living organisational reality is the invisible scaffolding made up of three elements – trust, purpose, and dialogue. Together, they form the compassion bridge that connects the formal and real organisations, enabling the formal objective to be delivered through the informal network. Grameen Bank embedded these three elements at every level of its operation.

Women trusted one another to repay loans because the system had trained them to see their fates as intertwined. Purpose was personal, shared, and urgent. It was about lifting a village together. Dialogue was a weekly habit, carried out face to face in open circles following agreed-upon principles.

Let's take each of these elements in turn to see how they can be made into repeatable patterns that enable compassion to become operational at scale, rather than staying as values on a poster.

Trust may well be the baseline of all functioning organisations, but the kind of trust that enables compassion to build at scale is not just about believing your boss or a colleague will deliver. It is about having the emotional safety to be confident to speak up, show weakness, or admit mistakes. As AI and data analytics are used to quantify performance, people start to worry about being measured more than they are seen. Systems make it harder to interpret intent. Grameen ensured people relied more on each other than on metrics.

Many organisations have purpose statements that tell you what the company believes, but how many of these truly drive behaviour? To be effective, purpose must be co-authored, localised, and adaptive by being constantly reinterpreted by each team and each individual in their own context. At Grameen, purpose wasn't printed on posters. It lived in the stories people told. Each borrower had their reason for needing a loan but, whether they wanted to feed their children, buy their own loom, or send a daughter to school, all those stories converged into a shared purpose of lifting each other. That collective clarity gave people something to strive for and grow with. Purpose without compassion is hollow. But compassion without purpose can be misdirected. What links the two is the space for meaning to emerge. That space is our final element: dialogue.

Without it, we default to assumptions. Dialogue is the fuel that keeps compassion alive. It is the way leaders check how people's needs are changing. It is the way teams reflect, correct course, and express emotional truth. This is where AI poses a danger. Given that conversational bots can simulate dialogue, capture employee sentiment, and help in ongoing conversations, it is easy to decide that they are now good enough to replace the hard work of conversing at scale. But simulation is not the same as connection. Humans, unlike AI, are transformed through conversations. In Grameen, dialogue was sacred. Weekly meetings were used as a form of emotional audits that allowed the system to adjust to human conditions as well as market ones.

When trust, purpose, and dialogue are active, compassion becomes systemic. It no longer needs the constant presence of a leader to flow. Grameen teaches us that compassion doesn't dilute with scale when it is embedded in the structure. The most powerful systems are those designed to listen to what people need rather than just to assess what they produce. AI cannot build trust, co-author purpose, or stage dialogues. It cannot live inside the real organisation. This is why leaders can't just stop at being compassionate; they must design organisations that can magnify the exercise of compassion beyond their personal impact.

In 2006, like Jane Addams before him, Yunus was awarded the Nobel Peace Prize, along with Grameen Bank, for managing to translate what the Norwegian Nobel Committee described as a vision that 'appeared to be an impossible idea' into actions that 'developed micro-credit into an ever more important instrument in the struggle against poverty'.[2] That's the power of compassion. It is a not only a success advantage but humanity's inalienable one.

That Muhammad Yunus's US$27 loan built a billion-dollar movement is not what makes this story impressive. What's more impressive is that, when people couldn't repay their debt, the system paused, listened, and rebalanced rather than punished.

This is why, in the next chapter, before we move on to practical tools to make compassion a reality, I want to explore the cost of disconnection, which occurs when the systems we trust become indifferent. I want to help you see how it emerges and spreads to give you a head start to avoid it. Because, in the absence of compassion, the only thing that scales is withdrawal.

Notes

1 First published by Kogan Page in 2007, *The Connected Leader* was fully revised into a second edition published by De Gruyter Brill in 2024.

2 The Nobel Peace Prize for 2006 press release. Nobel Foundation. 13 October 2006. Archived from the original on 19 October 2006.

24

The heavy cost of disconnection

In 1893, a mere four years after Jane Addams had first opened the doors of Hull House, George and Richard Cadbury decided to build a village. Bournville, on the outskirts of Birmingham, UK, was to be a community where factory workers could live with dignity, far from the slums and soot of the industrial inner city. More than just houses, they wanted to build a new social contract grounded in their Quaker values of equality, stewardship, and care.

By 1900, Bournville included over 300 thoughtfully designed homes surrounded by green space, with community gardens, clean water, and access to education, recreation, and healthcare. The idea – accepted today, if not always applied – was simple yet bold for its time. The Cadburys felt that people work better, not just harder, when they are respected as whole humans.

Workers received paid holidays. Medical services were free. Wages were fair. Cadbury refused to exploit child labour, even when rivals did. The factory itself was bright, spacious, and surrounded by trees. At a time when many industrialists saw their workers as expendable, the Cadburys were designing compassionate industrialism.

It worked. Productivity rose. Morale was high. Bournville was internationally celebrated as a humane counter-model to

DOI: 10.4324/9781003683124-32

Victorian capitalism. The village was alive. Sunday lectures, choirs, cricket matches on the green, story circles, and listening rooms created a culture of mutual attention. Yet what it offered was nothing compared with how it offered it. The real breakthrough was participation. Cadbury employees helped shape the community's rhythm. Dialogue was part of daily life. Senior managers and factory workers met at the same events and solved problems through their conversations. But, over time, something began to change.

In the 20th century, as Cadbury scaled nationally and internationally, its governance became more distant. The Cadbury family's hands-on presence gave way to formalised structures and professional management. Shareholder interests slowly took precedence over communal values. The amenities, the parks, the schools, and the trust funds remained, but something essential began to disappear. Conversations became more formal. Meeting frequency declined. Managers no longer lived in the community. Employees spoke more of being managed than heard.

Sure, people still took pride in Bournville. But the feeling of shared ownership faded. What had once been a collaborative, emotionally resonant system had become a polished machine. Cadbury remained an efficient and attractive business, but it was less alive.

Historian Carl Chinn had grandparents who worked in the factory. Writing after extensive research in the Bournville archives, he argued that, over decades, the village shifted from its lived, everyday ethos to a heritage experience that lived more in memory than in reality.

The factory was eventually absorbed by larger conglomerates. Decision-making moved even further away. Despite numerous efforts to retain the village's unique heritage, the relational fabric continued to fray.

This is the kind of disconnection that is so easy for leaders to miss. There is no big decline in numbers nor a visible crisis. Instead, it is the slow evaporation of emotional attention – people no longer speaking up because they've quietly checked out. With today's AI, automated, and hybrid-heavy work environments accelerating, many leaders are turning to digital systems to track engagement, monitor sentiment, and measure morale to try to anticipate a problem that isn't captured in metrics.

Bournville is a reminder that disconnection starts in silence, with the erosion of a shared story and the absence of real listening. Yet it is also a story that offers hope because the village did not fail owing to bad intent. It faltered because care, which was once embedded in proximity and practice, was no longer actively renewed. And this we can change.

Getting to the root causes of disconnection

Bournville was undone by the confidence that what had once been built with care, conviction, and proximity would continue to function without attention. It was undone by the confidence that dignity, once installed in the infrastructure, would self-perpetuate. It was undone by the confidence that the emotional resonance of the community would outlast the rituals that sustained it.

This is the nature of disconnection in organisations. It is rarely dramatic or crisis-driven. Most of the time, it is both silent and compliant. It is similar to people doing their jobs, showing up on time, and gradually disappearing on the inside. Disconnection is the absence of relationships masked by the appearance of normality. As such, it can go undetected for years, so much so that, by the time the system starts to falter, the very people needed to rebuild it have lost the will to bring their full selves to their work.

The three root causes of emotional disconnection are the dismantling of the three pillars of the compassion bridge between the real and the formal organisations we discussed in our last chapter, which were the foundation of Grameen's success.

Loss of trust

Trust is built from micro-interactions (the way feedback is given or conflict managed) between people. At Bournville, as the Cadbury's family presence faded, and corporate decision-making moved off-site, trust eroded. The new leaders were simply absent rather than malicious. Conversations became formal (a warning to all of us who are called to manage remote teams), and the real organisation weakened.

Modern organisations replicate this dynamic in subtler ways. When the pace of business accelerates, trust is often sacrificed for speed. Dialogue is replaced by directives, and enquiry becomes reporting. That's how most real organisations begin to fray today.

Erosion of shared purpose

Purpose is the sense of belonging to something larger, where one's individual actions connect to a shared outcome. When purpose becomes too abstract or too tightly held by leadership, it ceases to inspire. At Bournville, workers initially experienced purpose viscerally. It lived in their homes, their gardens, and their community halls. Over time, as purpose was institutionalised and depersonalised, it became more a source of nostalgia than motivation.

In many modern teams, especially in remote or hybrid settings, purpose must now compete with distraction, dislocation, and divided attention. When people cannot locate themselves in the purpose of the system, they stop showing up with meaning.

Breakdown of dialogue

Nothing sustains emotional connections like conversations. They create the space for uncertainty, emotion, and change. When dialogue evolves to become a round of status updates, agenda reviews, and reporting cycles, organisations lose their ability to self-heal. Hard truths get buried, and creativity collapses into consensus. Bournville's early days were full of dialogic rituals. These were community events, listening forums, shared planning discussions. When these faded, the culture unravelled, and care became theoretical.

In today's organisations, dialogue is often seen as inefficient. Leaders pay tribute to Elvis by singing 'a little less conversation, a little more action please'. With the rise of AI-assisted communication, we can even simulate responsiveness without actual presence, and this makes disconnection even harder to see.

A framework for REAL connections

By the time most leaders notice disconnection, it has already taken hold. This is where compassion becomes a strategic form of leadership. There are four components that allow trust, dialogue, and purpose to be reactivated across the system. I use the acronym REAL.

R is for restore psychological safety

Nothing reconnects people faster than safety. When people feel they can express doubt, emotion, or dissent, they connect physically and emotionally, as well as intellectually. In Bournville, as management became more distant, the village became a system of quiet compliance.

Restoring safety starts with leaders modelling what it looks like. Whether by admitting mistakes, inviting feedback, or acknowledging ambiguity, they can destabilise the current norm before turning it into something new. This is important, as even norms that no longer serve people can still feel familiar and safe. Leaders must break the silence by inviting emotional truth and reward it with presence rather than critique. With psychological safety, almost anything is possible.

E is for empathise across levels

When those at the top make decisions without emotional visibility in the lives of those below, the organisation splits. If, as I have argued, compassion is active empathy, the first act of reconnection has to be to ensure that empathy exists.

At Bournville's peak, community planners, workers, and leadership lived near each other. They shopped at the same stores, shared the same fields, attended the same events. But, as decisions increasingly came from corporate governance boards, the emotional distance grew, and empathy faded. Empathy must be engineered for reconnection to occur.

A is for align on shared purpose

People lose energy when they can no longer see how their efforts matter. When organisations grow, change fast, or operate in silos, people's sense of contribution erodes, and their engagement becomes mechanical.

Bournville teaches us that purpose must be felt to be followed. As market priorities began to dominate, purpose became something that lived in the organisation's history rather than being embedded in the daily rhythms of the village. Restoring purpose is not about writing better vision statements. It is about making people authors of meaning again. When people no longer know what they are part of, they can't show up as a part of it.

L is for listen structurally

In my experience, most leaders believe that listening is something they do. The key issue, however, is whether they do it actively and always rather than when they are asked or have time. Listening structurally means that your organisation has embedded opportunities for truth to surface.

Sustainable change only comes through cycles of reflection, dialogue, and adjustment. This is what active listening means. In Bournville, the loss of structural listening happened as spaces for informal exchange vanished, as decisions became encoded in memos, and as the system forgot how to hear itself. To listen structurally is to prevent this outcome.

The fact that Bournville drifted rather than collapsed reminds us that compassion needs to be sustained once it is installed. It shows us how disconnection is often quiet, sometimes cumulative, and always hard to measure. We saw how performance can remain high even as care drains out of a system. We explored how AI may accelerate this erosion by offering synthetic insights while numbing the human instinct to listen, feel, and respond. But disconnection is not irreversible.

The REAL framework shows that reconnection is a commitment to restore safety, empathise across boundaries, align purpose, and listen intently.

Over the last four chapters, we've built the case for a new kind of leadership rooted in what machines cannot replicate. In Chapter 21, we saw that emotion is foundational to leadership as it shapes influence, trust, and movement. In Chapter 22, we learnt that compassion is a practice that can be cultivated, structured, and made visible, rather than a trait. In Chapter 23, we explored how care scales through systems designed to hold connection. And now we have seen how even the most human systems can fray through neglect.

Together, these chapters form the architecture of Principle 5: compassion over calculation. They remind us that, in an AI-shaped world, leading with care is both human and differentiating. It is this designed, disciplined, and deliberate practice that separates those who manage systems from those who truly lead people.

Now we turn to the tools that can help build this practice into the fabric of daily leadership. The goal is not to standardise compassion but to ensure it survives scale, distance, and time.

25

Cultural architects

By now, we have seen that emotional resonance, deep connections, and care for others all differentiate humanity from AI. We have recognised that artificial intelligence without emotional intelligence stops compassion from enduring. Now, we must go into design.

This is why you will find below some thoughts on how to tackle the emotional foundations of leadership, the practice of compassion, the challenge of scaling care, and the high cost of disconnection. Together, they will help you become designers of culture.

As I have stressed in previous 'practical' chapters, the ideas below are not scripts. They are ways to test your assumptions, to reflect more deeply, and to create the conditions where others feel stronger and more capable as a result of your leadership. Given it is the systems we build that shape what people believe is possible, our responsibility lies in building systems that people can believe in.

The compassion inventory

Use this self-assessment to reflect on how well compassion shows up in your leadership practice.

DOI: 10.4324/9781003683124-33

Rate how often these statements apply to you, from 1 (rarely) to 5 (always):

1. I respond to emotional signals even when they're subtle or unspoken.
2. I make time to understand what matters to the people I lead, not just what they produce.
3. I reflect on the emotional consequences of my decisions.
4. I adjust how I lead based on what I learn from difficult conversations.
5. I ask, 'What is it like to be you?' more often than 'What's wrong?'.
6. I notice when someone is emotionally absent.
7. I give feedback in a way that protects dignity and promotes growth.
8. I have created systems or rituals that make caring a shared responsibility.
9. I resist automating conversations that carry emotional weight.
10. I recognise when my presence, rather than my experience or expertise, is what's needed most.

Instead of looking for specific scores, ask yourself the following questions: which of these did you find easiest? Which feel performative? Which will make the biggest difference? Your answers will point to the areas you need to focus on and the kind of practices you should try. In my experience, it is also helpful to reflect on these with a trusted colleague who can act as a mirror to your self-analysis.

Three design principles for compassionate systems

As we saw with Jane Addams, Dr Devi Shetty, Muhammad Yunus, and Cadbury, compassion builds at scale when it is embedded into system design. Here are three design principles to guide you:

1. Proximity is power: care travels through closeness. Whether physical, emotional, or attentional, leadership proximity regulates how people feel. Design rituals that create closeness even in remote or hybrid teams.
2. Emotion is data: too many systems treat emotion as noise. To build a compassionate system, you must make space for emotions to be surfaced, interpreted, and responded to, rather than just managed.
3. Reconnection is a skill: disconnection will happen. The question is whether your system knows how to heal. Build in check-ins, repair mechanisms, and listening forums that keep emotional feedback loops open.

Testing the strength of your compassion bridge

In Chapter 23, I introduced the idea of the connective structure that allows care to flow across the organisation through trust, purpose, and dialogue. I called this the compassion bridge that connects the formal and real organisations. Below are some ideas to test yours.

- Trust:
  - Do people bring bad news early or wait for damage control?
  - Is feedback shared peer to peer, or only up and down the hierarchy?
  - Are people willing to say, 'I'm struggling' as quickly as they say, 'I'm on it'?
- Purpose:
  - Do team members talk about what their work means to them and the organisation without being prompted?
  - Are decisions justified in terms of both performance and meaning?
  - Are people proud of *how* we do things as much as *what* we do?

- Dialogue:
  - Does disagreeing feel safe?
  - Do people speak more in meetings or outside them?
  - Does the system notice when someone withdraws emotionally?

Bridges always need maintenance. If your answers to the questions above feel mixed, it may be time to repair some of the elements of the bridge. Below are some examples of early signs of disconnection that can help you frame relevant interventions.

Spotting early signs of disconnection

As we explored in Chapter 24, disconnection can be hard to spot as it happens in small increments (e.g. quiet withdrawals, dulled energy, mechanical compliance). Here are five early signals to watch out for:

1. Surface-level positivity: no problem is a problem! Everyone is 'just fine', and there is no friction, no challenge, and no depth.
2. Decline in informal communication: if you hear fewer jokes and fewer side conversations, you will get fewer insights.
3. Engagement drops: people are showing up with no heart rather than not showing up at all.
4. Reactivity increases: if you see small frustrations escalating quickly, it is often a sign of emotional depletion.
5. Silence in response to change: if a new initiative is launched and no one asks questions, pushes back, or offers ideas, you know they are merely going through the motions.

As we have seen throughout this principle, disconnection is not a dysfunction. It is an indication that the organisational system has stopped listening to itself.

The CARE framework

To rebuild systemic compassion, try embedding the CARE lens below into your daily leadership practice to focus on areas that will make a difference.

Create conditions

What is the environment you are creating, facilitating, or hindering?

Examples:

- Do people feel safe enough to speak freely?
- Are there rituals that promote openness?
- Are power dynamics soft enough for truth to surface?

Ask about meaning

Do you know what matters to the people around you?

Examples:

- Have you asked what motivates others rather than what they want to deliver?
- Have you explored what's making it hard for them to care?

Respond with design

Have you changed a structure, or a habit, based on what you have heard?

Examples:

- Have you changed meeting rhythms to allow for better emotional connection?
- Have you adjusted team norms based on a feeling someone shared rather than an idea they suggested?

Embed for scale

Have you made compassion part of the system rather than just part of your personal repertoire?

Examples:

- Are there team rituals that don't rely on you to sustain care?
- Does onboarding, goal-setting, or recognition reflect emotional presence?

AI check

Given that AI tools are increasingly more 'emotionally' sophisticated, below are three checks to protect compassion from being reduced to code:

- Is this tool simulating care or extending it?
- Would I trust this system with my own vulnerability in full knowledge of the consequences of doing so?
- Does this decision leave room for human interpretation or erase it altogether?

Technology can enhance your reach, but only you can create the emotional conditions for others to trust, engage, and grow. That is not something you can, or should, delegate.

Weekly compassion prompts

Here are some questions you may want to consider adding to your weekly reflection prompts:

- When did I listen rather than just hear?
- When did I sense someone was pulling back from contributing and reach in to encourage them?
- What small gesture had a big emotional impact?
- What system/process/habit did I spot that made someone feel either more seen or more invisible?
- Where did technology distance me from a real conversation?

Commitment practices for compassionate leadership

Finally, here are some habits that, when done with presence and purpose, will create the conditions for others to bring their full selves to work.

1. Micro-reconnections: each day, reconnect with one person who seems distant; do so to understand rather than to fix them.
2. Emotion-first agendas: start one meeting a week by asking, 'How's everyone doing, really?'.
3. Compassion review: once a month, reflect on a time when you acted with compassion and a time when you missed the moment.
4. Silent listening rounds: create a ten-minute meeting ritual where people can speak without interruption.
5. Proximity pauses: before automating, delegating, or deciding, pause to ask if your presence would change the outcome?

Leadership was never about the volume of your outputs. Your value always lay in the emotional quality of your inputs. The ultimate test of your impact was always how many people you managed to make feel stronger, safer, and more capable because of how you showed up. Yet, given our reward structures, until now, you could get away with focusing solely on deliverables.

The compassion over calculation principle is a reminder that, unless you see compassion as structural, in a world increasingly managed by algorithms, you add little value. Compassionate leaders and systems are essential because, no matter how far AI progresses, only humans care about consequences. How you show up will determine whether you stay on, so we must now turn to our next principle.

Part 3

The heroic paper clip

As we move to the last part of this book and our final two principles, I want to introduce you to someone without whom Clippy would have never existed and Bostrom's 'paperclip maximiser' experiment would never have been possible.

The spiritual father of Clippy can be said to be Johan Vaaler of Norway. In 1901, he was granted the first patent for the invention that looked like a paperclip.[1] But it was World War II that turned the paperclip from a clever invention into a national symbol.

In Nazi-occupied Norway, where resistance was dangerous and free expression and speech were censored, the regime had banned uniforms, flags, and any symbol of national pride. But, in the autumn of 1940, students at Oslo University started doing something innocuous and inconspicuous enough to go unnoticed. They started to pin a paperclip on their lapel as a way to show unity and resistance to Nazi occupation. The trend caught on. Teachers did the same, shopkeepers joined in, and soon the paperclip had become a silent gleam of metal on wool that spoke louder than any chant or slogan.

The occupying Nazi regime, quick to suppress anything unapproved, banned the gesture. But, by then, it was too late. The paperclip had become a tiny, ordinary, utterly unbreakable symbol of defiance. In the Norwegian language, a paperclip is called a 'binder', describing an object that holds together. It was now binding the people of Norway. It was a whisper of resistance that reminded all those who wore it and those who banned

DOI: 10.4324/9781003683124-34

it too that, whatever the rules, humanity cannot be banned. Even in shackles, people can still be free in their own minds. The Nazis could ban the paperclip but not its meaning.

This is the third lesson of the paperclip. Leadership doesn't need to be loud to matter. It simply needs to be steadfast. Over the years, we may have come to define leadership in terms of control, but it is conscience that turns an ordinary person into an extraordinary leader.

Today's systems have erased the conditions for critique. Discomfort has been replaced by distraction. AI offers frictionless convenience and wears down our will to wonder. It is because of that slow erosion that the idea of radical humanity, or being alive inside, can seem naïve, soft, inefficient, or even obsolete. But we must remember that every AI system we implement is a moral choice. Every automation tool we deploy reshapes what it means to be human inside our organisations. The Norwegian people resisted because they cared. They refused to let others define their humanity for them. The same is true now.

The question is, what will signal your leadership? Will your lapel reflect your obedience or proudly display the paperclip of stewardship? You don't have to stage a revolution. But you do have to take a stand. This is why we need leaders whose presence highlights their intention and attention. This is our sixth principle, 'presence over performance'. Our modern-day equivalents of the Norwegian paperclip are the acts of leadership that bind people to a shared future. This is why we need leaders who can bind people together through a common story. This is our seventh and last principle, 'stories over structures'.

Together, these two principles give us our final imperative. The first imperative of being alive inside was to be more intentional in the way you express your voice and your values; the second was to stop optimising and start humanising. Our third imperative of being alive inside is the need, always, to choose to bind.

Note

1 I don't want to get all geeky about it but, for information, the paperclip as we know it today was in fact being designed at roughly the same time by the British Gem Manufacturing Company Ltd, which Vaaler couldn't have known about as it was not marketed in Norway. His patent was granted in Germany, as Norway did not have patent laws at the time. If you like this kind of thing, go to Wikipedia – the story is fascinating!

Principle 6

Presence over performance

Leaders aren't valuable because they're always visible.
They're valuable because they're fully present.

In our five previous principles, we looked at how emotions, ethics, instincts, curiosity, and care are a leader's advantage in the age of AI. With this sixth principle, we turn our gaze to how leaders show up, day by day, in a world that tries to pull people into data and away from each other. In the age of AI, where performance is increasingly automated and visibility easily manufactured, the most radical, rare, and powerful act of leadership is to give full attention. Your presence is neither performative nor just about being seen. Leaders who offer their attention create the conditions for clarity, energy, and alignment. Presence is how leadership is felt rather than observed.

- Chapter 26: to lead with intention, we must first understand that attention is the most powerful, and uniquely human, form of influence.
- Chapter 27: it is, paradoxically, the invisible channel through which energy, emotion, and alignment travel from leader to culture.
- Chapter 28: in uncertain, fast-moving environments, a leader's presence ensures creativity and resilience.

DOI: 10.4324/9781003683124-35

- Chapter 29: the fact that what leaders pay attention to gets done, rather than what they measure, makes presence the ultimate form of authority.
- Chapter 30: in a distracted world, where full presence is rare, it is precisely this quality that makes leadership transformative.

26

Intention is attention

In 2012, before Satya Nadella became CEO of Microsoft, he attended a meeting that would set out a new direction for leadership inside the company. It was a gathering of the company's Disability Employee Resource Group, a small internal community advocating for greater accessibility across Microsoft's sprawling portfolio of products and services.

Those in the room, used to senior leadership visits, were expecting a polished executive presentation. They were preparing themselves for a quick drop-in, with maybe a few prewritten words of encouragement, a slide or two about the company's future vision and their place in it, and a tightly timed departure managed by a group of assistants. However, instead of following a pattern set by his predecessor, and indeed most leaders inside and outside Microsoft, Nadella entered the room, sat down without ceremony, looked around, and simply asked, 'How does this work?'.

We're not used to a leader entering a room with no bulleted talking points, no script, and no posturing. We're not used to a leader asking just one question. And we're certainly not used to a leader staying silent. By simply offering his full, undivided, human attention, listening intently to the people in front of him, asking follow-up questions, and not interrupting, solving, or fixing, Nadella led rather than performed.

DOI: 10.4324/9781003683124-36

As Jenny Lay-Flurrie, Microsoft's chief accessibility officer, went on to recount, 'With that one question, all my nerves vanished, allowing us to have a very real and deep conversation about the ways technology can empower … and disempower people'.[1] And, just like her, the other employees in the room relaxed, making them able to voice their frustrations, fears, and unheeded ideas. It might have been a meeting that was unlike those many people in the room had experienced before in a corporate setting, but it was also the most real meeting they had been in.

This one question from one present leader went on to translate into real, structural change. Microsoft's investment in accessibility R&D, inclusive design principles, and the development of AI tools such as Seeing AI went up. All of this was enabled by one act of sustained, authentic attention. What made that moment so powerful is that Nadella never sought to dominate, to over-prepare, or to be right. This kind of leadership might seem small in contrast to the scale of challenges we've already explored in this book. After all, we've discussed navigating the murky territory of intuition in uncertain times, the moral weight of decision-making, the dangers of mistaking analytics for understanding, and the cost of automating human care. But all of the decisions made by the people we have met along the way depended on their ability to be fully present in the moment preceding their actions.

In an era when the need to perform is immediate, and real-time scrutiny is high, leaders are encouraged to be seen, to produce, to speak, and to do. Nadella's quiet, unwavering attention is a reminder that authority comes from presence.

If the earlier parts of this book helped us reclaim our authentic, emotional, ethical, and intuitive selves, this section invites us to inhabit them. It invites us to stop outsourcing our presence to our calendars, speeches, presentations, and dashboards and reflect on what we actually pay attention to and are present for.

Over the next chapters, I want to explore what happens when leaders reclaim this uniquely human capacity. First, we'll look at why attention itself is the true source of leadership impact. Then, we'll examine how presence becomes the conduit for human energy and alignment in organisations. We'll explore how the chaotic environments we now live in don't need more control, but instead need more presence. And we'll see how what gets a leader's attention becomes what gets the organisation's energy, alignment, and effort.

But first, let's stay in this particular room and see why a question, a pause, and a leader who chooses to listen rather than perform are the foundations of radically human leadership.

Attention is authority

Attention is the raw material of leadership authority. What a leader notices, and focuses on, shapes an organisation's culture far more than any declaration she may make. Attention is how leaders confer value. When Nadella asked his question, it was a sign that what followed mattered.

Attention isn't a single function but a set of interconnected systems. Neuroscientists Michael Posner and Mary Rothbart[2] describe its three components as the alerting network, which detects that something needs notice, the orienting network, which decides where to focus, and the executive control network, which manages how attention is sustained and modulated. Nadella's presence activated all three, both in him and in the room. His attention lowered the social threat level, redirected the group's focus, and invited a deeper form of presence from others.

This neurological activity is reinforced by Antonio Damasio's somatic marker hypothesis (which we discussed in Chapter 11 when we met Phineas Gage) that shows that decision-making is guided by feelings and bodily cues stored from past experience. These somatic markers act as shortcuts that help individuals focus on what matters most in uncertain or emotionally complex situations. Nadella's attention was a neurobiological posture that allowed emotional markers to surface within the team, shaping what was said and how it was received.

This form of embodied, human attention cannot be replicated by AI. Philosopher Evan Thompson's theory of 'enactive cognition'[3] shows us why this is a uniquely human advantage. In it, he describes how true attention is not only cognitive but emotional and embodied. Understanding needs to be experienced physically and emotionally in order to exist. Unlike one of his own machines, Nadella could and did choose to focus.

AI lacks the embodied feedback that gives human attention its depth. Artificial systems do not possess interoception (the body's ability to sense its internal state), nor do they have the capacity for emotional memory, hence their inability to weigh the human consequences of any decisions. A machine can flag a concern and be prompted to investigate it, but it will never understand its emotional gravity in the true sense of understanding. A machine can be programmed to 'read the room', but it will never have the experience, along with the understanding this brings, of being within it.

This is why true authority requires presence as much as competence. It requires leaders to tune into silences, perceive unspoken tensions, and validate the experiences of others without needing to fix these. This kind of attention is deeply active and, therefore, is not one AI can exhibit as, given its programmed nature, its attention can only be reactive.

Attention before action

Just as we do with compassion, we think of leadership presence as a personality trait. We believe it to be the product of charisma. True presence, though, is nothing of the sort. It is deliberately, repeatedly, and often invisibly, cultivated. It may appear effortless from the outside, but genuine attention is always the result of intentional inner work. Leaders who show up fully have prepared themselves.

It is easy to focus only on Satya Nadella's question, his pause, and attentive silence when, in fact, what made that moment possible and powerful was everything that came before it. Nadella walked into the room grounded in his own capacity to notice, to stay still, and to respond without defensiveness. That capacity takes preparation.

What Nadella demonstrated went beyond good manners and active listening; he displayed the ability to contain his own need for results to make space for others to contribute and achieve. This mindset of 'attention before action' requires leaders to align their emotional, cognitive, and physiological internal state with the needs of the moment. The neuroscientist Richie Davidson[4] suggests that this kind of attention is a skill that, through practice, leaders can develop by delaying reaction in favour of reflection.

We know that our decision-making capacity decreases when we are faced with too much information or too many demands. We know that we are less present and more likely to play a role when we carry internal clutter (mental noise, competing agendas, emotional residue) into external conversations. Therefore, if we are to develop attention, we must learn to reduce internal interference. Achieving that reduction happens through preparation.

Preparation is also enabled by self-awareness. Emotions are constructs based on how we interpret our body's signals. A racing heart may indicate fear, excitement, or anger, depending on context. Leaders who are skilled at reading their internal states are better able to regulate how they show up. Nadella's composed presence was embodied self-awareness.

Presence is cultivated through thousands of small choices that happen before meetings, speeches, or decisions. When we fail to create the room for this kind of attention, we default to performance. We speak before we've truly arrived. We react before we've ever reflected. We answer before the questions have been asked. The result is executive noise that drowns out insight, stifles collaboration, and substitutes speed for clarity. It is the noise that AI amplifies.

Presence cannot be simulated. It cannot be faked with posture, tone, or body language alone. It is felt because it is real. Teams can detect when a leader is half there, distracted, or preoccupied. They can sense when attention is fragmented, even if the words sound right. Conversely, when a leader is fully present, it creates a ripple. People feel seen. Dialogue deepens. Possibility expands.

The cultural anthropologist Edward T. Hall, known for his work on proxemics and the hidden dimensions of communication, emphasised that human interaction depends on far more than words alone.

One reason attention before action matters so deeply is that leadership decisions are made in environments saturated with pressure, ambiguity, and competing signals. With inner stability, leaders can cultivate a space of attention within themselves in order to create the possibility of clarity without assuming, rushing, avoiding, or controlling. Nadella led by relinquishing control for others to step in. That is how presence becomes not just grounding for leaders but galvanising for others.

Presence is not a luxury. It is more urgent in the age of AI than ever before. As algorithms take over more tasks, produce more answers, and anticipate more needs, the one thing they cannot replicate is attention formed through inner awareness. They cannot simulate readiness or presence. They cannot pause and listen to the tone behind the words or the emotion beneath the silence. Leaders, when they attend fully and with intent, can. That is the only way to lead so others feel invited to follow.

In the age of AI, when we are surrounded by systems that simulate understanding, only those who have trained their attention, rather than polishing their performance, will be followed. Attention is presence in motion which, once felt, changes the atmosphere. In the next chapter, we explore how presence, once grounded, becomes the invisible channel through which energy, emotion, and alignment move through a team. Where this chapter showed that presence creates space, the next will show how it generates momentum. Once a leader's attention is felt, energy follows.

Notes

1 Jenny Lay-Flurrie, 'Hitting Refresh on Accessibility', Microsoft Accessibility Blog, July 2017.

2 Michael I. Posner & Mary K. Rothbart, 'Research on attention networks as a model for the integration of psychological science', *Annual Review of Psychology*, 2007, 58, 1–23.

3 Evan Thompson, *Mind in Life: Biology, Phenomenology, and the Sciences of Mind*, Harvard University Press, 2007; Evan Thompson & Mog Stapleton, 'Making sense of sense-making: reflections on enactive and extended mind theories', *Topoi*, 2008; see also 'Enactivism' entry, *Internet Encyclopedia of Philosophy*, 2024.

4 Richard J. Davidson and colleagues have demonstrated that mindfulness-based practices can enhance structural and functional activity in brain regions associated with attention and executive function, particularly the prefrontal cortex. See Waisman Center, University of Wisconsin, 'Research of Richard Davidson shows how meditation changes the mind', 2007; APA Podcast, 'How meditation can help you live a flourishing life' (featuring Davidson); Center for Healthy Minds, 'How Science Informs Good Leadership'.

27

Human energy is contagious

In the 1940s and 50s, long before the sciences of team dynamics and neurobiology gave us insights to act upon, Viola Spolin was using games rather than fMRI scans to experiment with the human mind.

Working in immigrant communities and public recreation programmes in Chicago, less than ten miles as the crow flies from Jane Addams's Hull House, she developed structured improvisational exercises that helped people connect through spontaneous expression. Her games invited presence, attention, and the invisible rhythms that form between people when they are fully tuned into the same moment.

Her work eventually crystallised into what she called 'theater games', compiled in her seminal 1963 book *Improvisation for the Theater*.[1] The premise underpinning all of them was revolutionary for the time. Rather than train actors to act, she trained them to attend to themselves, to each other, and to the moment at hand. She would tell them, 'Don't initiate! Follow the initiator! Follow the follower'.[2]

Her games seemed playful on the surface but cultivated a form of group intelligence that could only emerge when individuals were attuned to each other's energy. One of her foundational insights was that the body knows more than the intellect

DOI: 10.4324/9781003683124-37

can plan. When well executed, her games would create focus in a room. An actor would make a subtle move that others would respond to instinctively, building an entire scene from their interaction. What emerged was presence, and that presence was contagious.

Spolin's exercises were adopted by the Compass Players and later by Second City, where her son, Paul Sills, brought them into the DNA of modern improvisational theatre. For decades, performers have credited her method with unlocking not just creativity but connection. To enter a Spolin workshop was to enter a kind of electric current in which you felt the energy of the group shifting as attention deepened. When one person was present, an entire room came alive.

What she intuitively tapped into is now well backed up by science. Spolin and her actors may not have had the jargon, but what they were living is what today's psychologists call emotional synchrony, interpersonal attunement, and co-regulation. This matters to us now because leadership, like improvisation, is a shared act.[3]

In the previous chapter, we saw how presence creates space and how attention, when full and undivided, enables clarity and authority to arise. Satya Nadella's quiet listening allowed people to show up more fully. In this chapter, we go one step further. I want to show you what happens when presence begins to move through the space it creates.

Although Spolin never used words such as 'transmission' or 'coherence', these were the things she was practising. Through her exercises, she created a system in which emotional energy can be shared. She demonstrated how, when one person is fully present, others align. Contrast this with AI. While machines function on energy, they have none of their own. They cannot shape a room's dynamic through their presence, given they have none. They cannot use silence or moderate their tone to encourage collective reflection. They can assist but can never attend. Only human presence can do this.

I want to share two ideas in this chapter. The first is that presence is not static. It is not the opposite of action. It is a channel through which emotion, energy, and alignment travel.

The second is that, in a world increasingly defined by artificial signals, the quality of human energy, of the kind that Viola Spolin invited, focused, and released, has never mattered more. Her 'theater games' were about enacting rather than acting. They were about becoming so fully present that others couldn't help but come to you. This is the sort of energy leaders need.

Presence as energy

Viola Spolin believed that energy flowed through a group via connections. In a way, her 'theater games' were rituals of attunement to the real organisation. Participants warmed up their bodies and voices, as any performer would, but they also warmed up their attention. One actor's focus would shape the group's focus as their presence became a centre of gravity.

We've already seen how the human nervous system is constantly scanning the environment physiologically for cues of safety or threat. We have already discussed how, when someone is calm, open, and grounded, their presence sends a neurological signal of safety to others. That signal is what is meant by co-regulation.

Spolin's workshops were masterclasses in co-regulation. Actors were told not to plan their lines but to sense the group and respond, accepting whatever was proposed as an opportunity to build. Spolin emphasised spontaneity for order to emerge. Her performers learned to wait, to listen, to react in rhythm with one another and the group. What emerged as a result was a collective, aligned, and responsive directional energy.

In workplaces, classrooms, hospitals, and boardrooms, the same dynamic is at play. Leaders create a climate by how they make you feel rather than by what they say. A calm leader entering a chaotic room can ground it just as much as a scattered leader can make a calm room chaotic.

This brings us back to Satya Nadella. In the last chapter, we saw how his presence during a meeting shifted the room. How it created an energetic field to which others could bring their full selves. It was attention becoming atmosphere. Presence offers a form of focus that shapes how others feel. Viola Spolin taught people how to sense energy. She trained actors to feel when a moment needed silence, when it was time to respond, and when it was better to wait. These calibrations weren't performed. They were perceived.

This act of energetic transmission is uniquely human. In practical terms, it means that a leader's presence is not just a style. It is the emotional architecture of the room. It is the difference between people waiting to speak and people who are ready to listen. Presence, then, is not the opposite of energy. It is its source. When a leader understands that her body, her attention, and her tone are all instruments, she begins to play a different kind of leadership. It is one in which energy is evoked and invited rather than imposed and controlled.

To better appreciate this, consider how teams interpret a leader's energy through rhythm and relational timing. Human beings are exquisitely sensitive to pacing. We are attuned to how long someone takes before responding, how quickly they shift topics, and how they hold silence. These cues shape the emotional tempo of the room. When a leader rushes, others accelerate. When a leader steadies, others slow down. If you don't believe me, try gently tapping a pen when someone is speaking to you and gently accelerate the cadence. You will see them speak faster without even noticing. This kind of metronomic gesture is proof of the power of presence and its contagion.

AI has no rhythm. It can neither hesitate nor pause. The tempo of trust and the dynamic of presence cannot be encoded. Yet we know that these are the very things that make people feel, thereby turning them into followers. As more communication gets mediated by tools, whether through automated updates, synthetic voices, or predictive analytics, these relational signals that regulate group energy risk being drowned out. In such spaces, the presence of a real, calibrated, focused, attuned, radically human leader becomes vital.

This is why your energy is directional. It tells people where to lean, when to hold, and what to trust. Presence is simply how that energy takes form. The most powerful leaders resonate, invite, and create the conditions for alignment to arise naturally.

Human energy in the age of AI

But energy needs to be calibrated. Just as unfocused energy can overwhelm, misdirected energy can divide. A leader's task is not just to bring energy into a room but to ensure that it aligns and moves in the right direction. This is where attention becomes orchestration.

Viola Spolin understood this without ever speaking in corporate terms. In her 'theater games', the most powerful scenes happened when players sensed the right moment to speak or stay still, intuiting the emotional arc of the interaction. This kind of calibration is often what separates good leaders who react from great ones who respond.

I am sure you will have experienced how the right tone, at the wrong moment, can feel manipulative. Great leadership requires a deeply human understanding of timing, which AI systems cannot copy. Their inability to modulate their own tempo means that they never truly calibrate. Studies in affective neuroscience (the study of the neural basis of emotions and feeling) show that empathy involves both automatic affective responses (involuntary, unconscious emotional reactions) and the extrinsic and intrinsic regulatory processes responsible for monitoring, evaluating, and modifying our emotional reactions. This is why, in an age where speed is prioritised, the human ability to read, regulate, and align a group's energy is a competitive advantage. Similarly, while maintaining one's own internal balance is the key to the kind of compassion we discussed in our last principle, energy regulation through presence is what transforms empathy into compassion.

Through her games, Viola Spolin created the conditions for this kind of emotional resonance. When a participant was anxious or distracted, the group generated the trust, space, and mutual attention that pulled them in. The ensuing energy became self-sustaining. This is the model leaders must embrace. Their role is to ensure that energy flows where it needs to go. This doesn't mean that they need to be upbeat, or smile, all the time. It simply means that they need to understand when to shift key. They need to be adept at using silences, pauses, and emotional regulation to step back in order to allow others to step forward or in.

Viola Spolin didn't give her actors maps, just as Miles Davis didn't give his band musical scores. Both remind us that the work of leaders today is to hold presence to align energy. We may lead in an age where performance can be simulated, but human presence that feels, listens, calibrates, and resonates cannot be faked.

By now, it should be clear that presence is something a leader practices rather than has. It is also clear that, when it is practised well, it generates energy. Viola Spolin knew this long before development professionals started to talk about emotional intelligence. She, along with Nadella, demonstrated the leadership truth that underpins our sixth principle: a leader's energy attunes a system.

Viola Spolin's legacy extended far beyond the rehearsal rooms of Chicago. Her methods laid the foundation for modern improvisational theatre, influencing the Second City and generations of performers. Her techniques became essential not just for actors but for educators, therapists, and facilitators of group dynamics. By the time of her death in 1994, she had transformed how we understand spontaneity, attention, and group dynamics. In the words of improvisational theatre, she offered us presence, and it is up to us to accept rather than block it.

But presence, even if it is calibrated and contagious, is not the whole story. Sometimes, energy is chaotic. Sometimes, a leader's job is not to hold stillness or even create alignment but to step into mess and ambiguity with speed to bring coherence. This is especially true in a world in which leaders are asked to move through complexity in real time.

Leadership today doesn't happen in controlled and stable environments. It happens in moments when presence must become something more than inculcating calm. Presence must also be capable of containing disruption, navigating unpredictability, and holding others without losing oneself. Leadership must reveal as much as regulate. This is why, in the next chapter, I want to focus on what happens when presence must be held in chaos.

Notes

1 Viola Spolin, *Improvisation for the Theater: A Handbook of Teaching and Directing Techniques* (Drama and Performance Studies), Northwestern University Press, 1999.

2 Viola Spolin & Carol Sills, *Theater Games for Rehearsal: A Director's Handbook*, updated edition, Northwestern University Press, 1985, p. 93.

3 There is no way I can do justice to the teachings of improvisational theatre for leaders. It would require an entire book. Luckily for us, my good friend, acclaimed improv performer, co-founder of The Comedy Store Players, and renowned executive coach and mentor Neil Mullarkey has written one I can't recommend highly enough: *In the Moment: Build Your Confidence, Communication and Creativity at Work*, Kogan Page, 2023.

28

Chaotic control

In 1943, at the height of World War II, a strange and secretive project was born behind a chain-link fence in Burbank, California. It operated with no official name, no standard oversight, and almost no bureaucratic constraints. What it did have was one man at the helm named Kelly Johnson, plus a mandate to do whatever it took to achieve something that had never been done before.

The US Army Air Forces had a problem. They needed a jet fighter and they needed it faster than any government process had ever been able to deliver one. Given how slow traditional defence contractors were, Lockheed Martin turned to Johnson, a blunt, chain-smoking engineer known for his ability to mix a heady intolerance of bureaucracy with unwavering precision.

He assembled a team of 23 engineers and technicians in a rented circus tent next to a smelly plastics factory and set out to build the XP-80 Shooting Star in 180 days. The team did it in 143. But it is the method Johnson used, rather than the machine he built, that is of interest to us here.

Johnson managed to create a culture where creativity could live inside chaos. The group iterated fast, changed course when needed, and operated with maximum intensity and total focus. And at the centre of this intensity was Johnson. He endlessly walked the floor, listening, watching, and sensing when to step in and when to get out of the way.

DOI: 10.4324/9781003683124-38

He had just 14 rules that would go on to become legendary in aerospace engineering. Rules such as 'A very simple drawing', 'A minimum number of reports', and 'Mutual trust and respect between team and leader' ensured that trust flowed in his team. And, because Johnson was fully present, deeply engaged without ever being overbearing, the team managed to thrive in an atmosphere that would have paralysed most other organisations.

And, if you think this is a one-off example of competent project management, know that Johnson went on to repeat what many saw as magic with the U-2 spy plane and the SR-71 Blackbird, both built in impossibly short timelines, in secret, with minimal oversight. Again, he did this by building teams who could perform in ambiguity and produce brilliance. Johnson was only human. But he had enough presence to never need to be omnipresent.

He would visit teams twice a day, curious rather than anxious. Engineers would later describe the subtle shift that occurred when he entered a room. They shared how much they respected how intently he paid attention and how he could see things they missed, because he was watching the work, not trying to control it. As he wrote in his autobiography, 'Listen: you'll never learn anything by talking'.[1]

In these chaotic, high-stakes environments, rather than fake certainty or clarity, Johnson modelled a different kind of control through his presence. He gave his teams confidence through his presence. Just as Viola Spolin taught us, he sensed and tuned the tempo. While it is tempting to think that complexity requires more control, Johnson's legacy is a counterpoint to the myth that leadership equals dominance. When leaders are increasingly tasked with operating in uncertainty, with teams under pressure, timelines that are becoming shorter, and inputs that shift hourly, how can we expect them ever to exert dominance? In these moments, the only source of power is presence.

The story of Johnson is the story of one man who led some of the most ambitious engineering feats of the 20th century by staying steady in the absence of clarity. Kelly Johnson didn't just build aircraft. He built environments where invention could fly (pardon the aircraft pun).

Nadella helped us see how, when leaders offer real attention, they create space for others to rise, making attention the foundation of authority. Viola Spolin then taught us how energy, when aligned, travels through teams and activates momentum, making presence contagious. What Kelly Johnson proves is that, when clarity is in short supply and momentum hits turbulence (no need for me to apologise, the plane pun wasn't intended), presence can be more than just attention and energy. It can help ground teams and liberate creativity. In the complex and idea-rich environments created by AI, leaders must channel, steady, and direct their presence. This is what I mean by chaotic control.

Grounding teams through ambiguity

Kelly Johnson's genius was never just about engineering. It was about orientation. In the unpredictable environments he led, whether wartime R&D, Cold War reconnaissance, or next-gen aerospace, he never provided certainty. Instead, he provided grounding.

Ambiguity has always been part of leadership. But the kind of ambiguity leaders now face is different. It's dynamic and shape-shifting. AI is accelerating information flow, shortening decision loops, and surfacing signals faster than we can process them. And, while it can help clarify the variables, it cannot remove the real challenge faced by leaders when the variables keep changing and no clear algorithm exists. That's not a technical problem. It's a human one.

So far, we have seen that leadership begins with focused, intentional attention, and that presence is the connective tissue through which teams align. For any of this to happen, leaders must first be able to hold ambiguity without becoming overwhelmed by it. Otherwise, presence becomes panic. This is why Johnson's story matters. The Skunk Works – a name the group chose to describe their unit inspired by the *Li'l Abner* comic strip by Al Capp, where the 'Skonk Works' was a dilapidated, smelly, and isolated location, much like theirs, where a mysterious 'skonk oil' was brewed – didn't operate under clear conditions.

They didn't know what enemy technology looked like. They were often given half-defined problems and absurd deadlines. What kept those teams grounded was the presence of a leader who could remain focused and flexible at the same time. Leadership in ambiguity requires the leader to become an emotional regulator for the room by absorbing tension rather than magnifying it.

In this way, grounding presence becomes a form of collective sense-making. Karl Weick, one of the foremost theorists of organisational behaviour, argued that, in moments of disruption, people don't look for answers; instead, they look for someone who can hold the questions without collapsing. Presence is that holding. It is letting go of the need to resolve, of the desire to predict, and, perhaps more importantly, of the pressure to look decisive.

Johnson understood this implicitly. When the U-2 programme hit multiple redesigns owing to unexpected altitude instability, he never let urgency dissolve into disorder. He asked, he listened, and he kept showing up. That steady rhythm gave his teams a psychological metronome. His presence became orienting. It allowed the teams to know which way was up when their work was going sideways.

This capacity to anchor without overwhelming is increasingly rare and increasingly needed. In a hybrid world where leaders are often managing teams they don't physically see, presence becomes more than body language. In these instances, the volume or proximity of your voice is replaced by its tone and cadence. To ground presence requires you to be attuned. What made Johnson exceptional, and what we can learn from him, is that he respected the chaos rather than trying to erase it. He knew that, for innovation to flourish, people must feel anchored, even when the environment is in a constant state of flux.

Presence as creativity enabler

In earlier chapters, we saw how attention creates clarity, and how presence can align and energize teams. But here, in the realm of chaotic creativity, we can see how presence allows leaders to create and regulate the psychological conditions to ensure that half-formed ideas survive long enough to become real. In high-speed environments, such as the ones we are all familiar with, ideas tend to be rushed, or pressured into being fully formed, and die as a result. Presence, in this context, is about creating a kind of buffered zone where imagination can work under pressure. It's a leadership function that does three essential things: it values ambiguity, absorbs pressure, and calibrates tempo. Let's take each in turn as Kelly Johnson's leadership at Skunk Works exemplified all three.

First comes presence as valuing ambiguity. Johnson's twice-daily walk-throughs, where he entered the space watching, and asking, meant that, when engineers were stuck, rather than their being pushed into premature solutions or conclusions, he was there to encourage them to see the value of the tension they experienced. This ability to recognise that the fragment of an idea targeted to the right issue is more valuable than a fully polished one that risks solving the wrong problem is what I mean by presence as valuing ambiguity.

To value ambiguity requires restraint. It requires a leader to hold back from the instinct to finish, to fix, or to frame too soon. It means allowing something to remain ambiguous, awkward, or half-formed while still taking it seriously. Leaders often think their value lies in offering solutions. But, in creative contexts, their greatest value is creating the space for ideas. Johnson's presence told his teams to keep going.

As well as valuing ambiguity, the second essential element of presence-driven leadership is the presence that absorbs pressure. Today's environment in general, and creative environments in particular, are noisy. They have too many deadlines, politics, and egos to be quiet. The kind of presence Johnson displayed absorbed that noise. He didn't let external urgency pollute internal exploration. He kept his teams focused on what mattered next, not what the outside world demanded now. In that way, he buffered the creative space so it could remain generative.

Absorbing pressure doesn't mean shielding teams from urgency altogether. It would be silly to pretend it is not raining while holding an umbrella. What it does mean is that a leader's role is to regulate how that urgency is felt. Without this buffer, ideas firm up too fast or shrink too soon. Leaders who are present in this way exercise a form of emotional containment by steadying the climate so that others can take cognitive and creative risks.

And, perhaps more crucially, the final key element of leadership presence is how it calibrates the tempo. Johnson had an intuitive feel for pacing cognitive rhythm. When a team needed time, he protected it. When it needed momentum, he applied just enough pressure to shift energy without crushing direction. This ability to sense and regulate the rhythm of invention can never be overlooked.

In fast-paced environments, there's a constant temptation to resolve ambiguity too quickly, or to grab at the first viable solution, rather than stay with the tension. Leaders who are present can feel that urge rising and offer deliberate breathing room as a counterpoint to the seduction of false certainty.

It is worth remembering that Johnson never designed or redesigned an aircraft himself. His role, as a leader, was to shape the conditions in which radical design could emerge. And this, perhaps, is the deepest expression of presence – presence as seeing rather than being seen. The power of his approach is that it only requires discipline. This is the discipline to walk the floor, to ask open questions, and to stop talking when the room is close to something real. It is the discipline to be in the moment consistently, attentively, lightly. That is the kind of leadership that makes creativity sustainable.

Kelly Johnson exemplified this with extraordinary clarity. His engineering genius lay more in the cultures he built than the planes he helped design. It was a culture of trust, pace, and permission. He showed that you can lead some of the most advanced innovation projects in a century without tightening control. You can walk among engineers and ask questions instead of giving answers.

By the time Johnson retired from Lockheed in 1975, he had led the creation of over 40 aircraft, including some of the most advanced ever built. But, perhaps more crucially, he left behind principles. His 'Skunk Works rules', rooted in autonomy, clarity, and attention, have become a blueprint for fast, focused innovation the world over. Despite all of this, for the people who knew him best, it is his presence they will remember. More than aircraft, it built allegiances, pace, and a way of leading that worked in the very conditions where control would have failed.

In the next chapter, before we move on, once again, to a set of prompts and ideas, I want to reinforce the importance of presence by showing you that, unlike what the old adage 'what gets measured gets done' would have us believe, it is, in fact, what a leader pays attention to that becomes what others believe matters most. It is the fact that attention shapes reality that gives a leader authority.

Note

1 Clarence L. Johnson & Maggie Smith, *Kelly: More than My Share of It All*, Smithsonian Books, 1989.

29

Attention as authority

Five years before Satya Nadella asked his 'How does this work?' question, Feike Sijbesma was asking another equally transformative, if somewhat more challenging, one: 'What does the world need now?'.

It was 2007. Royal DSM, the Dutch chemical company of which he had just become CEO, was known for its industrial products. It produced polymers, petrochemicals, and coatings. It was a profitable company, but Sijbesma, a biologist by training and a humanitarian by instinct, wanted something else as the company's future.

He began to ask himself and others more. What if the company's assets could be reoriented to fight climate change? What if innovation meant nutrition and bio-based energy, instead of more durable plastic? There was no expensive strategic review exercise. He didn't go for a grand, sweeping rebranding one either. Instead, he chose presence.

He walked the labs, sat with the R&D teams, and asked questions about biofuels and food equity in a way that, over time, led to DSM beginning to change. It changed because of Sijbesma's consistent and curious attention. And, as Viola Spolin would have predicted, where he lingered, others began to look more closely; what he asked about, others began to prioritise. As a result, what he refused to let go of (climate, health, micronutrients) became what DSM began to stand for.

DOI: 10.4324/9781003683124-39

By 2010, teams that once manufactured acrylic resins were exploring algae-based food supplements, as energy-intensive divisions were gradually being sold off. Nutrition, bioscience, and sustainable materials moved from being on the periphery of the business to the heart of it.

All of this happened because Sijbesma understood that performance is first and foremost about presence, and that presence happens through focused attention. He listened more than he spoke, which made people listen more intently when he spoke. His attention was steady. He kept returning to the same places, the same questions, with the same depth.

Many leaders I meet underestimate the fact that attention is a signal that becomes stronger over time. When it is repeated with clarity and care, that signal becomes culture. Sijbesma wasn't the loudest voice in the room, but his attention was unmistakable. It reshaped a multinational organisation from the inside out. Inside DSM, people began to tell different stories about what mattered.

By the time Sijbesma stepped down in 2020, DSM had tripled its market capitalisation, divested its petrochemical origins, and become one of the most respected sustainability-first companies in Europe.

That's the power of presence and what I want to explore in this chapter. I want to show you that what leaders pay attention to, consistently and visibly, becomes what others in the organisation value, pursue, and protect. I want to show you how attention, rather than metrics or mission statements, moves teams. I want to unpack the mechanics through which sustained attention becomes authority.

We've seen in the previous three chapters how presence shows up as grounded awareness, contagious energy, and a steadying force in chaos. I now want to show you how it directs effort. I want to outline how what you notice creates a culture that, over time, becomes the organisation's reality. When automation can process faster than any human ever will, this kind of presence, which holds and focuses attention, matters more than ever. A leader's presence determines what is chosen. Her attention is how that presence speaks. Sijbesma's story is the story of leadership as the disciplined craft of attention.

What gets attention gets done

'What gets measured gets done' is probably the dumbest thing ever said in leadership circles. Or, rather, let me be less hasty and judgemental: if not the dumbest, it is, at least, the most misguided. The only reason that what gets measured appears to get done is simply because most leaders, most of the time, only pay attention to what gets measured. The simple truth is that it is not what gets measured that gets done but what gets talked about the most, and what gets talked about the most is what gets the most attention from leaders most of the time.

What shapes how people make decisions and what they focus on is when leaders consistently return to the same themes and ask the same questions. This shapes what teams prioritise, what metrics they take seriously, and what stories they share in meetings, corridors, and town halls. Because Feike Sijbesma kept asking about health when showing up in the nutrition labs, it became what others believed mattered. Traditional leadership often assumes that influence flows through decision-making and directives, when, in practice, what most people in an organisation watch is what leaders focus on.

A recurring glance from a leader can carry more weight than a quarterly strategy document. This is why presence matters more than posture. Feike Sijbesma didn't perform sustainability but practised it consistently. Over time, people at DSM began to mirror that focus. When a leader joins an impromptu discussion and asks a follow-up question three weeks later, this is the moment you know that such attention will outlive any single conversation.

In a world saturated with optics and messaging, Sijbesma's approach was radically and subversively steady. He returned to the same rooms, the same scientists, and the same slow-moving problems over and over again. It is a leadership trap to confuse visibility with significance. Influence has never been about being seen everywhere. Influence is about being consistently present where it matters. That is the way teams begin to internalise what the focus is. Commands may well tell people what to do, but it is attention that tells them what matters. Over time, the latter is far more powerful.

DSM focused on nutrition long before it was profitable because Sijbesma started showing up in the company's emerging nutrition division. He didn't have to say it was important. He made it so by choosing to see it, ask about it, and stand beside it. A division that had once been peripheral now felt seen. And, if there is one thing organisational psychologists agree on, it is that, in organisations, what is seen grows. We align by attention. So it was when employees at DSM began to pre-emptively align their work with the values they saw reflected in Sijbesma's questions.

In a corporate world that is awash with KPIs and analytics dashboards, we must remember that data follow focus, not the other way around. Attention tells the organisation which metrics deserve interpretation and when. Sijbesma made sustainability important by focusing on it, not by measuring it first.

That capacity to notice, to choose what is relevant, and to feel the deeper texture of an idea is an act of prioritisation that is both deeply powerful and deeply human. Leaders who attend to things before the market does are often seen as visionary. But, in practice, it is often much simpler than that. They are the leaders who are just willing to notice what others overlook and to stay with it long enough that others start noticing too. At DSM, sustainability started as a way of seeing. And, because Sijbesma kept his attention there, it eventually became the organisation's mission.

Culture has never emerged from values posters or corporate slogans. It has only ever grown out of what people believe they are allowed to care about. That belief is set by watching leadership. It is a leader's attention that confers permission. When leaders don't stop paying attention, neither do followers. This is why distraction is such an insidious trap for leaders. When they chase novelty and shift focus after every meeting, they create ambient confusion. Teams who don't know what matters always return to what is safe, measurable, and only incremental.

A framework for presence

But how does this kind of real and intentional human presence translate into the kind of authority that others feel? As I have already mentioned, we make a mistake when we treat presence as a personality trait that only some people have. This misunderstands what presence actually is. Presence is not about being impressive but about being in the moment, focused on something other than reactions and responses. Presence is not about what you project but about what you pay attention to and how and for how long you do so.

What unites Satya Nadella's decision to listen before he acted, Viola Spolin's emphasis on responsiveness over dominance, Kelly Johnson's clarity under chaos, and Feike Sijbesma's patient reorientation of an entire global business is their shared discipline of attention. To show you that presence is not something mystical, I want to offer you a three-part conceptual framework.

Inner attention as the ground of authority

Presence is about the awareness a leader brings to each moment and, as such, it begins in the body.

Inner attention is the capacity to be anchored in one's own values, clarity, and ethical compass before even stepping into any interaction or decision. Sijbesma didn't react to quarterly market fluctuations. Instead, he returned, again and again, to the deeper commitments of climate resilience and nutritional equity. These were not just ground rules. They were his grounding truths. And, because he was grounded, his leadership had weight.

Inner attention creates coherence. When a leader is scattered inside, uncertain of her values or chasing the next validation, her attention becomes fragmented. By contrast, when a leader returns to a clear internal locus of meaning, her attention becomes magnetic. In an age where AI increasingly dictates tempo, urgency, and options, this kind of rooted, reflective attention becomes even more vital. Inner attention is the invisible posture that makes everything else possible.

Interpersonal attention as presence between people

The second domain of presence is what happens when a leader's attention enters a room. This interpersonal attention is the felt experience of being seen. For leaders, it encompasses the capacity to sense who is holding back, who is energised, who is overwhelmed, and who is unheard and to respond with presence.

At DSM, Sijbesma built this relational field through repetition. He followed up, remembered conversations, and noticed patterns others ignored. Interpersonal attention creates permission to care.

This type of presence is what anthropologist Edward T. Hall called proxemics to describe how space, orientation, and distance shape meaning. When a leader leans into a room with care and pauses long enough to absorb the unsaid, she generates coherence.

Cultural attention as the architecture of what endures

The third and final domain of presence is cultural attention. This is how a leader's focus becomes embedded in structure. This is where presence moves beyond personal awareness or relational space and starts to shape systems in terms of what gets measured, what gets repeated, what gets funded, and what gets left behind.

Sijbesma didn't just talk about sustainability. He restructured DSM's R&D priorities, shifted capital allocation, and rewrote the company's metrics. Sustainability became an operating principle only because the company's processes reflected the gaze of its leader. This is how cultural attention works. It develops through a repeated emphasis that signals, again and again, who we are, what we see, and, therefore, what we act upon.

Together, these three layers (inner, interpersonal, and cultural) form a framework for presence that is both practical and profound. Inner attention creates coherence, interpersonal attention creates connection, and cultural attention creates continuity. Feike Sijbesma never framed it this way, but his leadership lived it. Presence is an embodied practice of attention that orients others. In Feike Sijbesma's leadership, we discover how attention, held steadily across time, can restructure a global organisation through coherence.

Just as Muhammad Yunus became a founding member of the Elders, a group of world leaders working for peace and human rights, alongside Bishop Desmond Tutu, Feike Sijbesma became a key member of the Global Centre on Adaptation, alongside former United Nations Secretary General Ban Ki-moon. Just as Devi Shetty was appointed chairman of the COVID-19 task force in Karnataka, Bangladesh, Feike Sijbesma was asked to support the Dutch government's special envoy on the pandemic response in early 2020. Presence has a funny way of getting you noticed.

What you pay attention to doesn't just reveal your priorities but has the power to reshape organisations. What you choose to see becomes what your people begin to believe is possible and the broader world admires. Amid the complexity of modern leadership, presence must be not just understood but practised.

In the next chapter, I want to offer some prompts to help you live presence because sustaining it is about rhythm, returning, and remembering what you want others to remember. In the end, your organisation will focus on what you focus on. The coming chapter will help you hold that focus on purpose, on purpose!

30

Presence in a distracted world

By now, we've seen how presence comprises the kind of gravity that holds attention, keeps emotions steady, and focuses energy. In the age of AI, where leaders are surrounded by data, pace, and noise, presence becomes the distinctly human act of being somewhere fully and staying there long enough for meaning to emerge.

This chapter brings together the core lessons from our four preceding explorations of attentional focus, energetic alignment, creative grounding, and the architecture of presence. I have tried to translate these insights into practical rituals, prompts, and diagnostic tools designed to help you turn presence from an ideal into a practice.

As always, though, these tools are not prescriptive. They are just invitations to refine your attention, regulate your impact, and structure your leadership in ways that others can feel, trust, and follow. Use them as you wish but know that my intent is to help you ask better questions, reflect more deeply, and build the kind of presence that leaves a mark long after your actions end.

DOI: 10.4324/9781003683124-40

I am aware that some of the examples I share seem more momentous than what most of us are either capable of or have the opportunity to do day-to-day, yet it is worth reminding ourselves that all of us started out as children, and none of us were born with a special wisdom or greatness gene. We can all be present.

The leadership presence diagnostic

As is now fast becoming a habit, let's begin with a reflective self-assessment. This diagnostic focuses on practice rather than personality. Use our usual scale of 1 (rarely) to 5 (always) to determine how intentionally you show up.

1. I can sense tension in a room before anything is said.
2. I choose where to focus before I enter a conversation.
3. I return to the same priorities consistently over time.
4. I create enough space for others to speak before me.
5. I regulate my pace to suit the moment rather than my mood.
6. I follow up on issues long after they have surfaced.
7. I adjust my attention based on who needs it rather than who demands it.
8. I resist the urge to fix things and stay with tension long enough for solutions to emerge.
9. I notice when energy changes and respond accordingly.
10. I treat presence as a skill by practising to improve.

Here are some ideas about how to approach your score. If you scored 40 or above, chances are that your presence is felt and trusted. The question now is how do you make sure it is sustained? If you have a score between 30 and 39, this may mean that, while your presence is visible, it could be inconsistent. A score below 30 suggests your leadership may risk being reactive or fragmented, especially in high-stakes or fast-moving environments. Some of the practices below may be a good place to start.

Three practices to prepare inner attention

Presence begins before any action is taken. The three practices below will help ground your inner attention in order for your authority to be felt.

Pre-contact scan

Before any significant engagement, ask yourself the following questions:

- What emotion am I walking into the room with?
- What distractions do I need to let go of?
- What outcome am I looking for and why?

Two-minute stillness

Learn to build a rhythm of stillness. Take two minutes before any key interaction or engagement to sit in silence. Don't plan or review anything. Just arrive.

The anchor prompt

Choose one prompt from the three below to help you orient your presence:

- Who here most needs to be heard?
- What tension might emerge, and how will I hold it?
- What would it mean to show up with full attention?

The attention ladder

Use the table to help you assess the nature of the attention you give, what this teaches your team about what you care about, and what, as a result, they should care about too.

Attention level	*Indicators*
Passive attention	You are present but shift focus quickly
Episodic attention	You discuss something once but don't follow up
Repetitive attention	You return to key areas again and again
Embedded attention	Your focus reshapes conversations and stories

Energy mapping

As Viola Spolin's work taught us, your presence shapes the emotional tempo around you. Use the table to reflect weekly on what your behaviour may be telling your team.

When I …	*I might be signalling …*
Speak first and fast	That speed matters more than clarity
Pause and listen	That it is OK to think and reflect
Am consistent in the questions I ask	Focus and care
Shift topics quickly	Disinterest
Return to a theme repeatedly	That it is important to prioritise it

Regulating presence in chaotic environments

In Chapter 28, Kelly Johnson reminded us that presence regulates creative chaos. Use the questions below as a kind of behavioural triage when you are operating in ambiguity. They will help you keep your footing when clarity is still forming.

- Is this moment calling for speed or pause?
- Do I need to amplify or protect an idea?
- Who is emotionally 'off rhythm', and how can I bring them back?
- What pressure do I need to buffer so creativity isn't crushed or rushed?

Micro-presence flow

Presence is not about rehearsing for set pieces. It is felt in everyday interactions. The framework in the table will help you reflect on five small but important moments where your presence may either dilute or amplify your leadership. Try tracking one of these moments per week.

Moment	*Reflection prompt*
Start of an encounter	Do I arrive with clarity or carry chaos into the room?
Transitions	Do I allow for breath between segments or just power on through?
Listening	Am I truly listening or waiting to speak?
Interruptions	Do I model grace or signal impatience?
Closure	Do I summarise the meaning of what has been said or rush to the task?

The presence alignment check-in

This tool will help you align the three dimensions (inner, interpersonal, and cultural) of presence. Use it as a weekly or monthly check of where your attention is concentrated and what kind of presence you're cultivating (or neglecting). Choose one dimension to work on each week, along with one small adjustment (e.g., pause before speaking, repeat a message across meetings), and track its impact.

	Key question	*Signs that you are here*	*Signs that you are distracted*
Inner	What have I returned to that gives me clarity?	Clear sense of purpose, calm under pressure	Drifting, reactive focus
Interpersonal	Who have I made space for this week?	Active listening, follow-up	Rushed conversations
Cultural	What have I repeated enough for it to be remembered?	Your priorities show up in the team's language	Inconsistency between words and actions

Weekly presence prompts

- What did I pay most attention to this week, and why?
- When did I notice the energy shift in a room?
- Who did I make feel seen, and who did I miss?
- What urgency did I resist for the sake of clarity?

- What question did I return to repeatedly?
- Where was my presence felt strongest, and what made that possible?
- Did I practise presence or try to perform confidence?
- What did my attention give permission for others to pursue?

Commitment practices

1. Follow-up ritual: every week, return to an idea you touched on recently but didn't close. Your return will signal care.
2. Consistent theme: pick one thing to focus on and mention it in every meeting for 30 days. See how this reshapes conversations.
3. Energy reset: at the start of every day, decide how you want your energy to feel and give it a name (e.g. steady, open, focused); then, identify one thing that might disrupt this.
4. Attentional audit: at the end of every week, list the top three things you paid attention to that week. Then, check if these were the things that mattered most.
5. Presence partner: ask a trusted peer to tell you when you appear distracted, disjointed, or disconnected. Invite them to give you feedback regularly.

In this principle, we have seen that attention creates authority, energy invites alignment, and presence calms chaos. While these tools, by themselves, won't make your presence perfect, they will make it deliberate. In a world where AI optimises speed, clarity, and scale, this matters more than ever. Presence is the link between what you focus on and what others come to believe. But attention alone isn't enough to turn a group into a team of followers or inspire action. For that, leaders need something older and deeper than structure. They need stories. This is where we go next.

Principle 7

Stories over structures

Leaders aren't valuable because they build systems.
They're valuable because they shape belief.

With presence reclaimed, we can now turn to its most powerful expression: the human capacity to tell stories. In a world increasingly run by systems, it is easy to assume that structure creates results. But leaders are only followed when they are capable of offering meaning. Only stories can inspire beliefs.

With this seventh and final principle, I want to show you how leadership is the choreography of belief rather than the architecture of logic. It is through narratives that leaders engage emotion, navigate uncertainty, align strategy, and steward culture. Stories are the life blood of the real organisation and keep it alive. When algorithms generate language without understanding, it becomes even more vital for human leaders to ensure that what is said and how it is said comes from a place of intent.

- Chapter 31: leaders must learn to craft narratives that inspire, persuade, and move others because, before there is belief, there first must be a story.
- Chapter 32: A story is only as strong as the words that shape it, and this is why leaders must steward language as carefully as they do strategy.
- Chapter 33: when clarity is scarce, the courage to speak with honesty, humility, and hope becomes a leader's sharpest storytelling edge.

DOI: 10.4324/9781003683124-41

- Chapter 34: that is why strategy itself must be shaped as a story that links vision to values, and metrics to meaning.
- Chapter 35: it is the stories people tell when leaders aren't in the room that shape the culture of an organisation more than any structure or system ever will. We must lead accordingly.

31

The storytelling imperative

In 1851, in Akron, Ohio, the Women's Rights Convention had drawn a crowd of reformers, activists, and sceptics. The debate was fierce. Some argued that expanding women's rights too quickly would damage the abolitionist cause, while others insisted that white womanhood must take precedence. The room was thick with tension. And then, a woman rose to her feet to speak.

Her name was Sojourner Truth. She had been born into slavery in New York and grew up speaking Dutch as a child. She had walked away from bondage with nothing but her beliefs. That day, she decided to speak, and what she said became legend because no one can say for certain exactly how she said it. There is no recording, no official transcript, and no verified or verifiable script or footage. Yet hers remains a powerful story, passed on from generation to generation.

The version that has travelled through time, is quoted at marches, has been passed down through textbooks and assemblies, and is often performed by students during Black History Month was written down 12 years later by Frances Gage and included its famous refrain, 'Ain't I a woman?'.[1] It was stylised, reimagined, and possibly embellished. It showed the speech as having been delivered in a southern dialect Truth neither spoke nor used.

DOI: 10.4324/9781003683124-42

And yet, even the scholars who have criticised the inaccuracy can neither deny nor ignore its impact.

The earliest account of Truth's speech was written just weeks after it was delivered by Marius Robinson in the *Anti-Slavery Bugle*.[2] In it, Truth's voice is calmer, firmer, closer to how she sounded. In that version, there is no dialect, no repeated question, and no dramatic arc. But, even then, the power of her message still weighed heavy in that Ohio room.

She spoke of the physical labour she endured as a slave. She shared her grief over losing children to slavery. She lamented the silence of Jesus on the question of race or gender. She simply asked to be recognised and seen as a human being.

If our role is to create the conditions for others to engage positively with a goal, everything we have covered so far only becomes valuable if it moves people to act. And the primary way humans move is through stories. Stories are how we turn being into meaning and meaning into actions. They are how we convert personal truth into shared purpose. Stories are the substance of leadership.

Yet, in a world increasingly driven by generative systems, auto-generated content, and language models trained to simulate speech, the temptation is to think that storytelling is just another communication tactic to be scripted, automated, and broadcast at scale. This view relegates storytelling to mere language generation. However, its primary role is the generation of meaning. Stories, though, are not just about what is said. They are also about who says it, why, and at what cost. Only humans can assign consequences and carry truth.

Sojourner Truth didn't just speak. She changed a room by making the invisible felt. This is what I want to cover in this chapter. Leadership storytelling is neither the projection of emotion (we've covered that) nor just the transmission of energy (we'll come to that). It is the moment in which presence becomes narrative, and narrative becomes direction. Neurologically, we know that stories activate brain regions associated with empathy, memory, and sensory experience in ways data never will. We may like the data and the facts to speak for themselves but would do well to remember that they are mute.

Stories as human technology

There are moments that leave no transcript but still manage to rewrite the script. Sojourner Truth's intervention in Akron wasn't recorded but it was registered. Its power didn't lie in its linguistic form. Her story matters to us here not because of what she said but because of what it did. Storytelling is the human capacity to redirect attention to, reframe the meaning of, and place moral weight upon what has previously been invisible.

What Truth did that day was not scripted or machine-generated: instead, it came from lived experiences and conveyed their consequences. More than a communication tool, storytelling is an act of human authority grounded in experience, encoded in emotion, and capable of reshaping what others perceive to be true.

Throughout this book, we've traced the edge where human leadership diverges from artificial efficiency. Each principle has pulled a thread from that distinction, but stories are the loom that brings the threads together and weaves them into something durable. Stories are where authenticity becomes intelligible to others, courage takes voice, intuition becomes transferable, curiosity gains shape, compassion travels, and presence acquires gravity.

To tell a story as a leader is to become legible. Stories carry the narrative for choices, failures, and lessons. When we encounter a story, the emotional centres of our brains light up. Our sensory regions activate, and our mirror neurons simulate what the protagonist experiences. More than hearing stories, we inhabit them. Stories with tension, resolution, and emotional depth create physiological somatic responses in their listeners, releasing chemicals that increase empathy, attention, and trust. Facts don't do this. Data may trigger analysis, but stories trigger alignment.

That is why great leaders are narrators. The brain is wired to organise around stories. We've already seen, particularly in Principle 3, 'Intuition over instruction', how emotions allow us to reason when certainty fails. Stories tell us what matters, why it matters, and what should be done. A leadership story is a filter for action.

Long before we built cities, we built stories. They were the original infrastructure. Anthropologists have long argued that storytelling is what enabled human coordination beyond kinship. Stories carried rules and helped create shared identity. Myths are, and always have been, the operating system of a culture. Whether it is the origin story of a startup, the founding myth of a nation, or the informal lore of a team, it is stories that help groups explain themselves and make sense of their world.

In sociology, the concept of sensemaking is foundational. Karl Weick taught us that, in complex systems, people don't wait for clarity. They act based on the story that makes most sense to them in that moment. That's what leaders provide – not certainty but coherence. A story is a declaration of what deserves attention. We saw in Principle 6, 'Presence over performance', that authority grows where attention flows. When Sojourner Truth stood up, she reframed what was visible and gave it a new meaning that no one in the room could then unsee.

Leadership storytelling is the architecture of belief. It is the act through which leaders turn experience into insight, and insight into intervention. It is how leaders create understanding. This is why I call this principle 'Stories over structures'. I don't mean stories *instead* of structures. I mean that, without stories, systems cannot speak, and data cannot persuade. Only humans can make what happened mean something more than what actually did happen. Stories are the way we lead.

From story to strategy

When Sojourner Truth stood in Akron, she offered a story so rooted in lived experience that it altered the direction of the conversation and, eventually, of the movement. In corporate parlance, we would call this strategic because, at its most basic level, strategy is the art of choosing what matters, and storytelling is the tool leaders use to make these choices visible, shareable, and believable.

We often treat storytelling as something soft that comes after the real work of analysis and design. But leadership storytelling is not the opening scene of strategy. Instead, it gives it coherence and clarity when structure becomes too abstract to follow. A story is how leaders shape belief. Sojourner Truth turned a gathering into a movement by making strategy emotionally and morally inevitable.

Good strategies build bridges between where people are and where they need to go. Only a story has the tensile strength to bear the weight of fear, fatigue, history, and hope. The most effective stories answer three fundamentally human questions. They give shape to urgency (Why now?), coherence to priorities (Why this?), and meaning to identity (Why us?). They bind vision to emotions and link goals to shared values.

When Truth told her story, she answered these same questions in a more profound way than any programme or policy could have. Why now? Because the exclusion was present and visible. Why this? Because justice demanded consistency. Why us? Because no one else would say it if she didn't.

This is how leaders use stories to bring orientation that moves organisations through ambiguity.

We live in an age rich in data mining but poor in sense-making because we are missing the stories that place data in context and link results to values. By reframing, rather than replacing, the data with the introduction of her labour, motherhood, and faith into her story, Truth placed the human context, beyond the data points, at the centre of the policies that were being debated.

It's tempting to think, and indeed we are often taught, that the job of leaders is to bring clarity. But it is a mistake to think that this is achieved by removing uncertainty and doubt. Our role is to be able to use the tension created by multiple possible and plausible futures to a creative end. Stories are what help people progress even when there is no roadmap or it is incomplete. Stories make complexity coherent by bringing human context into the tension created by uncertainty. That is why Sojourner Truth became such a point of reference. She provided a moral compass to guide the conversation.

Stories shape cultures by outlining and reinforcing what matters and what is unacceptable. In this way, storytelling is how leaders inculcate the values that keep a culture aligned and alive. In times of pressure, uncertainty, and contradictions, it is this library of stories that determines whether a culture can adapt.

We don't know exactly what Sojourner Truth said. But the fact that a version of her story, albeit imperfect, paraphrased, and translated, still echoes over 170 years later tells us something about the strategic durability of stories, even when these are not precisely documented. The story was enough to last because the moment was lived, and its meaning stuck. It stayed even though it wasn't recorded. It endured because it was carried by the memories and myths of a movement. Her words survived through the feelings they generated. Her story became a truth that couldn't be ignored. That's what human storytelling does. It travels through people and endures because it is true enough to matter.

Stories are the mechanisms of meaning leaders use to align emotions with execution and directions with belief. Without stories, visions remain abstract, strategies stay procedural, and leadership continues to be impersonal. Stories are how human leaders make shared stakes visible and shared belief possible. It is because Truth led with a story that she shifted the frame of the debate, changed the posture in the room, and created an impact that lasted far beyond the day it was told.

Sojourner Truth's story made her a figure far beyond Akron. Though she was never formally educated, she went on to speak across the United States and became one of the most influential voices for abolition and women's rights movements, redefining, as she did so, what leadership could look like. Her story entered history as a reminder that, when words come from experience, they can move the world.

Leadership in the age of AI requires this same kind of storytelling that reframes what's possible by inviting belief. In an age of systems, templates, and simulated language, the real work of leaders is not to produce more content. It is to make meaning more visible. Storytelling is neither a soft skill nor mere stylistic flair. It is a human advantage in the age of AI.

But stories are not built from events alone. They are shaped by language. The words we choose, especially under pressure, construct the reality others will live inside. That is why, in the next chapter, I want to explore the strategic use of language. We'll see how metaphors, framing, and word choices are the muscles of leadership. Every story begins with a sentence in which every word signals what matters.

Notes

1 Frances Dana Gage, 'Ain't I a Woman?', *History of Woman Suffrage*, vol. 1, edited by Elizabeth Cady Stanton, Susan B. Anthony, and Matilda Joslyn Gage, New York, Fowler & Wells, 1881.

2 Sojourner Truth, speech at the Women's Rights Convention, Akron, Ohio, 29 May 1851; transcribed and published by Marius Robinson in *The Anti-Slavery Bugle*, 21 June 1851.

32

Leadership language management

Václav Havel led with paragraphs more than policies.

When he stepped into the presidency of Czechoslovakia on 29 December 1989, just weeks after the collapse of the 40-year Communist regime, Havel had a history of writing dissident essays and underground plays but no military record, no economic plan, and no bureaucratic experience. Despite, and maybe because of, all this, within months he had become the political leader of his nation and a key figure in his region.

In his first New Year's address as president, broadcast to a country still raw with uncertainty, he offered candour. 'Our country is not flourishing. The enormous creative and spiritual potential of our nations is not being used sensibly.'[1] In a single sentence in a single speech, he framed both the moment and the movement as a reckoning.

He spoke of the 'contaminated moral environment' the previous regime had created and left behind and described how it had appropriated the power of language using euphemisms, jargon, and slogans to pass on lies as truths. He rejected terms he eschewed such as 'rehabilitation' and 'brotherly unity' that the previous regime had used to claim legitimacy in order to oppress and coerce its people.

DOI: 10.4324/9781003683124-43

Havel spoke plainly and humanely. Having been an author, poet, and playwright before becoming a dissident, then president, he understood that language is more than just a tool for expressing thought. He knew that language shapes our thoughts. He knew that words shape worlds and that, therefore, you could change the future by changing the words.

Havel had learnt this long before taking office. As a playwright, he spent decades exploring how words function inside closed systems. His plays dissected how people used language to hide, to obey, and to collude. In *The Memorandum*, he had satirised a bureaucracy so obsessed with control that it invented its own incomprehensible language, robbing workers of autonomy and meaning.

In *The Power of the Powerless*, perhaps his most famous essay, he described the insidious way empty language could infiltrate daily life. In a scene reminiscent of corporate workplaces with meaningless posters claiming an empty purpose, he wrote about the greengrocer who places a state-mandated sign in his shop window claiming, 'Workers of the World, Unite!'. This Havel described as 'a shield … behind which he can hide his fear'.

He argued that semantic drift (the slow erosion of meaning through repetition, euphemism, and disengagement) was the core mechanism of oppression. He pointed out how, by colonising language, any regime could colonise thoughts and control behaviours. That is why he chose to simply speak the truth and, just like Sojourner Truth before him, he chose his words to match reality. The very truth that had got him banned, arrested, interrogated, and imprisoned by the previous regime had allowed the power of his words to stand as the regime collapsed around them.

His leadership style was, by traditional standards, unconventional. He spoke plainly, sometimes haltingly, but always deliberately. Every word was chosen to signal intent. Every phrase was selected to create distance from the language of fear. It was effective because it was coherent. Havel showed us that a leader's language can reset the moral compass of a nation, and how new metaphors, new frames, and new names can make sentences mean something again and reset a culture.

That is why we begin this new chapter with Havel as our guide. In an era of large language models that can generate fluent, persuasive output in milliseconds, leaders must reclaim what makes language human, because language has never been either neutral or just descriptive. Language that is embedded in memory, intention, and cost is the real language of leadership.

Framing the future

Language is a moral and strategic act. It gives leaders the wherewithal to name what matters, to frame what's happening, and to shape what comes next. That act of framing alters how others feel, think, act, and align. It is the infrastructure of meaning. Language generated by AI can sound precise, relevant, and on-brand, but what it might offer in fluency it lacks in accountability. Leadership language resonates when it is chosen, rooted in context and history, and carries a cost. This is in stark contrast to AI language that is just produced from patterns which carry only words, not responsibilities.

Václav Havel understood this long before the emergence of AI and long before he became a head of state. As a playwright living under a regime that had hollowed out language, he saw first-hand how words could enslave or set free. He watched the slow decay of public truth through repeated slogans that whispered falsehoods so softly that people forgot they had other ways of speaking. The risk of AI is linguistic abdication where good writing erodes the intent behind the words leaders use.

Before any decision is made, any direction given, or value shared, there is always a frame. Frames tell people what kind of situation they are in and what kind of response is required of them. Although frames are often equated with spin, they are only interpretation. They are a leader's way of expressing what is at stake and shaping the emotional posture of the group. Frames are best described as the mental structures we use to shape how we see the world. Just as you can change the world by changing words, you can change meaning by changing the way facts are framed.

If you choose to call a layoff a 'restructure', or a setback a 'lesson', or employees 'talent', you shape what others believe. The danger today is that much of this framing is being delegated to AI rather than being owned by leaders. Large language models have no concept of what words are for. They have no idea of a leader's (or her organisation's) history, context, or culture. Leadership language must be judged, not just generated.

Along with framing, leadership relies on metaphors to map the unfamiliar on to the familiar. Just like framing, metaphors are not neutral. They can invite action as much as they can shut it down, because any metaphor chosen will activate different assumptions about people, success, risks, and the nature of progress. Contrast 'moving the needle', 'putting out fires', and 'shifting gears' with 'planting seeds', 'building bridges', or 'lighting the path'. Where the former imply urgency, heroics, and speed, the latter signal patience, connection, and guidance.

Havel rejected the language of state ideology precisely because its metaphors betrayed its intentions. 'Normalisation' implied health, when it actually meant repression. 'Brotherly unity' disguised occupation. By exposing these metaphors, he was able to rewrite the emotional contract between people and power. Leadership metaphors represent a choice with consequences as the metaphors we use construct the culture we inhabit. This is why we need to be mindful of using AI models to generate them, as statistical interpretations of language cannot make a decision about which metaphor is emotionally aligned and appropriate or strategically useful to the future we seek. The difference between human and AI language is consequences.

Finally, language is how a leader stores institutional, emotional, and moral memory. Language is the thread that links today's decisions to yesterday's choices – and to tomorrow's aspirations. Leadership language offers continuity. Havel's voice remained consistent across the roles he was called to play. As playwright, prisoner, and president, he employed language that continued to be shaped by the inner coherence of his convictions. Your words are living memory and they are what leadership is made of, which is why you can't outsource them to a system and must choose them carefully.

Crafting collective meaning

Every organisation has stories, habits, and rituals that endure because of language. The words leaders use, permit, and repeat become the emotional and moral architecture of daily life. Over time, that architecture shapes what feels normal, what feels possible, and what goes unquestioned. Language expresses what an organisation believes, which is precisely why leaders cannot afford to treat language simply as a communication task.

Culture has never been defined by values on a poster or a set of beliefs and behaviours listed in a handbook. It is shaped by linguistics. You can spot a culture by listening out for what gets repeated, softened, omitted, or renamed.

Anthropological research has long shown that what we name shapes what we notice, and what we notice shapes how we act. Linguistic anthropologist Alessandro Duranti calls this means of producing and reinforcing social norms 'language as intentional action'. In effect, what we name shapes what we notice. In a leadership context, this means your words train attention. If you call your organisation a 'family', it sets expectations around loyalty and belonging. If you call it a 'machine', it signals interchangeability and efficiency. Neither is inherently right or wrong (although I admit to disliking both), but both shape what people will tolerate, expect, and reproduce.

In leadership, the way we name and define events establishes a frame that shapes the future. That's the reason oppressed groups throughout history have reclaimed names. Václav Havel understood this well, which is why he refused to use the dead metaphors of the Communist regime as one of his first political acts, reframing freedom as something achievable through language first. A leader's power comes from linguistic courage rather than institutional status. This is why I named this principle 'Stories over structures'.

The principle recognises that language is constitutive in that it initiates change. Václav Havel understood that refusing the regime's official vocabulary was resistance. By stripping falsehood from political speech, he gave people a new way to describe their reality and, in doing so, a new way to imagine their future. Sojourner Truth did the same. She named what had been excluded and, by doing so, reframed the terms of inclusion. In both cases, language was the start of what could happen. You can roll out new systems, policies, or priorities but, if the words surrounding them don't support meaning, they won't hold. That's why storytelling comes before structure. It's also why naming, framing, and language management are core acts of leadership.

In a noisy, distributed, and now machine-amplified world, the leader's voice becomes a source of coherence. Your language, when used consistently and carefully, becomes part of the cultural terrain people navigate by. Havel's speeches weren't grand but they were recognisable. His words echoed the language of his plays, his prison letters, and his essays. He spoke with conviction whether he spoke on a podium or not.

His story is an invitation to leaders to continue to speak by using their language to form a reliable narrative act that can be trusted because it is steady, even when it is not smooth.

Václav Havel left office in 2003 with little fanfare but with words that had outlived the regime which once tried to silence him. He died in 2011, but his language remains in the cultural memory of a country that had learned how to speak truth aloud. It also remains in the literature and legislation of a nation and in the graffiti and speeches of young dissidents across the world who still quote him.

For us, Havel's warnings feel oddly prescient, foreseeing, as he did, the slow erosion of meaning through repetition without conviction. For leadership to be alive, leaders should choose words that come with weight, that connect to context and carry moral continuity. They must recognise that metaphors matter, that framing directs action, and that every sentence is a cultural act. This is why language is a fundamental tool of leadership.

But the real test of language comes when everything is unclear and uncertain. This is why, in the next chapter, we will explore how leaders find their voices in what I will call truthful clarity, even when the story of what lies ahead is still being written.

Note

1 Václav Havel, 'New Year's Address to the Nation', 1 January 1990. English translation published in Václav Havel & Jan Vladislav, *Václav Havel: Or Living in Truth*, London, Faber & Faber, 1990.

33

Communicating in uncertainty

On 2 August 1985, at 18:05:52, Delta Flight 191 fell from the sky just moments and metres before it was due to land at Dallas Fort Worth International Airport. The plane had encountered a violent, downward rush of air that slammed it into the ground, killing 137 people: 136 passengers and 28-year-old William Mayberry who was driving his 1971 Toyota down Highway 114 as the aircraft's left engine skidded across the road at 200 miles per hour, killing him instantly.

Flight recorder data showed that the pilots never had a chance. The control tower had sent no warning. The radar had showed nothing unusual apart from a storm that was nothing the onboard systems couldn't handle. Yet something had to have gone wrong for tragedy to strike. That something was seemingly invisible, but it wasn't nothing. For one man, it was a confirmation.

Tetsuya 'Ted' Fujita, a Japanese American meteorologist based at the University of Chicago, had spent the previous decade trying to convince aviation authorities that there was exactly this invisible, silent, sudden, and deadly danger.

Ten years earlier, in 1975, Eastern Air Lines Flight 66, another commercial flight, had crashed on its final approach into John F. Kennedy Airport in New York, killing 112 people. The

DOI: 10.4324/9781003683124-44

circumstances had been eerily similar. The weather had been poor but manageable. The equipment was functioning, and no clear cause could be established. Fujita had been asked to assist with the investigation.

While examining the environment surrounding the crash site, he started to spot clues that were invisible in the data and to the instruments. What he saw matched a pattern he had observed before in tornado damage and high-intensity storms. It looked as though a powerful downward blast of air, not one that swirled like a tornado, had come crashing straight down.

That downward blast didn't have a name, so he gave it one. In that moment, Fujita gave the world the word downburst, along with microburst (its smaller, more violent cousin). The invisible something now had a name that was scientific enough to be credible and bold enough to be useful.

For nearly a decade after the Flight 66 crash, his theories were dismissed or treated with scepticism. No radar systems had ever detected microbursts. No pilots had ever seen them. The default assumption was that they didn't exist. However, Fujita persisted. He collected evidence, drew maps, and published reports in order to frame the fact that the atmosphere could turn on an aircraft with no warning. He knew that, without finding a language to describe a seemingly unreal reality, more people would die. He understood that ambiguity is removed through dialogue rather than data, and that dialogues can only be conducted where a language exists.

When Delta Flight 191 crashed, his ideas were finally vindicated. A NASA Doppler radar managed to record, measure, and confirm a microburst. Tetsuya "Ted" Fujita's words became part of aviation's lexicon. Detection systems and training routines were developed. Lives were saved all because of one man's idea that something only becomes clear when it has a name.

Sojourner Truth taught us that stories are the infrastructure of leadership. Václav Havel showed us how framing and metaphors are the very mechanisms through which culture is created. We now turn to the moments when the human voice is irreplaceable. Fujita's story sheds light on what happens when leaders are tested by a story that is unclear, and a frame is provided for unreliable data.

By giving uncertainty a name, Fujita created a new frame for others to act within. I want to show you how radically human leaders can speak clearly in unclear times by naming what is real, listening to what's not yet understood, and choosing language that holds others steady, rather than by claiming false confidence. I want to show you why clarity starts with a name.

Naming uncertainty

It is in uncertainty that stories are tested. While a leader's narrative shapes beliefs, her words frame reality when uncertainty takes hold and the natural temptation is to revert to vagueness or silence. We prefer to wait for clarity before we speak but that is precisely when words matter most.

To name the unknown is to help orient people so they are not being ruled by their fear of the unknown. By speaking, Sojourner Truth, Václav Havel, and Tetsuya Fujita helped others enter Yoda's dark cave, their words echoing in the silence. In developmental psychology, the cognitive and emotional impact of a name is called 'affect labelling'. Research using fMRI scans has shown that, when people verbally label what they're feeling, the activity in the amygdala (the brain's threat detection centre) decreases, while the right ventrolateral prefrontal cortex (associated with regulation) becomes more active. In other words, naming helps regulate.

When leaders name what others are afraid to say, or cannot comprehend, they offer a neurological relief valve. People don't just hear truth. Assigning a name lowers tension and increases both cognitive openness and the willingness to trust. Anthropologically, naming marks the start of shared meaning. Across cultures, naming organises ambiguity, defines roles, and ritualises systems. It gives a frame that stops people reverting to confusion or inference by offering a script for ways to behave. Fujita understood that to name what no one else can yet see opens the door to action, investigation, and, eventually, system-wide change.

And yet, in today's high-risk, hyper-scrutinised environment, many leaders hesitate to name what is real but unclear. The fear of saying the wrong thing overwhelms the imperative to say something.

Whether strategic, legal, or emotional, this fear produces leaders who say what is safe rather than what is salient. They end up sounding like machines because, increasingly, their speeches are being written by one. Fujita understood that to name what no one else can yet see opens the door to action, investigation, and eventually system-wide change.

AI has made it easier than ever to communicate without saying anything real. Generative language tools can now create content that is syntactically correct, tone-matched, and audience-appropriate but devoid of authenticity, ownership, or risk. Its output is a lawyer's dream (at least as far as language is concerned) but a leadership nightmare. Using flat, vague, and emotionally neutral language for the sake of safety leaves leaders without a human voice and their people with nothing worth listening to.

It shouldn't come as a surprise that, having come to associate strong leadership with confident declarations, leaders find it hard to say anything other than mere platitudes when facing uncertainty. Yet it is at these very times that people need to hear their leaders' real voices.

We know that, if we want people to act, they will need to interpret the situation they find themselves in despite not having all the facts. We know that, without clarity, there is no coordination. We also know, often from bitter experience, that, in the absence of a leader able to name and communicate in uncertainty, people will fill the gaps themselves. This is what, in sociology, is called narrative substitution. When there is no official frame or line, we fill the gaps with unofficial ones. Uncertainty, just like nature, abhors a vacuum. If the leader doesn't acknowledge a problem, employees will wonder if the leader might be the problem. Once that internal narrative takes hold, replacing it with a new one is even harder.

This is why Fujita understood that giving a name to microbursts was the key to their acceptance. By offering a frame within which reality could start to be shaped by those who could not see it, he was moving from theory to research. For leaders, the equivalent is to name fear and ambiguity. This can be as simple as saying, 'I don't know, but I will tell you as soon as I do'. This sentence may feel inadequate, but it has the benefit of being both clear and true. People respond better to messages that acknowledge uncertainty or call out reality than to those that hedge their bets.

People listen as much to why and by whom something is being said as they do to what is being said. The language of a leader only means something when the listener can sense the speaker has a moral relationship with the words she chooses. It's what Sojourner Truth did when she reframed the story of womanhood. It's what Václav Havel did when he refused to speak in euphemisms. It's what Fujita did when he described a wind that no one had yet seen.

Clarity is not certainty

One of the most enduring myths in crisis communication is that people crave certainty, when what they actually want is coherence. They need a clear frame they can trust rather than false reassurance or made-up answers. Fujita knew this instinctively. When he first described the microburst, he didn't claim total understanding. He simply named the risk and outlined the implications. His credibility came not from his clarity of thought but from his candid articulation of his current understanding of the phenomenon.

The same applies in leadership. Your role is to help people stay oriented in uncertainty rather than remove it. This kind of leadership communication requires precision in language, steadiness in tone, and a willingness to be emotionally present without making promises that cannot be kept. There are four steps to creating the resonance that creates coherence.

The first is to think about your tone. Human beings process tone before meaning. Our brain's emotional circuits interpret a speaker's intent based on vocal tone and facial expression milliseconds before the content of the message is understood. How you sound shapes how your words are received, regardless of what these are. Human leaders, by contrast to AI which can't know when to slow down, pause, or speak more softly or firmly, can carry emotions in their speech. In uncertainty, people are more likely to remember how it felt listening to you than what you have said. Tone is your care transmitter and what people remember.

The second step to creating resonance is listening. It is tempting in uncertainty, when everyone is looking at you, to have a fully formed message. But, when people are anxious or confused, language must be relational. It must respond to what people feel rather than what you assume they want to hear. In practice, this means inviting questions and naming the emotional reality in the room to let the the language of your message be shaped by what you've heard. Fujita didn't develop his theory in a vacuum. He studied damage patterns, but he also listened to pilot reports, survivor accounts, and air traffic communications. The way he explained microbursts was informed by the voices he had heard.

After tone and listening comes emotional truth. It's easy, when everything is in flux, to default to operational updates (what is being done, when results are expected, and who is in charge). But, in ambiguity, people are scanning for emotional truth more than they are looking for facts. They want to know if you're afraid too and whether you see what they're seeing. This is why honest language designed to name emotions matters.

Finally, the last step of creating resonance is to repeat the story. In moments of uncertainty, people may neither remember, nor indeed believe, everything you said the first time. Saying things again and again until others hear them properly provides rhythmic reassurance. Returning to the same message makes words credible through repetition. Fujita didn't publish his findings once and then stop. He revised them, reinforced his point, and restated his message until others could see what he had seen. For leaders, there is a simple message in his story. We should worry more about saying something true than about saying something new, and we should never worry about saying it over and over again.

You don't need certainty to speak clearly. You need courage, tone, and a willingness to stand inside the unknown while still naming it out loud. Fujita didn't wait for perfect validation before giving language to what others couldn't yet see. He had the courage, tone, and willingness to speak early, carefully, and steadily until processes to cope with what he had named had been incorporated into safety systems.

After the crash of Delta Flight 191, his theory, which had once been met with silence and doubt, reshaped aviation safety. New detection systems were installed at major airports. Doppler radar systems were adopted for weather detection. Pilot training was revised to consider downbursts and microbursts. The language of flying was changed. In the turbulence of uncertainty, human speech is the first form of care.

By the time Ted Fujita died in 1998, he was a globally acknowledged expert. In his honour, the American Meteorological Society held a tribute to him, *Storm Track* magazine released a special issue, and PBS broadcast a documentary about him. His research on severe thunderstorms, tornadoes, hurricanes, and typhoons revolutionised our understanding of each. To professionals in his field, he will always be best remembered for his Fujita scale of tornado intensity and damage, while meteorologists more generally would acknowledge his research on thunderstorms, hurricanes, and typhoons as revolutionary. For the rest of us, I would suggest that we should remember him, every time we step on a plane, as the man who saved countless lives.

So far, I have made the case that stories move people emotionally and literally, that language and word choices frame possibilities, and that speech in uncertainty ensures coherence. In our next and final chapter before the toolkit chapter, I want to turn from language under pressure to narrative as design and explore how leaders can shape organisational direction through stories that link goals to purpose, values to action, and plans to identity. I want to show how, regardless of context, the one thing that moves us forward is a story worth following.

34

Narrative as strategy

In 1833, a young engineer, not yet 30, stood before the directors of the newly formed Great Western Railway Company where he had just been appointed chief engineer. His name was Isambard Kingdom Brunel. What he did that day, with no technical plans, no timetable, certainly no budget, and absolutely no feasibility study, was simply to tell a story. That story would go on to define Victorian Britain and leave an indelible mark on its landscape.

Brunel proposed a vision that, at the time, defied credibility. He wanted to create a continuous, coherent journey that would connect London to New York. Passengers would travel by train from Paddington Station in London to Bristol in South West England and there board a steamship across the Atlantic, to arrive in New York having never stepped outside the Great Western experience. It would be a journey across two continents and one ocean, unified by one company and an engineer's dream.

At the time, Britain's railway system was still in its infancy, and steamship travel was risky and unpredictable. Investors were cautious. The public was sceptical. But, rather than rely on his technical capability alone, Brunel knew that the success of the project depended on whether people could see themselves in the story it told. So, he told it.

He described a future where the journey itself was seamless, comfortable, and luxurious. He spoke of stations that looked like cathedrals, locomotives that would glide rather than groan, and

DOI: 10.4324/9781003683124-45

ships that would make the sea feel civilised. He wanted every part of the journey to signal confidence in progress. His vision was about Britain moving forward as much as it was about goods and people moving across the world.

People who had been sceptical liked what they heard so much that previously cautious investors started to lend. Engineers and architects, bowled over by the vision, joined the effort. Tracks were laid across fields, bridges built over rivers, all spurred on by a vision backed up by a story that just made sense.

It was a story that helped navigate every obstacle placed in its way. When Brunel insisted on a broad-gauge track that made compatibility with other lines harder, when construction costs soared, when the SS Great Eastern, the largest ship ever built, became stranded on its launch day killing two workers, it was the story that absorbed the uncertainty. The story was so coherent that it made people feel part of something that mattered, and, because it mattered, it happened.

As we have already seen, the ability to tell a story is one of the oldest and most powerful tools of human leadership. It is how leaders shape meaning. We have also seen how the words leaders choose signal intent and build alignment. We have seen that narrative frames and metaphors shape culture in ways that strategic presentations cannot. We have also just seen how, despite our instinct to stay silent until clarity is achieved, it is when a leader speaks that a path becomes visible. In Brunel's story, the three strands of story, language, and uncertainty converge to weave a strategic narrative.

This chapter is about understanding that a good strategy is not a list of goals on a slide deck but a believable journey that connects what people do to why it matters. A strategy offers emotional coherence before it provides operational detail. This is what Brunel understood better than most. As a leader, he directed belief, aligning thousands of decisions across time, geography, and expertise with a story. Every choice made flowed from the logic of the story.

Strategy, at its best, is a story that moves, evolves, and learns but stays coherent as it does so. Such stories, with their abductive reasoning (i.e. logical inference from observation), moral framing, and culturally situated meaning-making, are ones that AI cannot generate. AI has neither tacit knowledge, nor social intuition, nor embedded context, nor any stake in the outcome. Strategies are stories, and stories are sentient.

Strategy as narrative direction

Strategy begins with direction but only becomes alive when it is felt. When we discussed Sojourner Truth, I mentioned Karl Weick's idea of sense-making in which he argued that the true function of leadership is to turn confusion into shared understanding. Strategy becomes a live act of narration. This is what Brunel did. His vision for a seamless journey from London to New York was not just a story with characters, obstacles, progress, and purpose but also one that aligned investors, engineers, and workers around a sequence they could believe in.

The function of a narrative in strategy is to turn intention into momentum. While it may be tempting to believe that coordination can be managed through systems and structures, this is not how human beings work. From an early age, we construct meaning through temporal logic (i.e. beginning, middle, and end). We use stories to locate ourselves in relation to others. We interpret before we execute.

Cognitive scientist Edwin Hutchins coined the term 'distributed cognition' to describe how performance is built from shared narratives rather than instructions. In his study of, rather appropriately given the story of Brunel, naval ship crews and, recalling Tetsuya 'Ted' Fujita, airline cockpits, he demonstrated that, in the absence of framing or a coherent narrative, coordination fails even if formal procedures are followed.

Brunel didn't leave that distributed cognition to chance. His narrative was the infrastructure of his strategy. Psychologists tell us that people are most engaged when they feel autonomy, competence, and purpose. By creating a narrative that linked purpose to activity, Brunel ensured that his employees could link their daily tasks to a larger company narrative and be significantly more motivated, creative, and collaborative as a result. Of course, a narrative doesn't replace operational clarity. This principle is not called 'Stories and no structures'. But what it does is provide the meaning that is needed alongside operational clarity. It ensures that the formal organisation becomes alive through the energy of the real one.

A narrative framework

A great strategy doesn't just tell people what to do. It tells them why it matters, where they are in the journey, and how to keep moving when the path is unclear. Creating a strategic narrative requires the ability to shape strategic thought into a form that others can carry, adapt, and believe in. Isambard Kingdom Brunel wove his vision into the very structure of his decisions. That coherence is what allowed his story to scale.

Leadership communication becomes strategy when it moves through four narrative lenses, each building on what we have explored across this principle.

The first lens is the story, which asks us to consider the emotional arc into which we are inviting others. Strategic leadership begins by establishing the emotional logic of the work. It looks at the tensions we are trying to resolve as well as the changes we are trying to embody. It is the story that gives structure to these aspirations. Brunel's story of connecting London to New York created emotional gravity by defining the stakes in such a way that it invited people into something bigger than construction and engineering.

The second lens is language, which asks us to consider how the words we choose will shape the culture and direction we seek. Words define the cognitive frame of the story. What we might choose to call a project, a phase, or a setback will alter how it is understood. Brunel used words with care. He spoke of progress, pride, and precision rather than efficiency or throughput. His story lived in his daily language, and that language shaped decisions. By calibrating words to moments, leaders give language its strategic force.

Our third lens is the lens of clarity, which asks us to consider how we maintain trust in ambiguity, because strategy does not move in straight lines, delays happen, and conditions change. In these moments, it is the story that becomes the glue. As we have already seen, clarity is about naming what's real and reaffirming the emotional arc when execution stalls, rather than having answers about how to get it started again. Whenever there were setbacks, and there were many, Brunel stayed true to his narrative. Each challenge was framed as a chapter of the story rather than a failure of the plan, keeping people aligned even through doubt.

Our fourth and final lens to turn communication into narrative strategy is the lens of direction, which asks us to consider how the story we tell informs the decisions and actions others take.

Strategy becomes real when people can use the story to make decisions without constant direction. This is when narrative becomes operating logic. Brunel's story was a system that shaped track gauge, ship design, even architectural aesthetics. All of these choices were made because they made narrative sense (even when they made no engineering sense). The coherence provided by the strategic narrative enabled innovation. Direction is the acid test of narrative strategy because, when the story leads to aligned actions without micromanagement, then it has become structure.

Once we have answered the questions asked by the four lenses (story, language, clarity, and direction), for the narrative to function as strategy, we need to ensure that it operates across three dimensions of alignment (temporal, emotional, and structural).

Temporal alignment – past, present, future

A strategic narrative must show continuity. It cannot ignore the past but it must ensure it carries the right frame. It must honour the present without being trapped by it. And it must offer a plausible and compelling version of the future. Brunel's story did this brilliantly. He invoked Britain's industrial heritage, defined the Victorian age as an inflection point, and offered the future as a unified transatlantic experience. His narrative made time feel like progress.

Emotional alignment – head and heart

People commit to meaning before they commit to strategy. Emotional resonance is the coherence between what is said and what is felt. Brunel's strategy worked because it felt like something. Whether awe, ambition, or confidence, it provided a kind of emotional logic that enabled trust. When a strategy is optimistic but the tone is cold, or when promises are abstract but the work is gruelling, emotional misalignment occurs and erodes belief.

Structural alignment – story in the system

Finally, the strategic narrative must live in the system. It must influence how projects are evaluated, how priorities are sequenced, and how success is defined. Brunel's story lived in his designs. From wide tracks for comfort to sweeping curves for grace, via architectural grandeur that built national pride, his work was his narrative made real. A narrative turns a vision into actions across distributed, complex systems.

A story becomes a strategy when it provides a shared emotional arc, a calibrated language, a stabilising clarity, and a unifying direction. These four lenses (story, language, clarity, and direction) are not steps. They are overlapping filters through which leadership decisions gain shape, credibility, and coherence.

Of course, Brunel did not follow this model. I could find no record, for example, of leadership development consultants working alongside him; instead, he simply embodied it. In a way, this is the most important aspect of the stories I have shared and the points I have made throughout this principle. What matters most is the ability of human leaders to see strategy as a story in motion. That is what makes them radical and alive inside.

Isambard Kingdom Brunel died in 1859 at the age of 53 without ever seeing his vision realised. He was exhausted by a lifetime of overwork, obsession, and public scrutiny. His ship ran late, his grand rail system was eventually narrowed to standard gauge, and most of his projects were over-budget and often politically fraught. But, despite all of this, his story endures.

He left behind an infrastructure but he built beliefs. The story Brunel told redefined what Britain thought it could become to such an extent that, in a 2002 poll of the '100 Greatest Britons' run by the BBC, his compatriots voted him second only to Winston Churchill, showing the power of strategic narrative to align systems towards meaning.

Stories trump structures because they bind vision to velocity, and purpose to process. When people understand where they are in the arc of a meaningful journey, they coordinate faster, commit more deeply, and adapt with more resilience. And only humans can create that arc.

In the next chapter, I want to bring together the key ideas from the last four chapters (story, language, clarity, and strategic narrative) into methods you can use to build belief, shape culture, and lead through stories every day.

35

How stories move cultures

There is a reason this is our last principle. Stories are the infrastructure of beliefs, and beliefs are the primary fuel of human leadership. In systems increasingly shaped by algorithms and scale, the need for real stories, spoken with intent, shaped through language, and carried by people, is what makes us alive inside.

In the previous four chapters, we explored how human leaders use stories to create meaning, use language to shape culture, use their voices to create clarity, and use narrative to structure strategy. As usual in this last chapter on the principle, I now want to invite you to pause to reflect on how to practise these insights.

I have already given you my usual warnings about the ideas below not being so much formulae but rather prompts for reflection. This time, though, I am not quite imploring you to stop and reflect but I am getting close to doing so. Stories are the most human leadership tool at your disposal, and your capacity to tell a story others can believe matters. After all, what is the point of claiming or reclaiming your agency over the future if you can't describe this in a way that engages the people you need to build it?

DOI: 10.4324/9781003683124-46

The strategic storytelling self-check

Let's begin, as always, with a small test. Use our usual scale of 1 (rarely) to 5 (always) to evaluate the following statements:

1. I can clearly articulate the founding story of my team or organisation.
2. I regularly use stories to explain my decisions and/or our strategy.
3. I know which stories circulate informally in my team and what they mean.
4. I make sure that I choose metaphors and frames in important conversations.
5. I change the narrative when it no longer serves our values or direction.
6. I avoid using overly vague or polished messages in times of uncertainty.
7. I revisit key messages repeatedly so that they are remembered, not just heard.
8. I adapt the story I tell to match the emotional state of my audience.
9. I resist using AI-generated language when meaning or emotion is at stake.
10. My team can repeat our story in their own words and still make it sound true.

I don't really have a range of scores for this one, but I would encourage you to ask yourself:

- Which of these come easily?
- Which feel performative or absent?
- What stories have you been telling recently – and why?

Five tests of leadership storytelling

To bring the principle 'Stories over structures' into practical focus, I have translated the ideas from the preceding chapters into five observable, adaptable, and actionable tests.

The coherence test: is there a single story?

Human coordination breaks down when people are asked to believe too many things at once. When messages conflict with each other, their energy will dissipate. The first responsibility of narrative leadership is coherence. So, can you write down (in 50 words or fewer) the story your strategy currently tells? How about if you ask your colleagues to do the same: do the versions align? If interpretations among your team members differ wildly, your story lacks structural clarity. A shared narrative is always a prerequisite for sustained coordination.

The language test: are your words intentional?

The metaphors, the verbs, and the tone you choose subtly construct the culture you inhabit. Leadership language, as Václav Havel showed us, is design. Review the last five messages, slide decks, or memos that you shared. What recurring metaphors or phrases stand out? What do these teach people to expect or to fear? Before you issue your next team message, try to replace one abstract concept (e.g. 'alignment') with a concrete image or action (e.g. 'pulling in the same direction') to see what happens.

The meaning test: what emotional truth are you holding?

Effective leadership storytelling is about honouring your own, and others', lived and felt experience. When leaders name the emotional texture of a situation, people feel steadier. Emotional truths build trust regardless of how easy or hard they are to hear. After a major announcement, privately ask individuals within your team how they felt when they heard your message. Their answers will show you whether your story resonated or merely landed.

The temporal arc test: does your story travel across time?

A strategy story needs to stretch. If it forgets the past, it risks losing grounding. If it ignores the present, it will feel abstract. If it doesn't describe the future, it can't possibly motivate. This is why strategic storytelling is a temporal discipline. With your team, sketch a narrative arc in three simple frames: the past (Where did we come from?), the present (What matters most now?), and the future (What kind of organisation are we trying to become?). Doing this together will help ensure your narrative includes memory, urgency, and aspiration as well as being collectively aligned, which gets us to our final test.

The ownership test: who carries the story?

If your strategic narrative only exists in your own head or on a slide deck, it won't survive the first minute of implementation. A story becomes real only when others can carry it forward in their own voice, without distortion. Ask a few colleagues how they would explain what the organisation does and why to a new joiner. The answers will tell you how much of the story is alive and how much is still waiting for clarity. A real story needs to be remembered.

The narrative contrast grid

In my experience, leaders who struggle to tell a clear strategic story do so because they have too many ideas or too many constituencies to please. The result is a message that tries to be everything to everyone and ends up meaning very little to anyone. Clarity comes from contrast. Use this tool to help sharpen your story by defining its negative space.

With your leadership team, fill in the 'What we are' column in the table based on your current strategy or cultural direction. Then, together, review the misunderstandings or outdated narratives that you need to explicitly move away from. Now, write the corresponding contrasts in the 'What we are not' column.

When you have done this, use the completed grid to revise your story, sharpen your framing, or prepare messages. I have provided some examples in the table.

What we are	*What we are not*
Purpose-driven	Seeking growth at any cost
Focused on long-term trust	Chasing quarterly wins
Curious and open-minded	Reactive or overly defensive
Built on lived experience	Dependent on AI mimicry
Seeking aligned action	Seeking individual compliance

The story to action ladder

A strategy without behavioural translation is just rhetoric, in the same way that a narrative that can't be acted upon turns into branding. The story to action ladder is designed to help you connect your overarching story to real decisions and behaviours at every level of the organisation.

Start with the highest-level narrative and ask yourself what it would look like if someone acted in alignment with that story today, this week, or this quarter. Write the core sentence that defines your current strategic narrative (e.g. 'We lead through presence, not performance') and then list at least five observable behaviours that would reinforce that message. Use these behaviours as the basis for role modelling, team charters, or performance reviews. The table shows a worked example.

Narrative	*Actionable behaviours*
'We lead through presence, not performance'	Leaders show up to frontline reviews with full attention
	Meetings begin with real check-ins rather than jumping to metrics straight away
	Leaders leave space at the end of meetings for reflection and questions, or to invite others to voice what feels unresolved
	Leaders pause before reacting to demonstrate their attention
	Time for listening sessions is protected

The narrative maintenance map

Over time, every story decays. Its meaning gets diluted, reframed, or appropriated. As a leader, your job is to make sure the story keeps its shape. Use the table to check for signs that your strategic narrative needs maintenance.

Narrative element	*Signs it is strong*	*Signs it is weak*
Purpose	People quote it unprompted	People are confused
Values	Trade-offs reflect our values	Decisions feel misaligned
Identity	Informal stories reinforce who we are	Disengagement, satire, or cynicism
Direction	Initiatives align with our strategy	Actions feel scattered and/ or reactive
Voice	Leaders sound distinct and recognisable	Language feels templated or generic

Story practice prompts

Here are my usual weekly questions so you can reflect or prompt a conversation with a trusted colleague. Some questions may feel repetitive from one principle to the next. This is by design rather than lack of imagination. Experience tells me that few people read non-fiction books from start to end as they do novels, and so, by repeating questions, I can make sure every 'toolkit' captures the main things that matter. The other reason is that the principles of radical humanity are distinct but also closely linked. Every principle feeds into and emerges from the others. These are my excuses, and I will stick by them!

- What story did I tell this week, intentionally or not?
- Who felt included in that story, and who didn't?
- What words or metaphors did I repeat, and what did they signal?
- At what points did my language hide more than it revealed?

- What moment could have become a story, but I let the opportunity pass?
- What version of our future am I reinforcing through my tone and framing?
- What competing stories are circulating, and what do they reveal?
- What's the one sentence that defines what we're trying to do?

Commitment practices

1. Tell one story per week: choose one moment of challenge, progress, or courage and tell it as a story in a meeting, memo, or other communication. Let your people hear how you shape what matters.
2. Choose words with consequence: when framing a new direction, ask yourself the following three questions: what does this word signal? What assumptions does it invite? Would I stand by this sentence if it were quoted back to me?
3. Rehearse your story, not your speech: before a major conversation, instead of rehearsing your talking points, start by rehearsing the story you are trying to land. What's the arc? What's the emotional turning point? What's the takeaway?
4. Build narrative muscle with others: each month, ask your team about the most important story they have heard recently and why it mattered. This will help maintain collective belief.
5. Resist synthetic coherence: when tempted to polish or auto-generate a message, ask yourself whether it would sound the same if you had written it. If it wouldn't, then rewrite it. If you couldn't be bothered writing it, why should you expect others to listen to or read it? AI can be a great editor, but you are the sole author.

Stories are the architecture of belief. When people know what story they're in, they show up differently. In leadership, belief is the primary force that turns ideas into motion. The ultimate test of a strategic story is not how well it's told but how deeply it is held in the organisation's psyche. That work is your work.

In the next and final chapter of the book, before we conclude, we'll step back. We've travelled through the seven principles in our last 35 chapters. Now, I want to turn to the leadership horizon and ask what kind of human leader does the future need? I want to share with you where I believe we have got to and where I think we should go in what I have called the ALIVE manifesto. It sounds grand but it is my way of helping you navigate the seven principles to reassert your humanity, find joy in doing, and energise or re-energise your organisation.

Conclusion: The ALIVE manifesto

This book is my tenth, so you would have thought that, by now, I would be used to writing conclusions. Yet I still find it difficult. My struggle does not come from not knowing how to bring the story to an end, but, rather, I struggle to find the best way to convey that the end of the book is really only the start of the journey. The end of my writing endeavour heralds the start of your interpretation and practice. So, rather than giving you a summary of the book in order to conclude, let me give you a challenge by way of a manifesto.

I hope I did my job well enough that, by now, you will agree with me that leadership in the age of AI is neither about catching up with, nor about competing against, machines. Instead, it is about making the choice to refuse to become one.

AI feels like a welcome acceleration. It is positioned as the ultimate enabler that frees humans to focus upon higher-order tasks. Data are analysed instantaneously, content is written more quickly, and insights are packaged with polish, leading to better decisions made faster. Yet, we never seem to stop to ask what those higher-order tasks we are now freed up to complete might actually be. Slowly, almost imperceptibly, the nature of leadership has begun to shift. It looks good but it doesn't quite feel like us. We can delegate the writing, then the planning, then the outlining of choices, and finally the logic of the decision itself.

Now, we sit in meetings with beautifully constructed decks on our desks, risk mitigation plans, and market maps expressed in tight and compelling words, but something is missing.

DOI: 10.4324/9781003683124-47

Leadership was never first and foremost about clarity, efficiency, or even tone. What brought people to follow was always presence, judgement, and humanity. We have optimised everything but, in the course of having done so, risk losing meaning.

This 'manifesto' is not written to oppose or criticise artificial intelligence. I firmly believe that the opportunities it offers and the possibilities it opens up are capable of reshaping our world for the better in ways we cannot yet imagine or comprehend. Instead, it is written partly because AI has enabled aspects of our leadership to become artificial, but also, more importantly, because AI has revealed that too much of what we have traditionally called leadership has already been automated.

We didn't have to wait for AI to take our jobs. We were all too willing to hand them over incrementally. It smoothed the rough edges, filtered out emotion, replaced dialogue with decks, and decisions with deferrals. We began to confuse flawless performance with felt leadership. We began to believe that, as long as things looked polished, they must be working. The risk is that, underneath this precision, people will continue to disengage emotionally and cognitively as much as they have already done physically. When cultures hollow out, leaders become replaceable simply because they have forgotten why they mattered.

Do not get me wrong. This is not a nostalgic cry for the old ways or for a return to the pre-digital heroism of the old days. This chapter simply proposes a structured, human, embodied response to the deeper question that AI poses: what is leadership for?

We are no longer competing with AI on intelligence, memory, or output. We are competing with our own diminishing humanity. We are learning to simulate answers faster than we are learning to discern which questions really matter. We are turning up with polish instead of presence. And we are slowly losing our capacity to feel, to notice, to hesitate, to reflect, and to care. A manifesto, by definition, is not a map. Instead, it is a declaration, a line in the sand, a set of first principles for a different kind of future.

The ALIVE manifesto is a mirror rather than a model. It will show you what you must bring back to your core if your leadership is to matter, not tell you how to lead. Each letter – A, L, I, V, E, – is drawn from the seven principles of this book. These form a synthesis that may be used as a way to rehumanise your practice. I hope they provide a simple structure that is easy enough to recall when your next meeting asks for clarity, when the next board report calls for efficiency, or when the next crisis tempts you to perform rather than connect.

The question is no longer whether AI can do what you do. It can. The real question is whether you can do what AI cannot: whether you can attune, lead, integrate, vitalise, and emerge. Can you be alive inside and lead from there?

A is for attune – listening to what machines can't hear

Leadership begins with attention, and attention begins with being attuned. To attune is not just to listen to what is spoken or stated but to notice the discomfort in a pause, the hesitation behind a yes, or the silence following an assertion. Only humans can sit with the discomfort long enough to wonder what is really going on. To be attuned allows leaders to sense weak signals, emergent tensions, and invisible risks before they become problems. It enables them to pick up on cultural misalignment and pivot before problems occur.

The two principles that underpin our ability to attune are 'Presence over performance' and 'Curiosity over certainty'. The former showed us that leadership resides in attention, while the latter reminded us that staying open to the unknown is more courageous than defending what we think we know. To be attuned is to enact both. It is about asking the real questions at the right time rather than having the right answers. Only attuned humans can understand what signals mean and translate data into discernment. Being attuned bridges the distance between analysis and awareness, as well as making others feel seen.

Here are three practices to remain alive inside:

- Be the quiet in the noise.
- Sense the signal beneath the script.
- Let others feel they matter.

L is for lead – clarifying direction in moral fog

To lead is to provide coherence. It is not about having some grand vision or claiming to know what the future holds. It is simply about owning the responsibility for the choices to be made. In an age of increasing ambiguity, this is no small task, which probably explains why too many leaders still defer decisions, outsource judgement, or hide behind process. Leadership begins when we ask what is right.

In 'Moral courage over mere compliance', we saw that ethics are a tension that leaders must be willing to carry irrespective of its weight. In 'Authenticity over automation', we learnt that people are looking for leaders who mean what they say and are prepared to live by this when it's hard.

Leadership in the age of AI is about being more transparent in your values, consistent in your standards, and courageous in your stance. When data fail to provide a decisive answer, it is your moral clarity that becomes your team's compass. Radically human leadership is about value alignment. When you are alive as a leader, your character shapes culture by setting a precedent others will follow.

Here are three practices to remain alive inside:

- Lead with your backbone.
- Make your values legible.
- Take the heat when it matters.

I is for integrate – using discernment, not just data

The future belongs to those who can live with paradox. Integration is the capacity to bring coherence by reconciling opposite propositions. It is the inner skill of resolving tension through synthesis rather than simplification. Leaders who integrate do not collapse decisions into either/or binaries but search for ways to allow multiple truths to coexist by holding space for competing values.

Radically human leadership calls for something slower, deeper, and more ambiguous than the optimisation and direction AI offers. In 'Intuition over instruction', we saw how discernment is the result of embodied experience, stored memory, and emotional resonance and learnt that it is only once we have the ability to feel that we can have the ability to choose.

Integration means feeling the full social, ethical, and emotional weight of decisions before any actions are taken. It is knowing that logic alone doesn't make something wise, and that values abandoned when tensions appear are not values at all. This is especially critical for decisions that are irreversible or involve cultural change. These are times when leadership must be lived from within.

Here are three practices to remain alive inside:

- Feel the weight of the logic.
- Trust the pause.
- Let the answer emerge.

V is for vitalise – generating emotional energy at scale

For the sake of full disclosure, I am still not entirely sure that 'vitalise' is the right word to use here. It feels clumsy to me, but I needed a word starting with V that describes the energy that comes from being alive. I am sure AI could have generated something better, but I thought I would stick with this rather than waste precious natural resources getting a machine to come up with alternatives. Anyway, the idea of 'vitalise' is to lead in a way that makes people feel more awake, more seen, and more connected to what matters.

'Compassion over calculation' showed us that cultures are built through the emotional climate created when people feel safe and heard. Being alive inside means leading in a way that pulls people towards shared purpose rather than pushing them to activity, and in a way that turns emotional resonance into organisational momentum. Alive inside is an invitation to lead in a way that puts emotional truth on the table. It is only when leaders create hope that energy flows, creativity returns, and people take risks again. Vitality comes from leaders becoming a more human presence.

Here are three practices to remain alive inside:

- Be the pulse in the process.
- Make care contagious.
- Turn culture into energy.

E is for emerge – leading what can't be controlled

Some things cannot be engineered. They must be allowed to unfold. Emergence is what happens when we make space for meaning to take shape. Only the kind of leadership that focuses on what might evolve is truly alive inside in a world obsessed with predictions.

'Stories over structures' showed us that systems shift through narrative. It outlined how they become alive through the slow, methodical, and shared sense-making that happens when people start to see themselves as part of something larger than their roles. To craft beliefs and build movements requires radically human leaders who create a sense of shared authorship that inspires contribution.

Emergent leadership is not passive. It is about having the courage to commit to what you stand for when you can't know exactly how things will go. It is about having the humility to let others shape the outcome, along with the discipline to keep the purpose intact. This kind of leadership asks you to shift from being in control to being in charge. It asks you to trust that, if the story is strong enough, the rest will follow.

Here are three practices to remain alive inside:

- Shape the story that shapes the system.
- Let the culture do the heavy lifting.
- Wait, watch, and nurture.

The traits outlined in ALIVE (attunement, leadership, integration, vitality, emergence) are not about being inspirational, natural, or even 'visionary'. Radical humanity is not about personality. To lead by being alive inside means leading from attention, making space for discomfort, and returning again and again to what is essential.

In the chapters you have read, I have tried to assert some truths about our humanity. Vulnerability is a strength. Moral clarity is non-negotiable. Stories matter more than structures. Questions are more powerful than answers. Presence changes everything. Data will never replace human decision-making. Taken together, they may feel somewhat overwhelming. They might convey the sense that there is a lot of work to do. But let me reassure you. To be alive inside does not require you to be either perfect or polished, but you do need to be present and willing to put in the work.

The five dimensions of this manifesto are ways of being that are available to anyone who chooses to show up differently. Whether you lead a team of two or a system of thousands, whether you're in the C-suite or on the front line, you and your team can become alive inside again.

The only preconditions for success are the refusal to outsource what makes you human, to hide behind certainty, speed, or structure, or to optimise at the cost of meaning. The only true test of leadership is whether anyone feels more human because of how you lead. That is probably the oldest truth of real leadership: it starts from the inside because the person you are shapes the culture you create.

I decided to set out on my own professional path because I couldn't shake off the belief that there had to be a better way to lead and build organisations. If you've made it this far (and I thank you for doing so), then I guess that you too may be wondering what this better way might be. Years of strategies without stories, data without discernment, and performance without presence have cost us trust, culture, meaning, and our humanity. AI doesn't take anything from us. We are willingly giving it away for the sake of efficiency when, instead, we should be reasserting our humanity to make that efficiency effective.

This book has never been about railing against technological progress. Instead, it is about reclaiming our seat at the table where decisions on the future are made. When everyone wants to rush, leadership is about slowing down enough to call out the metrics that ignore impact and to remind others that trust lives in culture.

We don't have to resist machines, but we must choose not to adopt a mechanical mindset. We need to be radically human for the sake of other humans. I never set out to write a book about technology. There are many out there written by people who are far more qualified than I to go into the technological depth of AI. This is a book about attention, intention, courage, and care. I wanted to write about what happens when leaders no longer want to perform, in the sense of playing a role, but want to be present and trusted because of their integrity and humanity.

You've read stories about ducks and chess-playing Turks, Go-playing machines, predictive models, and cultural metaphors. You've met philosophers, activists, actors, medics, bankers, politicians, technicians, engineers, and industrialists. I have shared with you stories of silence, regret, resilience, judgement, presence, and intuition. All of them have led us here, to this moment where a choice must be made.

We must not reject technology in the name of some romantic return to the past. We must embrace our humanity as a radical recommitment to shape the future. The future of leadership is neither automated nor automatic. It is activated by presence, by empathy, and by intentional resistance and support. It demands us to reconnect to what makes us alive inside. Will you follow the line or write your own sentence? Will you let the algorithm define the goal or will you hold the moral line?

While I hope that I have made a sufficiently informed case for you to be able to tell the difference and to care in order to answer Sam Altman's 'Can you tell the difference?' question that opened this book, in a way, it is an irrelevant question. The real question is, 'What difference will you make?'.

Index